# Who Runs the World?

# Who Runs the World?

## Girls, Leadership, and Women in the Public Eye

Michele Paule and Hannah Yelin

ROWMAN & LITTLEFIELD
*Lanham • Boulder • New York • London*

Published by Rowman & Littlefield
An imprint of The Rowman & Littlefield Publishing Group, Inc.
4501 Forbes Boulevard, Suite 200, Lanham, Maryland 20706
www.rowman.com

86-90 Paul Street, London EC2A 4NE

British Library Cataloguing in Publication Information Available

**Library of Congress Cataloging-in-Publication Data**

Names: Paule, Michele, author. | Yelin, Hannah, 1981- author.
Title: Who runs the world? : girls, leadership, and women in the public eye / Michele Paule and Hannah Yelin.
Description: Lanham : Rowman & Littlefield, [2025] | Includes bibliographical references and index.
Identifiers: LCCN 2024031134 | ISBN 9781538165423 (cloth) | ISBN 9781538165447 (paperback) | ISBN 9781538165430 (ebook)
Subjects: LCSH: Women in public life. | Women public officers. | Women—Political activity. | Leadership in women. | Role models.
Classification: LCC HQ1390 .P38 2025 | DDC 305.42—dc23/eng/20240820
LC record available at https://lccn.loc.gov/2024031134

*We dedicate this book to the late Jo Cox MP with
the kind permission of her family.*

# Contents

# Figures

# Acknowledgements

First, we would like to acknowledge and humbly thank our participants for their generosity in sharing their visions of the world that they would like to see and their experiences of the world that they would like to change. We also sincerely thank the tireless, committed, and unsparingly helpful education workers in schools and local authorities who gave their time to enable access to research sites. None of this work would have been possible without them.

While our names appear on the covers, no book is ever just the work of the authors but is the outcome of many collaborations, contributions, and communities. We recognise the support and solidarity – academic, practical, and emotional – of colleagues at Oxford Brookes University from the outset of this project, especially Joanne Begiato, Bill Gibson, Emily Brown, Mark Cain, Bev Clack, Alex Goody, Vicky Hatcher, Hannah Klein-Tomas, Simonetta Manfredi, Tina Miller, Leander Reeves, Kim Shadbolt, and Rachel Wilmshurst. Shelley Galpin provided invaluable support as RA, as did Kate Lonie for the pilot study. Academics beyond our own workplace – including Heather Mendick, Kim Allen, Laura Clancy, and Anita Biressi – have been hugely helpful and inspiring. Laura Coryton's energy and skill in turning our data into an activism course for girls have helped ensure the legacy of this project. The cover design was created for us by student Merle Greany.

Thanks, too, to friends and family who have supported us while we were working on this. Michele is particularly indebted to Juliette Adair, Linet Arthur, Shaista Aziz, Julia Blanchard, Sue Bell, Lizzie and Kate Bowe, Jannette Pollard, and the Sunday 'Triffids', a weekly group call between several staunch, funny, creative feminists, the persistence of which is one of the better legacies of lockdown. Hannah would like to thank all-round supportive hero Jack Royston, the cherub Arvo, Danielle Bird, Simon Foxall, Bridget Dalton, Natasha Corey Bell, Ruth Wye, Faraz Osman, the women on a group chat that, for reasons Hannah won't explain, goes by the name of 'The Prague Charter'. She would like to commemorate Fabian Buxton, Molly Nichols, and Rosalind Yelin: three of the most beautiful, inspiring, and beloved people Hannah has ever known, and sadly lost during the writing of this book.

\*\*\*

The inspiration for this project came from many sources. For Hannah, these include her many wonderful colleagues from her years working in the media and Su Holmes for her guidance towards what would become a lasting professional interest in the politics of visibility. For Michele, these include fellow Labour members in the Oxford East CLP, especially Ann Black, Anneliese Dodds MP, Trish Elphinstone, and Shereen Karmali and Ed Turner; Lubna Arshad, Oxford's youngest-ever lord mayor and first Muslim woman and the first woman of colour to hold that office; Aimee Winkfield, who continues to demonstrate that community is at the heart of leadership; and the World Association of Girl Guides and Girl Scouts (Europe), especially Amanda Medler, Marjolien Sluiter, Eszter Toth, Emma Guthrie, and Irene Rosales.

We are grateful to the Gender and Education Association and the Oxford Centre for Methodism and Church History for funding awards that supported the project, and to Oxford Brookes for a Research Excellence Award that made its expansion possible, and also for the Knowledge Exchange Award that supported our taking the findings out into the world.

# Introduction

## *May You Write in Interesting Times*

We completed this book just as Frank Hester, a prominent donor of significant funding to the Conservative, then ruling party of the UK government, was recorded saying that he hates Black women and wants Black, Labour Member of Parliament Diane Abbott to be shot (*The Guardian* 2024). Hester later released an apology, stating that his comments 'had nothing to do with her gender nor colour of skin' (@HesterObe 2024). Hester's initial comments and the character of his apology go to the heart of the themes in this book and of the concerns that prompted our study. They are illustrative of the hostile conditions of visibility for women in positions of power, especially Black women and those of minoritised ethnicities , and the ways in which these conditions are normalised, dismissed, and denied. Such hostility, and its elision in popular calls for girls to aspire to leadership, form consistent threads that we explore both in the accounts that girls in our study produced and in the discourses on which they drew. This work is framed within wider contexts of gendered inequalities in decision-making and leadership, the positioning of girls as the future solution not only to the gender leadership gap but to the wider ills created by neoliberal economic regimes, and of the increasingly restricted opportunities for community and civic engagement available to girls under long austerity in the United Kingdom. It investigates how girls conceive of leadership through their engagements with women in the public eye within wider discursive regimes of gender, power, and girlhood.

While initiatives to develop leadership in girls proliferate, there is to date little work exploring the discursive contexts in which girls form ideas associated with leadership – especially girls not already identified as future leaders and/or current activists. This work aims to address that gap. The research data on which it draws is from a project we conducted before, during, and after the COVID-19 lockdown era. The temporal context of the study was important in shaping its nature and findings, not only because the global COVID-19 pandemic created a hiatus in our interviews but because during that hiatus the media and cultural landscape changed. Not only did the pandemic bring discussions of gender and leadership into the media spotlight, but it necessitated a pause in our data collection during which we turned our attention to young women's online activities around leadership figures. In response to the challenges that lockdown created for us, and indeed for all empirical researchers in terms of access to participants, we traced themes that emerged in our pre-lockdown data into new participatory online spaces where girls and young women creatively responded to the heightened gender tropes in media representations of leadership.

## GENDER AND LEADERSHIP

The under-representation of women in decision-making roles is not just a matter of concern within the United Kingdom – it is a key focus of international bodies such as the European Commission (2018, 2024), the OECD (2023), and the World Economic Foru m (2024). In global terms, at the time of writing, the United Kingdom is placed at 18 in a league table of 146 countries in the 'Political Empowerment' category of the World Economic Forum's *Global Gender Gap Index 2023*, which may seem moderately respectable until one looks at how low the bar is set. And, taken alone, the UK statistics are depressing enough: A Fawcett Society review, *Sex and Power* (Marren and Bazely 2022), finds that 'Women are under-represented and outnumbered by men at a ratio of 2:1 in the positions that shape our politics, laws and culture' (2). While the number of women MPs in the UK House of Commons increased from 34% to 40.5% with Labour's 2024 General election win, women's representaion in local politics remains under 40%. Scotland and Wales do slightly better with 46% and 43% per cent respectively (fawcettsociety.org 2024). . A similar picture of gendered imbalance in the most important decision-making roles in our society emerges across all sectors – public and civil services, the arts, health, education, trade unions, and business.

Such gender-focused data on their own, concerning though the patterns they reveal are, conceal the supremacy of white populations in occupying power roles – the Fawcett Society ( Marren and Bazely 2022) reports that *where data is available* (our italics), 'Women of colour are simply missing altogether from the highest levels of many sectors'. This availability of data is key: the authors of the report found it 'difficult to access data to even establish whether women with intersecting characteristics such as ethnicity, disability, LGBT identity or religion, are missing' (3). We consider the problems of such a primary focus on counting the number of women in top roles in terms of its neglect of other key relations of domination and exclusion later in chapter 3, while we also recognise that it is evidence of a persistent gendered hierarchy that denies women cultural and economic power.

While unequal representation in leadership roles has been an ongoing concern in political and feminist domains since the mid-twentieth century, the call for more women leaders emerged into the popular arena following the global banking crash of 2008. This call was not, however, made on grounds of equality: it was rationalised in terms of specific traits associated with ethics and caution that it assumed women would bring to leadership roles (Prügl 2012; van Staveren 2014). These traits, it was imagined, would save the (capitalist) world from future disaster. They are prominent in models of 'inclusive capitalism' (Randa 2022; de Jong 2021) which seek, in the face of looming crises in climate and world poverty that have grown out of unbridled free-market neoliberalism, to bring 'a new private sector-based approach'. This approach promises profitability while simultaneously delivering a better quality of life for the poor, a respect for diversity, and 'a sustainable approach to ecology' in order to save the planet (Hart 2005, xlii). Who better then to deliver such salvation than women leaders, already culturally endowed in the public and corporate imaginary with the qualities of empathy, inclusivity, and connection with both fellow humans and the natural world? (Chin 2004; Median-Vicent 2020). When the COVID-19 virus spread to become a global pandemic, the figure of the woman leader as saviour entered the public sphere with an urgency driven by unprecedented fear; women leaders were seen as 'the real heroes in the fight against COVID-19' (Sky News 2020), and medics argued in the BMJ for the need for 'cultivating and harnessing the advancements of women's leadership globally and implementing a gender inclusive lens in pandemic preparedness' (Meagher, Singh, and Patel 2020). This female leader/saviour figure illustrates how the concept of leadership itself perpetuates the values of masculinity through its masculine definitions of femininity (Calás and Smircich 1991, 299). Calls for governments to expand female representation and for companies to appoint more women directors work to sustain this kind of gendered 'knowledge' about leadership precisely because of the complementary, feminised leadership traits that women supposedly bring to the role. The implied requirement to demonstrate feminised behaviours to justify claims to masculinised power roles combine to make leadership an 'impossible space' (Tseëlon 1995) for women even as such calls increase.

At the same time, conditions that might promote women's leadership have been eroded. In the name of 'necessary' austerity since the 2008 crash, increased privatisation and drastic cuts to public services and facilities have meant that the community routes to decision-making roles that women are most likely to follow have been effectively cut off, as we discuss in chapter

1. Nicolas Rose (1999) explores the shift, under neoliberalism, from addressing economic inequality to a focus on promoting equality of opportunity; this shift entails a focus on the individual as responsible for taking advantage of such opportunity, but also as responsible for failure to thrive in a system where entrepreneurialism has replaced state structures ensuring wellbeing, and optimism has replaced security. The resources necessary for constructing the successful self are increasingly hard to access (Scharff 2016, 110), while entrenched structural inequalities that dictate such access are elided. Leadership roles, one might argue, represent the apotheosis of successful selfhood. They are the highly visible totems of the neoliberal individualist model of the entrepreneurial subject. As Mary Beard (2017a) notes, power is 'an elite thing, coupled to public prestige, to the individual charisma of so-called "leadership", and often, though not always, to a degree of celebrity'. It is this relationship with public prestige and visibility that has helped produce what Lorna Finlayson (2018) describes as a fetishisation of representation, whereby the presence of more women in high-profile roles is seen as evidence of success in resolving wider gender inequalities at the same time as excluding them from the agenda.

As calls for more women leaders proliferate, the issues that such women face have come into sharp focus in contemporary political contexts. These include the rise of public misogyny as an adjunct to the increase in populist, authoritarian leaders (Kaul 2021) – this we witnessed in the terrifying circus that was Donald Trump's presidency in the USA (Robson 2020). Also of concern is the vilification of women politicians online, particularly women of colour (Bigio and Vogelstein 2020), the online abuse suffered by women activists (Hess 2015; Lumsden and Morgan 2018), and the predominance of hostile, sexist representations of political leaders in the mainstream media, when they are represented at all (Ross et al. 2013; Tischner, Malson and Fey 2019).

## MISOGYNIST MEDIA CULTURES

The risks of visibility are unevenly distributed (Yelin and Clancy 2021), and celebrity culture in particular is a punitively gendered 'theatre of punishment' (Tyler and Bennett 2010, 380). Scholars of gendered media have robustly evidenced the 'stark differences' in the treatment of men and women in the public eye, where women are under unrelenting and vicious scrutiny underpinned by normative 'cultural consensus about "out of bounds" behaviours for women' (Holmes and Negra 2011, 2). Highly visible women are constantly policed and are more harshly judged than famous men in a misogynistic media culture. This culture is founded upon the judgement of famous women 'that brings into play gender norms [to] determine what is "appropriate" for women and girls more widely' (Kavka 2014, 71 and 60). This manifests in aggressive surveillance of women's bodies, 'the key terrain upon which discourses surrounding female celebrity are mapped' (Holmes and Negra 2011, 7), as those bodies are presented to audiences with the suggestion that women should judge both women in the public eye and themselves (Wilson 2010, 30). This misogynistic culture also manifests in the threat of harm to those bodies. Due to 'a gendered dynamic of popular interest and pleasure in the misfortunes of female celebrities' (Holmes and Negra 2011, 1) and cultural misogyny in which men are let 'off the hook' for their violence against women (Patterson and Sears 2011), harm to women is paraded for entertainment appeal (Boyle 2011; Yelin 2020). As such, even media representations of women who hold significant power often reveal 'the weight of convention upon them and point to the limits of the field of representational possibilities for highly visible women in contemporary culture' (Yelin 2020, 269). It is this hostile arena that girls are being exhorted to enter, as the saviours of the future.

## GIRLS AS THE FUTURE SOLUTION TO THE GENDER LEADERSHIP GAP

The figure of the girl as a totem of neoliberal optimism is well attested (Ringrose 2012), the feminised qualities of self-responsibility, reflexivity, and diligence attributed to her making her the 'ideal late modern subject' (Harris 2004, 6). Even as the burden of austerity hits girls and women hardest (Allen 2016; De Henau and Reed 2016), they bear the responsibility not only for saving themselves but for revivifying national economies (Roberts 2015). Following the global economic crash of 2008, it might have been anticipated that such a demonstrable failure of existing systems would shake faith in neoliberalism both as economic policy and guiding ideology. In fact, both became more entrenched as the crisis was mobilised as an occasion for increased austerity measures in the United Kingdom (Mirowski 2014), and increased focus on the individual's own responsibility for their wellbeing (Clack and Paule 2019). While, as McRobbie (2008) observes, neoliberalism in the earlier part of this century saw female citizenship directed away from political participation and towards self-actualisation through consumer citizenship, as the failings of such neoliberalism become increasingly apparent, calls to girls as potential leaders redirect their citizenship to that of compliant, heroic activism in the service of inclusive capitalism. This can be witnessed in the proliferation of girl-focused texts in the media from the 1990s onwards (Harris 2004; Gonick 2006) positioning girls as 'idealised citizens' (Projansky 2014, 11). The 'girl leader' in particular is a site where powerful discourses associated with post-feminism, neoliberalism, and capitalism converge under the guise of empowerment. In a similar fashion to the ways girls are seen as the key to advancing progress in the Global South (Bent 2013), girls in the Global North are an increasing focus of attention as the solution to not only gendered inequalities in decision-making roles and thus the depredations of sexism (Hopkins 2002), but to wider global ills (Koffman and Gill 2013). Already imbued with girl-power and post-feminist narratives of women's success in making change, the 'can-do' girl (Harris 2004) of the affluent West is now tasked with the mission of saving the world through the 'feminisation of responsibility' (Chant 2006). Jessica Taft (2020) observes how 'Girlhood, as a social and cultural category, has multiple associations that make the figure of the girl activist especially desirable in the contemporary context of profound inequality, structural violence, and climate crisis', making what she terms 'the girl activist saviour' peculiarly fitted to deliver the promises of 'inclusive capitalism', and thus 'functions to symbolically resolve public anxieties about the future'. It is not all girls, however, who are called to such leadership. While the 'helpful, harmless heroic girls' of Taft's (2020) analysis and the 'good girl' of Anita Biressi (2018) exemplify how girls from outside the magic circle of privileged, middle-class whiteness are summoned as compliant 'endorsers of political agendas and as agents of change', the mobilisation of such figures works to 'elide, occlude or sideline, from the public conversation' ways in which less compliant and more marginalised girls are excluded from the mechanism of agentic citizenship.

## ROLE MODELS FOR GIRLS AS THE SOLUTION TO THE GENDER LEADERSHIP GAP

In the United Kingdom, the late 1990s saw girls start to outperform boys in national exams and to enter university in greater numbers than boys. These same girls will now be entering their forties, but one would have to look hard to find them in government or in other leadership roles. An absence of visible role models in girlhood is popularly cited as a root cause for the paucity of women in decision-making positions in adulthood; this narrative has been widespread in popular, girl-focused, and corporate media realms over the last decade – for example, *The Guardian* national newspaper (Fraser 2014) ran an article claiming 'Young women need female role models to inspire success'; a Forbes (Warrell 2020) website headline states that 'Seeing Is Believing: Female Role Models Inspire Girls to Think Bigger', while skincare website BraveInBloom (2024) offered a blog titled 'How Women Are Inspiring the Next Generation: Great Role Models'. A burgeoning range of popular campaigns seeks to stimulate girls' leadership aspirations through a combination of exposure to role models and boosting individual confidence

(Biressi 2018). These include Sheryl Sandberg's 'Lean In Girls' (https://www
.leaningirls.org/ 2023) and Edwina Dunn's 'The Female Lead' (2017), which
aim to address this shortage through providing a range of adult-endorsed role
models that will, it is hoped, stimulate girls to aspire to leadership themselves.

As we argue in chapter 2, such 'role model' solutions for girls are often
based on problematic assumptions. In their simplistic ideas of gender-
matching, the complexities of relationships that young people may have with
media figures are reduced to a matter of inspiration = imitation. There is a
lack of recognition of the importance of the cultural contexts in which girls
encounter media figures, the meanings girls attach to them, and how encounters and meanings are embedded in girls' everyday lives and media practices.
They elide structural inequalities in their reliance on individual aspiration.
Importantly, in calling for more women leaders to be present in the public
eye as role models for girls, they do not recognise the wider context of hostile
media representation of those women leaders (van Zoonen 2006). Finally,
while role models are held to be important, the models themselves are those
endorsed by adults. This fails to recognise the range of spheres, from politics
to celebrity, that girls might draw upon when formulating their ideas about
leadership. Young people are consistently instructed that they should not base
their aspirations around celebrities (Mendick et al. 2018), and even when
celebrity role models are offered to them, the ways in which they are expected
to admire such models are heavily policed within celebrity discourse itself
(Yelin 2016). Role models function on the assumption of a powerful affective influence in the fostering of aspirations, yet the concept itself is poorly
defined, as is the theorisation of how such role models might work. The
popularity of role model solutions is one we interrogate further in chapter 2
as a mechanism by which, under austerity cuts to youth services, the responsibility for developing girls as leaders is redirected away from the provision of
structured opportunities within communities and towards the individual girl.
We consider the exemplar role model interventions we discuss as representing the apotheosis of a particular set of girl-orientated discourses rather than
as resources that girls are necessarily engaging with.

Our research aimed to challenge the problematic assumptions of role-
model interventions through a focus on girls' own preferred women leaders,
whether from celebrity, politics, or their own communities, and on the diverse
ways in which they respond to these women. We were interested in how
girls' choices, and the meanings they read into them, are shaped by contextual and intersectional factors, as well as by potent prevailing discourses of
gender and power. The project was conducted with participants from groups
poorly represented in leadership along intersecting axes of gender with race,
class, religion, disability, sexuality, and UK regionality – elements that
combine and reinforce one another to create specific and intensified forms

of marginalisation (Crenshaw 1991) and that have hitherto too often been 'tokenised' in studies of girlhood and leadership (Fraser and Hagel 2016). As a project invested in girls' self-determination, our definition of girl encompasses and respects the self-identification of non-binary and trans-youth. We endeavoured to centre participants as socially situated makers of meaning around media representations of women leaders (Kim 2004), and identify ways in which their engagements with those leaders are framed by both wider discourses and their local experiences of gender and power.

To do this, we conducted twelve semi-structured group interview workshops with ninety-four participants aged 13–15 in diverse geographical and socio-economic settings. Our twelve sites included nine comprehensive state secondary schools, one independent girls' school, one special educational needs and disability (SEND) school, and one Local Authority Youth Office. These were located across rural and urban settings in England, Wales, and Scotland. Girls had access to devices connected to the internet during the focus groups so that they could search for and share images and memes relating to concepts and public figures they wished to discuss. (See the appendix for a more detailed account of the research design.) The images comprise additional data, illustration, and counterpoint throughout this book. The public figures discussed in this book were brought up in conversation or searched for online by the girls themselves and demonstrated the extraordinary breadth of popular discourses, people, representations, references, and examples on which girls are drawing when formulating ideas about gender, visibility, and power. The wide-ranging conversations traverse diverse cultural fields. As such, we shall consider how family, teachers, peers, politicians, sports stars, fictional characters, and a wide range of singers, actors, TV personalities, influencers, and other modes of celebrity feature in the dialogic process of girls forming ideas about power and opportunity through the interrelations between their media engagements and lived experience.

## OUTLINE OF CHAPTERS

In chapter 1, we explore ways in which girls drew on wider popular discourses of girlhood, feminism, and leadership to form their ideas about gender, power, and who might wield it. We identify discourses associated with confidence, listening, and voice as central to girls' conceptualisation of leadership. We examine the selective address of such discourses in terms of the ideal classed and raced subjects they imply, how they regulate girls' claims to voice and space, and identify ways in which they reframe and recirculate entrenched gendered tropes and reinforce hierarchised binaries. We contrast the ''shared typical' of the prevailing discourses on which girls across the twelve research sites drew with the particularity of participants' experiences of leadership. Girls expressed anxiety over their lack of understanding of both routes to and institutions of power and leadership at all levels, whether community, political, or corporate. They described the necessity of experience in order to develop the competence they saw as particularly incumbent on women leaders to articulate as well as demonstrate, but their own experiences of responsibility and decision-making were, with few exceptions, confined to domestic spheres. We find evidence that this limitation of experience can be attributed both to uneven, uncontextualised citizenship education provision in their schools and to the loss of opportunities under austerity within their communities.

In chapter 2, we identify the underlying assumptions of solutions to the gender leadership gap that suggest that offering more visible role models to girls will inspire them to become the leaders of the future. These include the reliance of such assumptions and solutions on having more women represented at top levels as constitutive of equity in itself, and indicative of gender equality having been achieved across all social and economic strata; their assumption of 'media effects' and their basis in neoliberal tenets of individual aspiration and the entrepreneurial self while eliding the structural factors that foster or inhibit girls' possibilities of ever inhabiting such roles. We offer data from our 'Girls, Leadership and Women in the Public Eye' project to show how girls' choices of and engagements with women in the public eye challenge such assumptions in their blurring of the celebrity/leader divide, in their own recognition of the role of privilege, and in their debilitating awareness of the risks for women in the public eye that act as a deterrent to any latent desires to wield power they may have.

Chapter 3 examines the attitudes of participants under contexts of neoliberal austerity at a moment when discourses surrounding inherited privilege and race intensified in popular culture, coalescing around the marriage of Prince Harry to Meghan Markle. We examine attitudes towards Meghan as a public figure, institutional royalty as a concept, and Meghan's symbolic ability to bridge tensions of progression and regression around the royals. In so doing, we shed light on how girls respond to and internalise ideas about power, work, and inheritance. We offer new understandings of monarchy and celebrity, and also girls' negotiations with popular discourses of meritocracy and privilege. We address a dearth of empirical analyses of public perceptions of royal celebrity and provide insights into the mediation and reception of Meghan as a new member of the monarchy and the broader interpenetrations of the race and gender she represents. The girls' feelings about Meghan are viewed alongside celebrities who the girls discussed through royal rhetoric of queendom and bloodline: Oprah Winfrey, Nicki Minaj, Queen Latifah, and Beyoncé. Around Meghan's celebrity dynamism, the girls construct economies of royal 'work' and related meritocratic ideas of 'deserving' or 'undeserving' royals. Consistently, the girls' discussions disrupt ideas of hereditary power, ultimately calling to rescind public funding of the monarchy.

In chapter 4, we consider ways in which girls are enjoined to imagine leadership in terms of the aspirational, individualist leadership models in the high-profile campaigns, 'Ban Bossy', 'Lean In Girls', and 'The Female Lead' as examples of the contemporary turn to the agentic, aspiring girl as the solution to the gender leadership gap in the future. We consider these campaigns within a framework suggested by Janet Newman's (2015) distinction between individual 'aspiration' and collective 'hope' in political contexts of austerity, and contrast their address with our findings suggesting girls' preferences for collaborative leadership models and motives for leadership as a means of achieving wider social change. We show how girls' own envisionings of leadership are developed through their local experiences and their encounters with wider leadership discourse, particularly as represented in highly visible women across a range of media. We suggest that the concept of 'leadership' presented to girls needs to be challenged in terms of its gendered individualism and its failure to capture ways in which they desire to participate in decision-making.

In chapter 5, we explore the ways in which girls and young women, as the already luminous subjects of leadership and empowerment discourses, responded to the emerging media formats, heightened public authority, and increasingly polarised gendering of power in the COVID-19 era. In response to what we term the *leadership theatre* of the UK daily lockdown state briefing, we identify the emergence of ven*troll*oquism as a resistant and critical means of articulating girls' and young women's otherwise unheard and unsolicited critiques of ineffective, performatively masculine state power. Drawing on data collected in focus groups with teenage girls across England, Scotland, and Wales before and after lockdown, and on a newly emerging COVID-19 era genre of TikTok lip-synching, we show consistent patterns of girls' and young women's disquiet with populist, androcentric risk-taking and the feminisation of caution. This disquiet found expression in the specific conditions of lockdown media and the transmedia affordances of the freshly booming TikTok platform. This (e)merging genre utilised ventriloquistic practices of remediating state broadcasts and drag impersonation of male politicians to evade the strictures upon girls' and women's voices. We locate this resistant practice within chronic wider concerns surrounding gender, voice, and visibility rendered acute by COVID-19.

# Chapter 1

# Girls on Leadership

## From Confidence to Competence

Girls recognise that leadership is not, in the public imaginary, *for* girls; that in fact the world that exhorted them to 'girl power' is loath to grant them any power at all and indeed is threatened by the very idea. This was clear in two of our Glasgow participants' discussion of media treatment of the teenage climate activist Greta Thunberg:

> *Ruth:* Aye, I think it is because some men will be threatened because she's a female child.
>
> *Charlie:* They think that she's a delusional child, but in reality she is trying to make a difference. Aye, because one she's a child and two, she's female. A female trying to tell a strong man how to do his job and then she's a child as well trying to dictate how to do his job.

The ways in which girls in the study understood leadership as a concept were shaped by both the blandishments and the hostility inherent in discourses surrounding girlhood and leadership. This exchange encapsulates various themes which we will explore in this chapter: namely, the confidence required to 'dictate' to others, the competence required to know 'how to do' things, and the backlash anticipated when seeking to hold this kind of power from the locations of gender, youth, and their intersections. These themes emerged from our initial questions in the focus groups, where we asked girls how they understood leadership and its operations, what they saw as key traits, and which of their own experiences they understood as leadership. The discourses on which girls drew in their responses constitute a part of a larger formation of knowledge about power and who might wield it in terms of gender, and also in terms of intersecting axes of dis/advantage such as class and race. Discourse, of course, is not neutral; it creates systems of knowledge that frame how personal experiences are validated or marginalised (Foucault 19888). We examine how these discourses provided girls with a framework for understanding leadership within global media, local, and educational contexts. In doing so, we tease apart some of the intertwining popular discourses constructing both girlhood and leadership and consider the extent to which they are adequate to represent girls' situated experiences.

In conducting the interviews, we worked from the assumption that the opinions that the girls produced would largely be formed in the process of the research conversations. (See 'Notes on Methodology' in the appendix for further discussion of this.) This could, of course, be said of all interview encounters when viewed from a dialogic perspective, which recognises that 'the researcher, by specific questions, and even by her or his observing presence, instigates self-reflections' (Frank 2005, 968), and thus that participants' stories must be heard not as surrogates of their lives outside the interview but as acts of engagement with researchers (Mishler 1991). It is, however, particularly pertinent to our study because girls were selected as broadly representative of the populations that their schools and youth groups served, rather than identified or self-identifying as (potential) leaders. With the exception of some of our independent school participants, they were not participants in leadership programmes, although some schools did offer skills development as a part of classroom learning and extra-curricular provision; thus, we did not anticipate their having previously engaged in reflection on women and leadership , although we could deduce some interest in the topic from their having volunteered to take part in the study. Our girls were not, then, the self-identifying activists, feminists, and young leaders of, for example, Jessica Taft's (2011), Anne-Marie Enderstein's (2018), or Sue Jackson's (2021) studies. Moreover, because participants were teenage girls, many of them from groups under-represented in decision-making roles, leadership was a domain of which few had any first-hand experience. As Taft (2011, 9) notes, girls are 'excluded political subjects, marginalised within formal politics and within social movements', as our Glasgow participants above recognised in relation to Thunberg. Thus, the girls' ideas often necessarily drew on second-hand experiences and wider representations which, as Taylor, Gilligan and Sullivan (1995, 4) observe, can be complex and contradictory, while their own experiences of decision-making and responsibility hinged on opportunities that were themselves dependent on local resources or were culturally gendered activities of a kind that precluded framing within their understanding of leadership.

Teen girls, however limited their experience, are nonetheless the focus of popular discourses that interpellate or 'hail' them as future leaders. The concept of hailing, as Althusser (1971) explains, functions in the sense of being tapped on the shoulder by a police officer and realising that one is specifically being addressed by a compelling authority; this works because it helps secure the subject's sense of who she is. Such hailing represents one of the ways in which young people 'are increasingly called upon to participate in the polity and in civil society' but via discourses of choice and freedom that target them as consumers 'rather than in any more politically meaningful sense' (Harris 2008, 484). Despite the popularity of entrepreneurial 'girl boss' narratives across legacy and newer media (Fradley 2022), and prominent educational campaigns addressing girls as potential leaders, such as 'Lean In Girls' and 'The Female Lead',[1] there were no definitive models of girls' leadership on which participants drew. Rather, they assembled their ideas from the diverse array of attributes and traits associated with girlhood and gender, with power and responsibility (Taft 2011, 181) that circulate in the 'youthscape' – a term coined by Maira and Soep (2004) to describe the social, cultural, and environmental landscapes specific to young people, encompassing their mediated and material experiences, perspectives, and activities – and, more specifically, the 'girlscape', in which the identificatory figure of 'the girl' is placed 'at the centre of a consumer culture conceived of as both utopian and egalitarian' (Yoda 2017, 173).

Many of the attributes and traits identified by participants were those of the pervasive popular feminist discourses exhorting girls to confidence, voice, and visibility noted by Sarah Banet-Weiser (2018). Alongside girl-orientated discourses, participants also drew on mainstream media representations of leadership. Such representations themselves are informed by existing cultural stereotypes and by a range of corporate and other texts, for example, self-help guides and popular presentations such as TED Talks (Eagly and Carly 2003; Gill and Orgad 2017; Enderstein 2018), as well as by celebrities and opinion leaders (Meyer 1995; Klapp 2017). These amorphous elements combine to constitute 'leadership' in the social imaginary: that mostly unexamined set of beliefs and assumptions that shape our social world and provide a normalising framework for its structures and roles (Castoriadis 1987; Taylor 2004).

This is not to imply a difference or separation between discourses of girlhood and those of leadership; elements such as the advocation of confidence, self-promotion, and self-responsibility circulate across both. While popular feminisms promote neoliberal principles of individualism and personal autonomy, corporate capitalism promotes entrepreneurialism and women's entry into the workplace, including corporate leadership roles (; Gill, 2007; Gill and Orgad, 2017; Rottenberg 2018) as elements of what Nancy Fraser (2009 p.114) terms a 'dangerous liaison' between feminism and neoliberalism. Thus, both wider political discourses and those of popular feminism provide girls with tools for constructing leadership. Within this discursive milieu, participants struggled to form cohesive ideas of the leadership possibilities for women, especially marginalised women, and in media spheres where, despite the current luminosity of feminism, 'women's identities,

gender, and bodies are routinely tied together and attributed meanings anti-
thetical to leadership' (Sinclair 2013: 242), and in local conditions where
routes to power are shrouded in mystique.

## 'CONFIDENCE IS KEY' (DENISE)

It is confidence that emerged most strongly among the leadership qualities
that girls identified as important. It was described as an essential characteristic by participants in all groups: while there was a variety of definitions and
clarifications, there was no disagreement. That girls should so readily evoke
'confidence' is unsurprising given its discursive reach (Banet-Weiser 2018,
92). Gill and Orgad (2017) describe how

> Exhortations to female self-confidence are everywhere in contemporary culture:
> in education, confidence is hailed as an answer to what is formulated as girls'
> low self-esteem; in the workplace it will help women to 'lean in' and feel pow-
> erful; in consumer culture it is claimed as 'the new sexy' and as 'more important
> than beauty'. (5)

The prominence of this call to confidence is rooted in a cultural interest in
the perceived self-esteem crisis in girls that has been growing since the 1990s
(Gonick 2006; Hains 2012). As Jennifer Baumgardner and Amy Richards
(2004, 65) observe, 'girls went from being invisible to being vulnerable'.
This new visibility grew from girls' increasing presence as economically
active subjects (Johnson 1993) and the emerging status of 'the girl' as a
barometer of success and totem of optimism and progress under neoliberalism (Harris 2004). Public attention to girls' self-esteem in particular is attributed to the combination of second-wave feminist psychologists' creation of
a new 'psychological knowledge' of girlhood within patriarchal cultures,
with public interest in girls' underperformance in science and mathematics
(Gonick 2006, 18). These conditions fostered 'a frenetic proliferation' of
empowerment initiatives and promotions that cast girls as being in a state of
crisis due to 'insecurity, or lack of self-confidence, or a lack of leadership,
among other things' and 'marshals entrepreneurialism and feminine capacity as a response' (Banet-Weiser 2018, 4–47). While popular parenting and
education guides, girl-focused programmes, and motivational texts frame
confidence in girls as an individual, psychological trait, diminished by wider
gendered cultures but restorable through therapeutic intervention (Aapola,
Gonick & Harris 2005, 54), Banet-Weiser (2014) theorises confidence as
a discursive, consumer, and performative phenomenon that intersects with
broader structures of power and privilege, arguing that

while self-esteem is ostensibly a psychological issue of the self, it is also mar-
shalled in surveillance practices that are raced and classed. . . . The white, middle-
class girls who fit the category of what Anita Harris (2004) calls the can-do girl
– potentially empowered, entrepreneurial, media savvy – are the targets for a
variety of moral panics and public discourses about their low self-esteem. (, 87)

Confidence discourses were strongly present in participants' talk in
ways that reproduced the therapeutic tenets of popular 'self-esteem' narratives (Gonick 2006; Rimke 2020) and also operated as the Foucauldian
'technology of self' (Foucault 1988) noted by Gill and Orgad (2017, 6) as
'a technology within and through which women and girls across age, race,
sexuality and class are exhorted to think about, judge, and act on themselves'.
This emerged in girls' perceptions of lack of confidence as a personal issue
treatable through intervention and in their regulation of their own and one
another's claims to confidence within parameters of acceptable (classed and
racialised) femininities. However, while they saw lack of confidence as a
problem specific to women, they did not attribute its lack solely to internal,
individual traits. They identified hostile gendered cultures as inhibiting the
development and expression of the confidence central to leadership but did
not see any resolution available other than work on the self.

Denise expressed the centrality of confidence in a way typical of girls
across the study:

I think confidence is key, because if you're not very confident, people are not
going to see you as a leader, but if you have a little bit more confidence, then
people see you as leader material.

Susan's response immediately framed confidence as a gendered problem:

I always think that (women) don't believe in themselves as much and don't have
confidence because, like, they can come up with something really good like the
men, but I just think they don't have the confidence to do it.

Kelly made the link between the internalisation of patriarchal values and
confidence deficit:

And because men have, like, brought up the idea [that men are more suited to
leadership] then the women start to believe it. And so they start to doubt themselves and they start putting themselves down and doing worse because they just
been brought up thinking they can't do good enough. So they do it themselves
because they just get that idea in themselves.

This casting of confidence as an issue pertaining to girls and women
while attributing its lack to wider gendered inequalities marks a change

from the cultural conditions of the 'can-do' girls of the preceding generation. For girls at the turn of the twenty-first century, success entailed a disavowal of feminism and a promulgation of a post-feminist discourse of equality-as-achieved (McRobbie 2009). In 2004, Madeleine Jowett (9–95) noted a 'cultural proscription' surrounding assertions of inequality among young women in her focus groups on feminism. This proscription, she argues, emerged from the historical contingence of neoliberal self-responsibility, of girls growing up with the equalities legislation passed in the 1970s in the United Kingdom and of the optimistic discourses of social mobility and progress that characterised the then New Labour Government. These conditions produced in young women a sense of entitlement to equality that in itself removed the right to be restricted by, or indeed speak about, inequality. Twenty years on from Jowett, at the time of writing, girls inhabit a world in which feminism, far from being the 'unsayable', has 'undeniably become popular culture' through celebrity feminisms and popular feminist movements (Banet-Weiser and Portwood-Stacer 2017, 884); these feminisms overwhelmingly interpellate girls (Jackson 2021). As noted above, the girls in this study were not selected because they identified as feminists, but contemporary girl culture is so imbued with popular feminism that its discursive tenets and tropes nonetheless permeated their discussions. While popular feminisms have rendered the recognition of gender inequality fashionable, the confidence needed to overcome such inequality is obligatory (Gill & Orgad 2017).

Popular feminisms have, as we discuss in chapter 4, been extensively critiqued for their persistent neoliberal individualism (Gill 2016; Banet-Weiser 2018) and for promoting awareness of gender inequality only as a problem surmountable by appropriate aspiration and attitude adjustment (Rottenberg 2014). Our data show how this cultural impasse leaves girls in the position of having simultaneously to demonstrate awareness of gendered barriers to power but to take responsibility for overcoming them as individuals. As Anita Harris and Amy Shields-Dobson observe, 'it remains difficult for young women to be recognized or to produce themselves as agents whilst claiming to be affected at all by patriarchal power structures' (2015, 153). This tension was present across multiple research sites in girls' descriptions of confidence as an individual leadership trait that is cultivatable through work on the self, while its absence is produced by a cultural climate hostile to women leaders.

The following is typical of girls working out ideas about the centrality of confidence to leadership. Their talk reveals conflicting perspectives on the possibilities for women of overcoming discrimination and disadvantage through attitudinal adjustment:

*Inaya:* I think . . . some women are, like, too shy to . . . to put themselves forward and give their qualities, so they might just stay back and not take the next step.

*Maryam:* Many women like to point out other people's good things, but they don't know what their good things are. They just focus on their insecurities, so we should try not to do that.

*Faiza:* I think only because of the high criticism that they've already faced in the past. So, they could see when a woman tries to stand up and say proudly what she's good at and what she's bad at, she's just neglected and said that she's bossy and she just wants to, you know, just show who she is. And she doesn't really care about anyone else.

*Nadia:* I agree with the idea that there's a link between the two and with that I believe that we can encourage women by having more activities for them to understand their own skill set and to figure out themselves in a sense.

*Faiza:* I think because there's a lot of stereotypes when it comes to femininity. And also when females go they know that they wouldn't be taken seriously to be a leader, because men are usually seen as higher than women. . . . So I think women know that they are going to face the consequences if they try to speak up.

*Jinani:* [When] your voice is heard like, not on TV or what not, like what you say and what you do can like influence people worldwide, but I feel like it does come with like lot of negatives . . . people might not agree with you and I feel like you might get a lot of hate and people might like try to put you down for what you do.

This exchange shows how girls made connections between confidence, visibility, and misogyny. Their references to women's 'skill sets', 'qualities', 'what they're capable of', and 'what they're good at' indicate that they did not see women as lacking capacity but as inhabiting cultures of visibility which require reflexive articulation of that capacity. Such visibility becomes a political end in itself (Banet-Weiser 2018, 23) and confident self-promotion a demonstration of equality achieved. But the girls also recognised the entwined relationship between feminism and misogyny and how this plays out in spaces of visibility. Faiza's reflection, 'women know that they are going to face the consequences if they try to speak up', exemplified their recognition that women's attempts to enter a masculinised field of power will inevitably invoke hostility; leadership's traditional domination by men, its underpinning by essentialist beliefs about men's fitness and right to inhabit it, its public visibility, and the political, financial, and cultural power it represents making it a ground-zero for the cultural misogyny identified by Banet-Weiser as the counterpart to women's increased claims to competence in spaces of power (2018, 137).

## THEY NEED TO BE ABLE TO CONTROL THAT CONFIDENCE (EVA)

Within the discussion groups, participants policed what they saw as transgressive or appropriate forms of confidence, negotiating a careful balance between self-promotion and attentiveness to context, between enhanced visibility and endorsed femininity. Their talk exemplified the encultured modes of development through which girls' maturation is marked under patriarchal cultures via their capacity to create and sustain successful social relationships (Gilligan 1992). In these contexts, confidence becomes a managed performance. Eva's contribution emphasises the performativity of a display that must be disciplined:

I was going to say confidence, but they need to be able to control that confidence into doing what's right rather than being too confident in themselves and then coming across a bit big.

The following contributions demonstrate ways in which girls experience these boundaries and find strategies for navigating them via amplification/ affirmation of one another's skills:

*Maryam:* So the fact that there's less female leaders it means that lots of people are not being able to see what females are actually capable of and, like, they're good. Like, how we said that it's easier to see someone else is good and then that's the reason why other females can't stand up and say about themselves that, yeah, we can do this as well as men.

*Serena:* Because you know yourself, sometimes you know yourself better than you know your friends, but I don't know, sometimes showing off doesn't feel right sometimes. It depends on who you are. . . . It depends, if you're one of those people who, like, you know, who likes to hear the compliments. Who, like, in a way quietly asks for them, or whether you are shy and don't want to be complimented because it gives you attention. It's kind of like bigging yourself up isn't it? . . . Yeah blowing your own trumpet.

The use of 'big' was a recurrent pattern across the groups in describing their reluctance to occupy positions of power and visibility, occurring more than fifty times. Making oneself small was, for the girls, a way of managing visibility, surveillance, and ultimately safety in climates hostile to women's power. For example, in southwest London, the following exchange showed Desta opting for a role of reduced visibility and a safer caring' role:

*Desta:* Yeah I don't really see myself as like a *leader,* leader, but like . . .

*Interviewer:* What's a *leader* leader?

*Desta:* Like someone who will guide people, or help people, I mean I would like to help people, but not like, it's not like very big, like I don't want to, I just want to be part of it and not like a leader. . . . I like helping people, just, like, I don't want to be like the centre of attention.

While 'bigging yourself up' represented a problematic challenge to endorsed feminine behaviours, and courted the dangers of visibility, affirmation and amplification strategies enabled girls to promote one another's visibility safely through endorsing friends' claims to leadership qualities. Such strategies have achieved growing prominence within media and professional feminisms (Cavalieri 2019; Eilperin, 2016; Peterson, Pearson, and Moria 2020) and they are also common in girls' social media peer engagements, where they manifest as complex codes of practice for 'liking' and commenting on one another's posts within participatory communities (Harris 2008; Hansen, 2019; Eek-Karlsson 2021; Rogers et al. 2021). Peer affirmation offers support for girls in navigating the visibility that 'confidence culture' demands of them (Harris 2004; Gill and Orgad 2017) and in countering the individualism inherent in popular feminism's address (Rottenberg 2014). Tempting though it is to celebrate such activity, however, it is important to recognise that it also constitutes a form of emotional labour falling on women, an element of the nurturing and communicative skill set ascribed to them in leadership roles (Chin 2007). It is also a gendered form of labour in digital economies: Laurie Ouellette and Julie Wilson (2011, 549) identify how some social media sites rely on the affective labour of peer-affirming engagements in sustaining interactivity in ways that not only may not prepare them for 'serious' or public forms of 'political activity' but emerge as a reworked form of the traditional casting of women as the 'invisible helpers' (McGee 2005, 1–14). Girls' discussions indicated how this kind of emotional labour constitutes a kind of shadow behavioural curriculum in schools to help them navigate classroom visibilities. In the pilot study, such affirmation was a prominent strategy which participants mobilised in their discussion of leadership and confidence in terms of themselves. Noting this, we included a question asking girls to describe leadership qualities in friends and to reflect on the experience of doing so in contrast with claiming such a quality in themselves, in subsequent focus groups. This example is from a

rural comprehensive school where girls describe leadership qualities they see
in their peers:

*Natasha:* She always listens to other people's ideas and she's not afraid to, like,
tell people that's what she thinks.

*Samantha:* She can almost tell people off if they are arguing with their ideas in
the group, if they're not considering other people's and tell them that you need
to listen to each other.

*Isabel:* She's very confident and, like, does have her own opinion, but then does
also, like, share stuff as well.

*Serena:* At the same time as taking in other people's ideas, she can reflect on
her own and change them and alter them and then make them better.

*Isabel:* It's just easier to speak about your friends and stuff.

*Serena:* Yeah it's easier to make them feel, you know, good about themselves
than feeling like you're just, you know, like, cocky.

In these contributions, in each case, a girl identified and affirmed a potentially risky leadership behaviour – but in a friend, rather than in herself.
These risky behaviours represented facets of confidence and behaviours
traditionally coded as masculine and thus likely to draw negative attention
to women: assertiveness; enforcing boundaries; giving opinions; influencing
the opinions of others. The final two contributions relate peer affirmation
directly to the management of their own visibility: reciprocity in affirming behaviours ensures the individual's strengths will in turn be rendered
visible.

Confidence thus emerges in girls' conceptions of leadership as a performed
demeanour attaching to women's leadership in particular and one that must
be appropriately managed and tempered with feminine behaviours. Writing on the female voice in public contexts, Deborah Cameron (2006, p. 16)
describes how, while men are judged for actions and achievements, the status
of women in the public eye is dependent on 'symbolic resources' such as
appearance,[2] demeanour, and speech and that women therefore pay forensic
attention to these. She argues that women's positioning within public life
can be understood through this public focus on symbolic resources, a focus
that men largely escape. Girls recognised the importance of developing
such resources in determining the ease with which they might navigate the
complex restrictions and conditions of female visibility that, as Anita Harris
(2004, 11) observes, normalise surveillance.

## SOMEONE WHO CAN SORT OF GET THE DICTUM
## OUT (NADIA)

Speaking was closely entwined with confidence in girls' discussions across research sites. Nadia (East Midlands) described a good leader as 'Someone who can sort of get the dictum out in a sense. Like, they can explain things well and they are really confident'. Kerry (Bradford) described the best way to go about making change as 'Speaking out . . . if you speak out hopefully then others will follow eventually'. Mary (Glasgow) extended the idea of confidence as both an attribute and a product of good leadership:

> I feel with leadership all the time you have to be confident of your own people. It could be, like, teachers, they would be confident of talking to kids. Or it could be, like, of Government, you have to be confident talking to people. So, I feel if you haven't confidence, it doesn't give other people confidence. So, when you're talking it probably makes them more nervous than you are.

All the girls recognised that confidence in the public sphere is closely associated with speaking modes that imply masculine forms of power (Walkerdine 1990; Cameron 2009). For example, Sarika (Cardiff) offered an understanding of women's current and historical exclusion:

> I think that women don't have as much of a voice as men might do, because, like, earlier . . . like, years and years ago I feel like women were kind of looked down on. So, and it's not completely changed yet, so that's probably why.

The girls' discussions also revealed how school curricula and classroom cultures shaped the possibilities for developing the kind of speaking they associated with confidence. For example, few participants felt comfortable talking in public, and only one class in one school was described by the girls as specifically promoting their speaking abilities. The importance of educational contexts in developing or suppressing particular kinds of confident speech is well attested: engagement in classroom debate is seen as a masculinised performance (Walkerdine 1990); it derives from historical associations of masculinity with rationality (Battersby 1988) from the development of which women have been traditionally excluded (Le Doeuff 2005). Cameron (2006) describes how

> In 21st Century English Speaking societies . . . leadership roles and the associated linguistic practices are, in theory, available to both sexes, but there remains both prejudice and internalised anxiety about the female voice in public contexts. (p. 6)

This prejudice and internalised anxiety is evident in classroom contexts where speaking behaviours, even those endorsed through curriculum or teacher approval, can militate against the maintenance of feminised identities and earn peer disapproval (Francis, Skelton, and Read 2010; Paule 2017). As Gonick (2003, 131) observes, making claims to speaking space within the classroom can be laden with social risk for girls. Meanwhile, boys' social discursive practices are built on their historical cultural advantage and work to help them develop valued modes of public speech. This is a persistent pattern: Swann and Gradol in a 1988 study find that boys are given more opportunities in school to develop 'the sorts of competitive speaking skills that are necessary for participation in many formal contexts' (137) while Judith Baxter's 2002 study of classroom talk shows how boys 'appear to be more powerfully positioned than girls within a range of classroom discourses' and that their ability to mobilise specific, gendered discursive practices offers them 'more opportunities than girls to constitute themselves as "effective" public speakers' (83).

Success and authority in public speaking are associated with privilege and class as well as gender (Fabricius 2000; Beal 2008; Tan et al. 2021). This is manifested in the United Kingdom in the negative bias attached to regional accents in contrast to a valorisation of received pronunciation – a bias that persists well into twenty-first century according to a recent Sutton Trust report, which finds that received pronunciation is 'the dominant accent in positions of authority' while 'regional, working class and minority-ethnic accents are heard less in some careers or positions of authority, reinforcing anxiety and marginalisation for those speakers' (suttontrust,com 2022no page ). Accent, of course, stands in for class, and as Julie Bettie (2014, 144) observes, schools are 'key shapers of one's perceptions of class difference' in an ongoing process. Girls at the independent school described how they altered their accents to fit in with the elite school setting as a part of the classed identity work they undertook:

*Darryl:* I change my accent, from when I'm at home. I'm a lot, well, I'm much more well-spoken. . . . I have, like, the worst accent possible.

*Alicia:* I think that's the same that happened to me. I remember doing that even when I was younger, I changed because my school friends . . . were, like, from different backgrounds, so I changed. I changed my accent.

However, it is not just accent that conveys authority in public space, but familiarity with rhetorical modes of formal debate (Kay 2020). In a south-coast comprehensive serving a largely middle-class local population, girls described how they were rehearsed in these modes in the context of their lessons. The participants here reflected the majority of the school's cohort; all were white and spoke with the received pronunciation associated with privilege:

*Interviewer:* So does there tend to be debate, do people argue with each other?

*Rachel:* Definitely. But we all kind of learn from it and I think that's really important.

*Interviewer:* How do you feel when you offer an idea in class and somebody disagrees with it?

*Bea:* Um well it doesn't really knock you down, but you sort of think about it, um maybe their opinion is the opinion that could be right. But then again there's not really a right answer.

*Interviewer:* How do you respond when somebody disagrees with you in a debate situation?

*Laura:* Well you come back saying something else that sort of . . .

*Bea:* I was going to say that yeah.

*Rachel:* Well, it's when we have debates, it's just funny, because I feel like you kind of contradict each other and then you're like, really both of you are getting really passionate about it and it doesn't cause arguments most of the time, it's just you walk out of the classroom and you think you know your opinions were great, like that's what, you learn from other people, I don't think that should make . . .

*Interviewer:* It's very much the mode of governing in this country, you see the Houses of Parliament. Do all of you feel comfortable in that mode, that arguing?

*Sophie:* I think it depends on the subject and how confident you are yourself on knowing that subject and if you don't know your points or you don't really know what they're going to come back and say to you, then I feel like it can knock your balance a little bit. *Laura nods vigorously.*

These girls' comfort with debating, their claims to confidence in the face of disagreement, prompted the interviewer to make the link with debate conventions in the UK government, conventions which are 'defined by the norms, values and linguistic practices of middle-class men' (Kay 2020, 154). Given the continuing importance of such formal modes of speech in public life, the development of speaking skills as a part of curriculum specifications in the United Kingdom is unsurprising. There is some divergence across the regions of statutory requirement: in England, the National Curriculum for the Teaching of English (2014) and in Scotland, Education Scotland (2016) both specify the teaching of formal debate; The Welsh Government's Curriculum for Wales (2016) specifies debate as an example of speaking skills development but does not mandate it. Education Scotland also recommends that 'some young people may also be given the opportunity to be selected for leadership opportunities which is an ideal context to use presentation skills' – although it does not specify which young people should be selected for such opportunities. This omission is important because it elides ways that enabling student 'voice' in schools can 'act as a practice that separates those with privileged voices from those who do not have access to the capital that voice offers and represents' (Finneran, Mayes and Black 2023, 2), exacerbating existing inequalities of access to influence. It was not between the three countries that we saw the biggest difference in claims to confidence in speaking but between the positions of girls along axes of race and class, as well as gender.

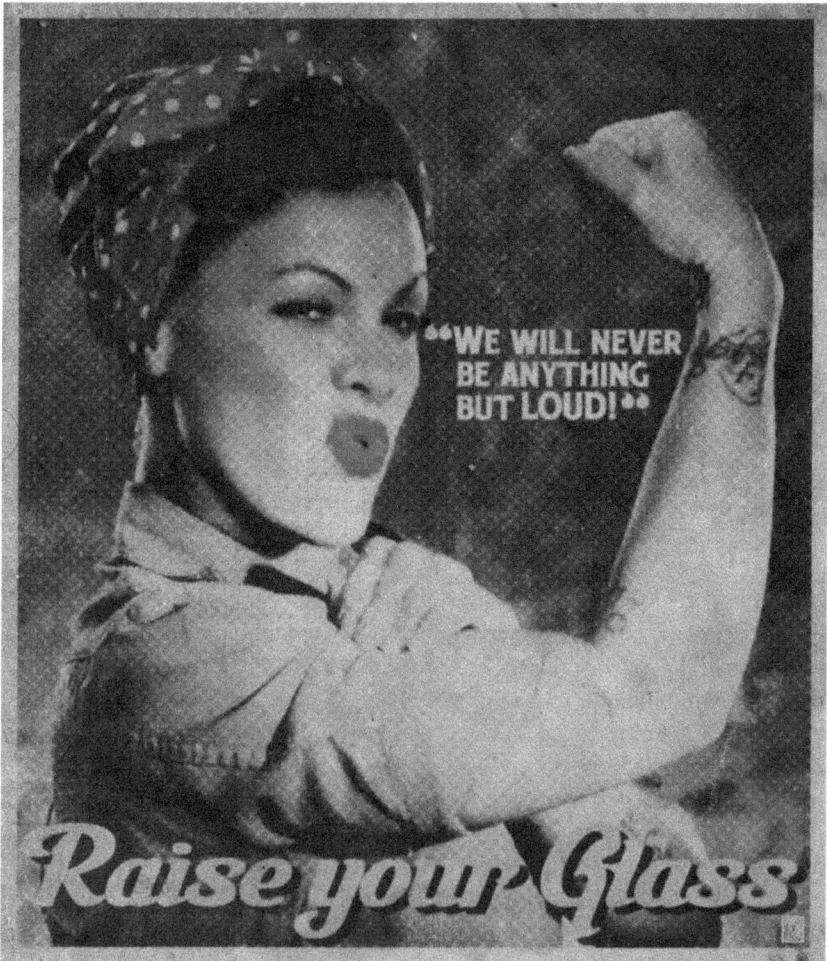

**Figure 1.1    Image of American Singer Pink Found Online by a Participant.**

The image of iconic singer Pink found online during and shared by a participant during our group interviews was particularly interesting to us in its celebration and containment of voice in specific contexts (figure 1.1). Pink (Alecia Beth
Moore) is posed as the iconic Rosie the Riveter, an American figure from the Second World War exhorting women's participation in the workforce, specifically
in the blue-collar manufacturing sector. Although the song ('Raise Your Glass')
it advertises is not nostalgic, the image draws on a cultural figure from the past.
It is hard to think of a contemporary popular image available to girls that represents working-class womanhood. The image was hugely popular in its time and
has since been evoked – not uncontroversially – in a range of feminist contexts,
including by other figures admired by participants, such as Beyoncé, Michelle
Obama, and Hillary Clinton, and in a teen girls' mural of Malala Yousafzai (Du
Plooy 2021). Pink, reported to be the most played female artist of the twenty-first
century (BBC News 2021), is a cultural figure who represents nonconformity and
activism for young women; her song 'Raise Your Glass' specifically celebrates
the pleasures of loudness among 'underdogs' and the 'nitty-gritty'. The poster
includes the line 'we will never be anything but loud'. The image is indicative of
ways in which girls are exhorted to give voice, to take up aural space, but our data
suggests that girls' experience of doing so – especially the working-class girls of
whom Rosie is a figurative antecedent – are constrained in terms of the 'voice'
available to them. Pink's evocation of Rosie in this image can be seen as a kind
of citation feminism – the 'practice of referencing popular feminine and female
emblems as an intergenerational expression of women's solidarity' (Vesey 2018,
73); however, it also draws attention to ways in which women's power and voice
are contained within specific contexts – whether mobilised for a war effort or
evoked in popular commodity feminisms.

## AND SHE LIKES TAKING TOO MUCH (TOYA)

While the middle-class girls quoted above described their pleasures in debate,
for Black girls and working-class girls, speaking up in assertive ways can be
perceived as aggression, as transgressing endorsed femininities, and as a threat
to authority (Morris 2007: Currie et al. 2007; Tyler 2008; Eagleton 2017).
Demonstrating 'voice', for them, can compound other ways in which they are
perceived as not conforming to ideals of middle-class femininity (; Malveaux
2015). The experiences described by participants underscored the limits of
empowerment discourses exhorting girls to voice because such exhortations
are, as Nicola Gavey (2012, 719) describes, 'untethered to the situation of their
lives or the meanings ascribed to them, their bodies, and actions'. Our focus
groups revealed girls being silenced in three distinct ways – through racialised

labelling as aggressive, through status-based silencing of working-class girls of colour in care, and through Islamophobic stereotyping.

Girls we interviewed in the Care sector had difficulty in describing formal or learning occasions on which they were encouraged to develop speaking or given opportunities to be heard. Instead, their examples focused on arguments with teachers and responding to peer aggression. 'Looked after' girls experience 'contested vulnerability', where they are infantilised by labels and interventions which presume their deficiency (Ellis 2018). This compounds their negative social status. The 'looked after' girls we spoke to were of Black British and South East Asian heritage; they reported being ignored, silenced, or being punished when they did speak up – this was often in the cause of protesting against what they saw as unfairness. In one instance, a girl described her experience of protesting a teacher's tardiness:

> *Susan:* Um, you know what? When you do become, like, when we got late for the, when we go to, like, school or college, they always say 'Why are you late?' They ask the question, right, 'Why are you late?' And when the teacher comes in late, they don't care, because yesterday in my maths class, my teacher didn't come for half an hour. We were waiting for him and then we were just like 'Where is he, where is he?' He came and I said, 'Sir, why are you late?' because we were waiting, and he was like, 'Don't talk.'

Another protested the mispronunciation of her name:

> *Denise:* And he was like, 'Who do you think you are?' and I was like, 'Sir, that's not nice,' and he goes, 'If you think that's not nice then you can get out of the classroom,' and I did. I left.

The 'who do you think you are?' and 'don't talk' responses to girls' speaking out about what they experienced as unfairness in the behaviours of those with power over them underscore the attachment of allowable 'voice' to acceptable bodies. 'Who do you think you are?' is a rhetorical question; in unequal power relations, such questions are problematic in that the anticipation that they will not be answered reinforces the hierarchy between the speaker and the addressed. Further, they can be deployed as a means of veiling an unsayable premise that is nonetheless understood by both parties (Frank 1990, 724) – here, that girls like her should not speak as though they inhabited more powerful bodies. The exacerbation of inequality experienced by these girls in the care sector was marked.

Bodies are signifiers of status, and thus of the right to speak and be heard. As Mikhail Karikis argues, conceptualising human speech 'without taking into account the body that produces it . . . undervalues the embodied "who" that speech emanates from' (2015, 79). In the exhortations to voice prevalent in popular confidence discourses addressing girls, that 'embodied who' is invisible beyond being gendered. Its classed and raced elements are missing, and such omission elides the silencing and invisibility of some while conferring the right to speech and visibility to others – those privileged bodies from which assertiveness is recognised as the expression of authority rather than resistance.

Black participants in a North London school recognised and lauded their own and their peers' confidence in speaking, but also recognised that this could be perceived as problematic. They described how they felt silenced by wider culture in the following exchange:

*Ada:* Oh she can talk! She knows how to get her point straight, like, she's a good public speaker and she's good at getting people involved.

*Tani:* She could be a good lawyer.

*Ada:* A good lawyer.

*Toya:* And she likes talking too much.

*Ada:* She's the one who talks too much, she talks to the . . .

*Tani:* . . . is honest, a little bit too honest, she'll say the honesty, making it sound, like, rude.

*Ada:* She's too rude.

*Fara:* I think that's because most of us are, like, if I go back to my first point . . . just because you don't know my story, it don't mean I have no voice. I believe because most women don't actually speak out loud about what's happened to them and they keep to themselves. Men believe we don't have a voice at all, men believe that we are just quiet and that we don't have no power to take over the country. But to me I feel like just because we're not speaking don't mean that you can do a lot of things outside.

The nature of the voice made possible within popular feminisms is one of optimism: it is that of the 'happy, confident girl', emanating from a default white, privileged body (Shields Dobson & Kanai 2018, 13), while the silencing of girls across political and media spheres intensifies along intersectional axes. Working class and Black participants shared the experience of their speaking out being perceived as 'too much', as inappropriately 'rude' rather than confident, as aggressive rather than self-assertive. This is not just because they did not have the 'right' kind of voice – accents in this group were 'Black London', a regional variation prominent in public consciousness and tied to location, race, and class (Kerswill 2013; Drummond 2017), but because 'Black girls' agency has been treated primarily as a social problem, rather than a strength' (Taft 2020, 4). One of the most frequently admired female leaders among all participants was former US First Lady, Michelle Obama. It was Black participants, however, who specifically valued her as representing the possibilities for Black women's voice:

> *Toya:* Because she knows how to talk. Because I watch her and she's like, 'I'm a Black woman, I'm here talking to you here, you can make a change'. That was quality, when she was talking so much, she was telling them to make a change and she was talking about how she was going in university and now she's married to the President of America. Adding to that as well, like she's a Black woman and in society that isn't as big as a white man, and so I think that makes, like, whatever she says and, like, her views which are all really positive, it makes a bigger impact on people, because it just shows that someone who came from a background or was born as a minority, can have that opportunity to be, like, in the spotlight and make in a good way, I think that makes her be a leader.

Anticipation of not being heard can contribute to a reduced perception of being valued and of having agency in contexts where gendered hierarchies are entrenched; these perceptions intensify with exclusion along intersectional axes. Such anticipation can reinforce power imbalances (Muragishi et al. 2022), as repeated experiences of negative cues increase vigilance and awareness of exclusion (; Steele, Spencer and Aronoson 2002; Murphy and Taylor 2012). Our Black participants' experiences of not being heard shaped ways in which they anticipated their own voices being perceived and in which they sought to regulate others' speaking. As Tani described:

> Because you (the leader) have more power than them yeah and, like, you're here and they're there and, like, you're being rude to them, but it makes them feel tinier, it makes them feel horrible. Because you have way more power you can do anything you want.

For girls in a Muslim faith school, claims to voice were framed within a wider awareness that Western stereotypes see them as silenced by their religion (Janmohamed 2016), a stereotype that they were keen to dispel. Similarly to young Muslim women in Sanghera and Thapar-Björkert's (2007) study, they saw their faith as supporting women in negotiating between the demands of public and private roles in their desires to effect change. They distinguished religion from culture, locating oppressive effects in the latter, and pointed out the historical role of religions in general, not just Islam, in limiting women's public roles:

*Nadia:* In my opinion rather than it be religious, I think it's more of a cultural thing. It slowly is starting, slowly like, it is slowly changing, but obviously change is a bit slow.

*Shamina:* I feel just really, it's a stereotype as well, but also in religion, some religions it's not that they prevent you from being a leader,

*Nadia:* I think some religions they usually say that it's usually a man's position to be outside of the house and doing stuff there and usually a woman will just be inside the house and looking after kids and that sort of thing. So, I think, it's just how the standards have just been set in here, so it's just people, people find it weird if a woman tried to do something that wasn't intended for them to do.

Harris (2004, 141) draws attention to ways that, in girl empowerment programmes, issues of voice and silence can be overly psychologised and homogenised, while socio-economic inequities are ignored. She draws attention to 'class, race and culture' needing to 'emerge as issues in young women's experiences of being heard'. Participants recognised that being heard on their own terms, about their own experiences of exclusion and hopes for the future, is intrinsic to their having 'voice'. Amanda, whose family settled in the United Kingdom from Ethiopia, drew our attention to the relative freedom to speak she felt in the United Kingdom, and reflected that the cornerstone of leadership was being heard:

And like your voice is heard, because like I said like in some places it's very hard to speak up without being targeted in, like, society and the fact that we can speak in here, in this country, it gives us an advantage and not only that but we have people that will listen. Obviously, if, for example, I was to become a president, you know how, like, presidents always have like speeches and they go to parliament and they talk, loads of people all over the world, it doesn't have to be only in this country, but online, like on TV, you are watched everywhere and your voice is heard. . . . Even though it might come with negatives as like your opinion might be mean and stuff like that, but all in all, at least you are heard and that is the most important thing.

It was not surprising, therefore, that 'listening' emerged as a key trait for leaders among participants across the groups.

## SHE'S QUITE CONFIDENT AND SHE'S A GOOD LISTENER (LIZZY)

The next most commonly mentioned attribute for leadership described by participants was that of listening. Discourses of listening attached to gender and to power in the public imaginary present a complex interweaving of authority, gender, and inclusion, and participants' discussions reflected this. The woman as 'good listener' is a persistent historic trope (Briton & Hall 1995; Szameitat et al. 2015), one that has been dated back to ancient myth informing European civilisation by Mary Beard (2017a). Historically in the United Kingdom, 'listening' is a common theme in the conduct literature addressing young women in particular (Dahmer 2016): for example, John Bennett's *Letters to a Young Lady* (1795 n.p.) reminds the young female reader that 'nature has given you *two* ears, and only *one* tongue'. It even appears in proto-feminist Mary Wollstonecraft's (1787) guide to educating daughters. Twentieth-century magazines frequently gave advice to women on being a 'good listener' , and the trope persists into the twenty-first century in popular media representations of evolutionary biology and neuroscience – for example, a *Daily Mail* (Greenaway 2014) article headlined 'Women are better listeners, study says' – in ways that reanimate and reinforce traditional gender hierarchies (Hasinoff 2009; Pickersgill 2013).

While subordinated listening is lauded in traditional models of femininity, 'not-listening' appears as a masculinised trait and a performance of domination (Solnit 2012) – for example, it circulates online in the popular neologism of 'mansplaining' (McClintock 2016). Modes and performances of listening/ not listening can thus be both indicative and constitutive of gender hierarchy (Pratto et al. 1994; Santoro and Markus 2021). Not-listening, for the girls, emerged not only as a masculine trait but one typical of elite, unrepresentative leaderships. Failure to listen was described by participants as a significant marker of bad leadership both in their local experiences and in the public figures they drew on, and these were exclusively men. For example, Susan described how

> Near my house there was, like, leader in a group, but he always thinks because his ideas are more better and really good because he's a leader of the group. But at the end, everyone left the group, because he didn't work out, because he doesn't listen to other people. He just think oh my, because I am the leader you have to listen to me, but it's not that, because the leadership is you have to understand other people and you have to listen to other people, so to make more better around you, so yeah. . . . It's not about showing off, it's about understanding other people. . . . You have to understand the people, that's what a leader is.

Moving from the local to the global, Laura found that former American president Donald Trump, who at the time of writing was found guilty of thirty-four counts of falsifying business records yet still running as a Republican presidential candidate, 'doesn't really seem to interact as much, like, with people or a wider range of people. He's more just his group or the people he wants to represent, instead of the whole country that he's representing that he should be looking after.' Rachel made a similar complaint of Rishi Sunak (UK prime minister at the time of interview):

He's pulled out of the Climate Change and that's not really, like, that's a big change that a lot of people want to make and he's not really helping, and he's not asking other people. Like he's not taking people's opinions really. So, he's only representing the interests of a particular group, not of everybody, which is going back to the first thing about being representative.

The kind of listening participants saw as essential to leadership was not the traditional, subordinated feminine performance that exists in a causal opposition to popular discourses of 'voice' addressing girls, but rather an active means of engaging central to their ideas of representative, ethical leadership. Listening, for them, was an attentiveness to the needs and views of others. As such, it offered new dimensions to the confidence they deemed necessary to leadership: there must be confidence that the leader's actions are representative; the leader is then not just a performer of confidence, but a figure of confidence-as-trust and a receiver of confidences as disclosures of vulnerability, as the exchange between girls in a rural comprehensive illustrates:

*Chloe:* She's like really good at listening and will always like think about your needs as well as their own and also they also put responsibility on you like with their trust.

*Lizzy:* She's quite confident and she's a good listener.

*Penny:* Very, very confident and talks to everyone.

*Bella:* Yeah, listening and making, going in the right direction.

*Dawn:* Confident.

*Anna:* Like listens and can give advice.

*Amy:* Like she's able to give really good advice and she makes me laugh all the time. She always, like, considers my opinion and if I'm worried about something. She knows when something's wrong or right so she can accept the atmosphere.

*Chloe:* Because you see it in other people because you're listening to them and it's how they react with you whereas when you're reacting, it's just you, it's just you doing something, so you don't necessarily evaluate how you deal with situations.

In their descriptions of the local leaders they named, such as teachers, the same theme was evident: those who held direct power over their daily lives were judged according to their ability to listen, as in this exchange:

> *Laura:* Teachers don't understand that children are, like, now, because all the teachers have these rules and stuff, but they don't understand what the children really want or need to learn properly.

> *Diana:* That is coming again to what we were saying earlier about do you really represent, do you really understand what the issues are for people that you are representing?

> *Rachel:* And also, teachers I feel like they can say oh yeah well I was a student too, but it's different because obviously the times have changed.

> *Shameem:* I think you'd go to like the Head of this school and then tell him what you want as a change and then hopefully because he's a good leader, he should listen.

Girls at a Muslim faith school in the Midlands opened their discussion with similar views:

> *Faiza:* Someone who understands, like, different people, so like, people who come from, like, poorer backgrounds, or richer backgrounds, so someone who understands how they feel.

> *Inaya:* I think a good leader is someone who makes everybody heard, so like a leader, they are leading a team and they make sure that they're all . . .

> *Shamina:* I think a good listener, so something similar to what they said, like if they listen to everyone, everyone should have a chance to give their ideas and the person should consider all of them.

Rather than a performance of demure passivity, such 'listening' is a means of affirming and including others' views with the aim of meeting their needs, and thus a means of balancing hierarchies (Bodie 2012; Fischer 2013; Parks 2018). For participants, listening was a step towards an inclusive 'speaking for', which they saw as an essential characteristic of good leadership.

A commitment to inclusivity and equality has often been identified as a key concern of youth, but also as utopianism,[3] a temporary stage and political rite-of-passage (Broome 1990; ; Harrington and Dillahunt 2021; Piispa and Kiilakoski 2022). Girls' focus on listening does not just demonstrate youthful idealism, however: it resonates with shifts in wider public discourse where inclusivity is increasingly seen as central to economic flourishing. As the neoliberal project is recognised as failing to deliver economic prosperity, as creating social instability, and as failing to resolve environmental challenges, there are calls for a more 'inclusive capitalism' to address these failings (Randa 2022; de Jong 2021). This requires alternative, post-heroic leadership models of which listening, empathy, and valuing different viewpoints are defining characteristics (Billing & Alvesson 2000; Kelan and Wratil 2018; Pullen and Vachhani 2021); meanwhile, relational leadership models are more in demand in increasingly digitised and service-orientated economies in the post-industrial West (Enderstein 2018, 3). In these economic contexts, listening as a valued leadership behaviour has emerged in popular and corporate discourse since the early 2000s as a feature of the so-called 'woman's advantage,' for example, enabling Hillary Clinton to claim that women are better listeners and therefore better leaders in an interview for a best-selling book on women in politics (Newton Small 2016).

Listening becomes particularly prominent in the mass media during times of crisis as a key element of feminised, ethical decision-making: this was observed during the global financial crisis of 2008 (Elliott & Stead 2018) and, as will be discussed in detail in chapter 5, during the 2020 pandemic in representations of women leaders in both corporate and political contexts (Alcadipani 2020). Typical examples include a story in *The Guardian* (Dudman 2020 n.p.) with the headline, 'Female leaders make a real difference. Covid may be the proof', while a BBC News (Goswami 2022 n.p.) feature asked, 'Have female CEOs coped better with Covid than men?', a piece in which women corporate leaders agree on the existence of a 'female playbook' of leadership skills that includes 'championing empathy' and 'upping communication skills' as opposed to the 'combative, individualistic and cut slightly macho' expectations of male leaders. Girls drew on such media discourses in their discussion of leadership in the post-pandemic interviews: for example, our Glasgow participants reproduced the oppositional gendered tropes in their descriptions of Boris Johnson as an irresponsible leader and Nicola Sturgeon as caring:

*Ruth:* Boris Johnson was obviously the Prime Minister at the time and he was opening the UK back up, but she was like no, we're staying in lockdown.

*Tamsin:* She was trying to protect. . . . She was trying to prevent us trying to get more sick.

Coverage of women leaders such as New Zealand's female prime minister, Jacinda Ardern, who became a public icon for empathetic leadership (Edmondson Chamorro-Premuzic 2021; MacKenzie & Garavan 2023) were popularly cast in binary, feminised opposition to Donald Trump and Boris Johnson's ego-driven, macho leadership in the popular press and across social media (Johnson 2022; Nerlich 2022; García-Beaudoux 2023).[4] Among participants in a Muslim school, Ardern was also named as a good leader for her ethical response to Islamophobic terrorism (the Christchurch bombing).

> *Zainab:* Yeah, I think the President of New Zealand, she's a female and she's made such a huge change in New Zealand like I remember there was an attack in a Mosque in 2018 and she even wore a hijab for, like, two weeks. So, she definitely wanted to create a good change and she felt really apologetic of all the things that happened back then. So, she has all the characteristics of being a good leader and she's humble and she's kind and she's made New Zealand economy . . . and she's also creating New Zealand to be stronger too.

Here, Zainab is reproducing the wider media narrative associating feminised leadership, inclusivity, and economic prosperity. However, while women leaders deploying these skills enjoyed particular prominence during the pandemic, their subordinate status is underscored in the 'glass cliff' phenomenon, in which women leaders and the skills attributed to them are valued in times of crisis, while preferences for male leaders are restored in recovery/prosperity (Bruckmüller and Branscombe 2010). As a *Forbes* article put it: Data Shows Women Make Better Leaders. Who Cares? (2021). Girls' prioritising of listening as an attribute of effective leadership thus taps into and recirculates wider discourses of gender and power in which the feminised leadership skill of empathetic communication is prominent. While it is tempting to applaud this as a challenge to phallocentric models of leadership, it also plays into a gendered complementarity which reinforces gender stereotypes and patriarchal divisions of labour, transforming emotional labour into capital (Enderstein 2018).

## YOU HAVE TO FEEL IT'S SOMETHING YOU'RE COMPETENT TO DO (CANDACE)

While there was a marked similarity across the focus groups in the discursive elements on which girls drew in imagining leadership, when describing their experiences there was more divergence, notably along axes of privilege as we saw in their accounts of 'speaking' opportunities. If prevailing discourses present a 'shared typical', turning to a focus on experience can offer perspectives on particularity, enabling understanding of how experience can both 'be rooted in particular prevailing forms and trends' (McIntosh & Wright 2019, 449), and 'occur within and reflect a variety of socially and discursively determined practices' (Scott 1992, 34).

Before we explore the divergence of girls' experiences, it is important to note that when we specifically asked about their leadership experience, the majority of participants denied having any. However, when we changed the vocabulary to ask what experience they had of being *responsible* for something or of being a decision-maker, we got a different range of answers. Almost every girl claimed some form of domestic responsibility – this included household chores, care of younger siblings, supervising homework of siblings, shopping, and budgeting. Some also reported emotional responsibility, when they had been assigned an explicit role for keeping a family member happy or for making sure everyone was looked after at a family event. Wider economic discourse has traditionally failed to recognise domestic labour as productive work (Folbre 1991), and this translates into leadership vocabularies that do not enable girls to frame their experiences as meaningful, in the same way that adult women might hesitate to claim household management as work experience. The limiting of girls' responsibility and decision-making to the domestic reflects the historic gendering of public and private spheres (Rendall 1999) and draws attention to the need to look 'outside of traditionally defined sites of leadership and in those places that are usually designated as informal and private' in seeking to understand young women's leadership (Lee-Koo and Pruitt 2020, 2). It has particular implications for girls' restricted opportunities to participate in public life under ongoing austerity, as we discuss below, and offers evidence that girls experience additional and significant barriers to participation in the public sphere to those already facing youth (Lipsitz 2013).

Our participants expressed the desire for more experience to build competence-based confidence, rather than the psychological labour required to create subjective self-esteem. Cadence observed that if you want to 'have, like, a large impact on, like, the world or something . . . you have to feel it's something you're competent to do.' Amina agreed, asking, 'Yeah, how do you get competent at stuff?' and Maya responded, 'Experience'. Girls made this distinction in their discussions on women leaders too – for example, Chioma described Alexandria Ocasio-Cortez, the youngest woman ever to be elected to the US House of Representatives, as someone who 'knows what she's talking about', saying that while 'there are some people that just go there and just talk and talk and talk for the sake of talking' Cortez 'knows, like, what she's doing, do you know what I mean?' In the final part of this chapter, we show how experience was unevenly distributed across the groups represented among participants, and also how the girls understood their own exclusion.

## I HAVEN'T BEEN TOLD WHAT IS INSIDE, WHAT HAPPENS ON THE INSIDE (SERENA)

Notable areas of difference between the groups were those of learning leadership skills and familiarity with institutions and routes to leadership roles.

These are recognisable as core elements of citizenship education, a subject that has been a focus of educational reform since the late twentieth century in the United Kingdom (McLaughlin 2000)), when it was found by the 1998 Crick Report to be 'an unfulfilled expectation in a national agenda', delivered through 'uncoordinated local initiatives which vary greatly in number, content and method'. Couched in urgent terms, the report recommends that citizenship education deliver:

> no less than a change in the political culture of this country both nationally and locally: for people to think of themselves as active citizens, willing, able and equipped to have an influence in public life and with the critical capacities to weigh evidence before speaking and acting; to build on and to extend radically to young people the best in existing traditions of community involvement and public service, and to make them individually confident in finding new forms of involvement and action among themselves. (7)

Crick's concern is not, however, a new one; Mary Wollstonecraft, for example, made the case for the value of citizenship education both to girls and to the wider nation thus:

> To render women truly useful members of society, I argue that they should be led, by having their undertakings cultivated on a large scale, to acquire a rational affection for their country, founded on knowledge, because it is obvious that we are little interested about what we do not understand. (264)

Citizenship education is now mandated in the distinct national curricula of England, Scotland, and Wales; it is a broad and contested terrain and is developed differently according to national political contexts and the kinds of subjects it wishes its education system to produce (Haste 2010). While there is not room here to offer a critical analysis of the citizenship promoted through curricular iterations in different UK nations, each includes knowledge of national and local democratic processes and institutions and recommends some kind of community engagement. Such curricula constitute a key apparatus for bringing into being particular kinds of young citizen subjects. Given the national importance attached to citizenship education and the specificity of content, in these varying specifications, it would be reasonable to anticipate some familiarity with aspects of public life, with the functions of power, and with routes to civic engagement among participants. However, girls across the three UK nations represented in the study expressed a lack of understanding of systems of government at both local and national levels and also of ways to engage with communities to effect change. For example, Serena, a Black student in North London, describes how

I don't know whether it's because I haven't got to that stage in my education yet, but I haven't been told barely anything about the Government. I haven't been told what is inside, what happens on the inside. What you see on the outside we know because it's on the news, but what happens on the inside, isn't talked about I feel. . . . I think they are drawing from. . . . Yeah because it's drawing from you know people that are relatives or friends of people that have already done it or you know they're already up high status so they, you know, don't care.

Serena's comment is interesting not only because it suggests a failure in formal citizenship education but also because it indicates her awareness that such education in itself may not provide access to corridors of power; that who you know might be more important than what you know, and that those in power roles are not concerned with the lack of access for girls like her. The ignorance of 'what happens on the inside' appears as a reverse image of the elite boys' schools such as Eton and Harrow that see their role as preparing boys for elite power roles and whose alumni dominate the British government's cabinet – the most powerful decision-making roles in the country (Epstein 20144).[5] Serena's sense of exclusion is not just produced by her feeling that the operations of power are obscure, but by a perception that such obscurity indicates a wider lack of concern about, or even hostility towards, her inclusion. Other girls described similar perceptions. For example, Becky, a working-class student in the rural West Country, stated that

If you're higher up, people are more likely to listen to you. So, like Michelle Obama she can speak her word and something will happen about it, but if one of us was to be like, we want this to happen, I don't, kind of how society works, you wouldn't really get, like, much recognition for it.

In Becky's statement, again we see her awareness that her ignorance of 'how society works' is tied to being 'one of us'; her lack of understanding of how to effect change is tied to her powerlessness to do so. Girls at a Bradford school expressed their awareness of the relationship between region, class, and power when discussing government:

*Callie:* If you take people from, like, posh areas, they'd have all this (opportunity) . . . because Bradford is not like a very posh place.

*Cadence:* Oxford, they're posh people, right?

*Amina:* We're not one of the best areas.

Understanding of the relationship between power, institutions and processes expressed in poorer schools and regions was mirrored in the participants interviewed at the girls' independent school. These girls were aware of their difference from, and advantage over, their state-educated peers. Comparing herself to girls who had just described the additional pressures they experienced when they transferred from state schools, Felicity said, 'I know that I've only ever been to a private school my entire life, I'm one of *those* people'. Darryl recognised that they were being prepared for future leadership through a range of activities provided by their school, describing how, 'We're all part of this bigger organisation that's national called the United Kingdom Youth Parliament. And basically, it's just, we have campaigns and we are just like working on them'.

They had regular access to local elected representatives and democratic institutions and were given advocacy training in a range of settings. Annabel told us that she was sent to that particular school in part because it would prepare her for (corporate) leadership: it is interesting that the location of the school in the United Kingdom was also important, as her family viewed the United Kingdom as context friendly to women's leadership:

> I'm actually, my grandparents own a business abroad and I'm, they want me to take over . . . which is why they sent me to this school partially . . . and because it's abroad they have different kind of views on leadership, like where we live in that country, the women aren't . . . they don't have very many leadership roles . . . well to be honest I lie actually, the Mayor is a female, but she got a lot of backlash from it and a lot of people don't respect her opinion and a lot of people take her to court over it actually.

It was not only the advantages and skills that Annabel's family expected her schooling to confer that are notable but also her perception that she was being educated in a national context that promotes gender-inclusive leadership. This is in stark contrast with Black and working-class girls' experiences of exclusion, elitism, and obfuscation of routes to power both in school and on a national stage.

This pattern of contrasting experiences among participants highlights ways in which discourses and mechanisms purporting to increase participation and power, such as national curriculum specifications, are in fact 'complicit with ongoing inequalities of access, resources and representation between students in schools and between schools' (Finneran, Mayes and Black 2023, 12). Writing in a US context, Wendy Smooth and Elaine Richardson (2019, 152) argue for the tailoring of citizenship education to recognise ways in which race, gender, and class shape Black girls' perceptions of themselves as non-leaders. The responses of participants in this study suggest a similar need to adapt curricular provision to intersectional gendered contexts across the United Kingdom: it is not only inconsistencies in delivering curriculum specifications that render routes to power a mystery to girls, but a failure to recognise that citizenship education itself needs to address structural barriers to leadership. In not doing so, it ultimately works against the aim of Crick report in producing citizens who are 'able and equipped to have an influence in public life' (QCA 1998, 7) and instead actively maintains barriers to girls developing such influence.

Where citizenship education was successfully tailored to their needs, it emerged strongly in the girls' discussions. Some state schools serving minoritised and disadvantaged populations were invested in preparing girls to participate in decision-making processes and leadership roles. This was not always successful: while some of the girls took pride in roles of responsibility and saw school councils as an important means of representation, others were frustrated with what they saw as the trivial nature of decisions school councils could make, such as allowing water bottles in lessons or making minor changes to school dress codes, when they wanted input on bigger issues such as adapting curriculum content to reflect their concerns about the climate crisis. One school in particular stood out, however, an all-girls Muslim faith school serving an impoverished, post-industrial catchment area in the East Midlands. Students described their school's provision of skills training, creation of formal decision-making roles for pupils, mechanisms for election, and learning how to mobilise their representatives to address issues important to them. They spoke with familiarity about processes and roles in terms of power, and these processes and roles resembled those of institutions outside of school:

*Zainab:* So this year we have like, there's lots of school councillors, so there's two from each class I think and they all have different roles, so this year we have like Head of Student Council and then a Treasurer, a Secretary, an Assistant and lots and lots of different roles and then we got to, like, vote who we think would be best for that role, which represents how we are democratic.

*Nadia:* So for last year what we did was each week we would give our ideas and if we did have anything for that week that the school council was in charge, then they would also expand on how they can help out, which roles they can take for that event, or that time period.

*Zainab:* So whichever class we're in, we ask them, like, what changes you would like in the school and what can we do to improve our school and make it better and then we go and deliver these ideas to the teachers.

In asking girls to identify roles and responsibilities in their schools that enable them to participate in its power structures, it is important to recognise that such roles themselves rarely afford equal opportunities or representation. As Finneran et al. (2023, 2) observe:

Students are not consistently or comprehensively afforded the opportunity to participate in decision-making about issues that affect them: rather, student voice has often exacerbated an uneven distribution of access to voice and influence. Student voice initiatives can provide contexts that recognise the voices who are already privileged.

Even in settings where *all* students might belong to groups marginalised in terms of broader representation in leadership, those students who are older, more popular, more articulate, or more academically successful are most likely to be given opportunities to participate in the power structures of a school (Silva 2002). In this school, however, girls who were outside these usually favoured categories described being chosen by teachers to undertake leadership roles. For example, Shamina (whose attendance record was poor) tells us how

> There was one time in one of our lessons when we were just doing separate group work in science and my teacher placed me forward to be in charge of our little group. But it was a bit nerve-wracking because I hadn't really been there for any of the lessons, so it was, I was a bit surprised. . . . Yeah I was a bit surprised that she would have chose me, but at the same time it was nice thinking that my teacher thought I had the skills to be a leader.

In this school, while confidence figured prominently, as it had in other sites, as a key leadership attribute, leadership was also framed by girls in terms of democracy and community responsibility in ways that were directly tied to their school experiences. In conversation with a teacher after the interviews, she described how it was a school priority to give girls tools to make change, because changes important to their democratic participation in the wider world were not otherwise going to be made.

## YES, THIS IS CORRECT (LIFE IN THE UK TEST 2024)

It is not only schools that can provide leadership development; community-based activities have traditionally provided opportunities for girls. While there is no unified theory or defined curriculum for girls' leadership education (Ely, Ibarra, and Kolb 2011; Eva et al. 2021) participation in such activities is frequently found to be a factor in the fostering of leadership skills such as decision-making, collaboration, and taking responsibility (Hancock, Dyk, and Jones 2012). However, opportunities for girls to engage in such activities have been drastically reduced. The implementation of neoliberal austerity economic policy in the United Kingdom from 2010 onwards has seen the closing down of youth services and privatisation of leisure spaces. The YMCA (2020) 'Out of Service Report' on local authority expenditure on youth services reports that in the decade between 2010 and 2020, more than 760 youth centres closed, and youth service cuts were made totalling over a billion pounds in real terms; this has had a profound impact on the opportunities for youth to engage with their communities. Harris (2008) describes how neoliberal policies of minimal state involvement in public life result in 'reduced participatory opportunities in the public sphere' for youth, undermining the development of 'collective and civic identifications'; for girls, this is particularly significant as without community activities, they are more likely to be confined to the home – unless they can afford privatised leisure activities (Hall 2019). This was reflected in our study, where girls reported limited opportunities to take part in activities and clubs outside of school that did not require payment. For example, Jill on the South Coast complained that a lack of suitable volunteers to help run her local youth club meant its closure, while in other areas, girls said opportunities outside of school were simply non-existent.

Exclusion from leadership development in girlhood should be considered particularly significant when one considers the age gap in women and men's interest in politics and the significantly later age at which women enter political leadership (Sanbonmatsu, Carroll, and Walsh 2009; Randall 2016; Fraileand Sanchez-Vitores 2020). Women are also more likely to emerge into leadership roles from backgrounds in community activism, rather than as career politicians (Cassell et al. 2006; Zaslow and Schoenberg 2012). The ongoing impact of austerity in communities is noteworthy as local activism is often gendered, with women more involved in local activism and community groups (Martin, Hanson and Fontaine 2007). Under extended austerity, then, generations of girls in the United Kingdom are losing opportunities to develop the community activism and leadership skills that would be their most likely route to leadership.

In the absence of youth clubs and community activities, involvement in extra-curricular sports emerged as the most likely opportunity for girls in the study to develop leadership skills: participants involved in such sports described taking responsibility for organisation, for coaching other players, for motivating peers, and for deploying players and deciding strategies. Sports also provided (alongside school councils) rare instances where girls had the experience of being elected or selected – routes to leadership more typical of men's careers than women leaders' 'emergent trajectory' (Cassell et al. 2006). Girls so elected described concern for feelings and awkwardness in competing against peers, but also surprise in the pleasure that winning gave them. Claire, her school team's rounders captain, described getting chosen:

The team chooses you, so they vote for you. . . . I mean, I wanted to get chose, but I felt a bit bad because obviously she wanted it as well, so it was kind of awkward . . . but they all said my name. . . . It felt quite nice actually.

Such opportunities, however, tend to depend on economic resources, whether at the school, community, or family level. As Collins (2004) found, while sport itself is a way of developing citizenship skills, poverty is core to exclusion from sport. We found girls' access to such extra-curricular activities as sports and music to be unevenly distributed across the groups represented among participants, broadly following socio-economic resources. Our findings echo those of a UK survey conducted by the World Association of Girl Guides and Girl Scouts with the University of Essex, which found that only girls in independent schools were likely to have any kind of identifiable leadership experience through enrichment activities (WAGGGS 2017). The normalisation of extra-curricular activities as an embellishment rather than a core of the school experience, and one that is dictated by economic resource, can be witnessed in its inclusion as an element in the 'Life in the UK' citizenship test trial. This test aims to establish candidates' familiarity with British culture and history and its questions are, in principle, based on assumptions and facts presumed to be common among UK citizens. Candidates, when faced with the statement: 'Many schools organise events to raise money for extra equipment or out-of-school activities', rather than select 'No, schools get money from the government', must choose, 'Yes, this is correct' (The UK Test 2024)[6]. The normalisation of unequal opportunity to develop citizenship is thus enshrined in the way citizenship itself is defined.

## CONCLUSION

Inviting girls to discuss leadership reveals how wider prevailing discourses shape their understanding of ways in which power is embodied and demonstrated in contemporary society. It reveals the distance between the notional 'girl' of neoliberal optimism and consumer feminisms and socially situated girls' perceptions of the exclusions and restrictions that shape their civic and political identities and aspirations. The dominance of 'confidence' discourse in particular is indicative of its successful permeation into girlhood subjectivities, and of how the longstanding focus on symbolic resources in women leaders is intensified through contemporary cultures of visibility and surveillance in girl-focused popular feminisms. It illustrates concerns that visibility has become a political end in itself, suggesting that a focus on symbolic resources and performance as essential leadership traits diminishes girls' critical political literacies because it locates responsibility for the development of such traits within the individual girl: even while recognising that hostile gender cultures are responsible, it fails to engage with the structural and economic causes of inequality.

Confidence discourse provides a frame for girls' conceptualisations of leadership that is both problematic and limiting. It is problematic in its elision of structural exclusions that intersect with gender, in notionally exhorting all girls to 'voice' while failing to recognise cultural hostility towards the speaking-out of girls with the 'wrong' voices emanating from the 'wrong' bodies. This discourse is tied to educational practice in the implementation of speaking and citizenship curricula that, while aiming to develop pupils' abilities to participate in public life, are not delivered consistently; nor do they recognise dimensions of gender, class, and race that shape pupils' capacities to develop the required skills to achieve those aims. Confidence discourse has to be stretched to accommodate girls' complex, ethical, and intersectionality-situated envisionings of leadership; for them, it must be more than performance/demeanour – it must be a receptive role. In girls' hands, confidence becomes a useful, multifaceted heuristic, compared with the single-dimensional, individualistic exhortations of confidence culture.

Girls' accounts of their opportunities to develop leadership skills reveal a disjuncture between 'the girl' as a highly visible totem of cultural and consumer optimism and as a future leader who will resolve inequality and save capitalism – and a failure to resource provision for girls. Curricular provision needs adapting to contexts across the United Kingdom, as in its current state, it fails to solve the mystery of power roles and institutions and fails to address structural barriers to leadership for girls. A lack of opportunities to develop leadership skills through community roles and activities, combined with a lack of familiarity with processes and institutions of power, is particularly significant for girls as it means their most likely routes to power disappear, and they are increasingly confined to domestic spheres. Neoliberal economic policies, then, paradoxically render less likely the realisation of the neoliberal ideal in the figure of the powerful girl. In the next chapter, we turn to the idea of the role model as neoliberalism's substitute for experience under austerity.

## NOTES

1. We examine the resources for girls produced by 'Ban Bossy', 'Lean In Girls', and 'The Female Lead' initiatives in chapter 4.

2. We discuss girls' attention to the importance of appearance for women leaders in chapter 3.

3. See chapter 4 for further discussion of utopianism in contexts of collective hope and individual aspiration.

4. We discuss the gendering of leadership in public discourse during the pandemic in chapter 5.

5. The success of these schools in engendering a hostile exclusivity was witnessed in 2022 when Eton pupils booed and shouted misogynist and racist slurs at a group of visiting state school girls ( Atkinson2022).

6. The test's questions are drawn from the Home Office (2023) publication *Life in the United Kingdom: A Guide for New Residents,* a book that has been a cornerstone of British immigration policy since its launch in 2005 (Brooks 2019, 22) and has been criticised for its propagation of a neoliberal model of citizenship relying on 'strategies of responsibility, empowerment and self-improvement' (Turner 2014, 332).

*Chapter 2*

# The Limits of Role Models
# and the Risks of Visibility

An absence of role models in girlhood is a popularly cited cause of the shortage of women in decision-making positions in adulthood. The power of leadership exists in a close relationship with public visibility, and this relationship is regularly foregrounded in adult interventions that seek to stimulate girls' leadership aspirations through the public pedagogy of role models. In this chapter, we explore the problematic nature of such popular solutions via a framework suggested by feminist critique of the 'fetishisation' of representation, by their media effects foundations, and by their alignment with neoliberal logics. We argue that role model solutions offer an overly simplistic view of girls' engagements with public figures and that they recognise neither the contemporary conditions of women's visibility nor how such conditions regulate girls' imaginings of power along axes of 'race' and class as well as gender.

As the gender imbalance in decision-making roles garners increasing attention in the public sphere, a lack of role models in girlhood is popularly identified as a key factor in the shortage of women leaders in adulthood (Pereira 2012; Fraser 2014; *BBC.co.uk* 2016; Warrell 2018). The prevalence of this way of thinking can be understood within the wider discursive positioning of the 'agentic girl' as an emblem of social mobility and change (McRobbie 2009; Switzer 2013; Paule 2019; Biressi 2018), and simultaneously as vulnerable to the influence of mass media (Gonick 2006; Gill 2007: Ringrose and Barajas 2011; Paule 2017; Mendick et al. 2018). Role model solutions addressing girls are, we argue, attempts to shape a specific element of the 'public pedagogy' of media texts (Giroux 2004). In their intervention into the relationship between girl audiences and representations of women, they seek to regulate the meaning-making and identity work that characterise girls' relationships with celebrity figures (Duits and van Romondt 2009, 43).

A range of high-profile projects, such as Sheryl Sandberg's (2014) 'Ban Bossy' and Dunn's (2023a) 'Lean In Girls' – the girl-orientated spin-offs from her 'Lean In' initiative in the United States – and Edwina Dunn's (2017) 'The Female Lead' here in the United Kingdom mobilise role models including celebrities and women from professional fields in popular campaigns that aim to stimulate girls' leadership ambitions. The concept of leadership itself and its traditionally individualist, authoritarian, and masculine connotations is not, in general, challenged within such campaigns; rather, their tendency is to encourage girls to function more successfully within its terms (Harris 2004). There is a vast array of similar initiatives and programmes (Banet-Weiser 2015; Biressi 2018) and it could be argued that they are needed; some studies suggest that access to role models plays a key part in the development of girls' leadership aspirations (Salmond and Fleshman 2010; Archard 2012; Wolbrecht and Campbell 2017), while national and international surveys find that girls struggle to name female leaders they admire (Estrada, García-Ael, and Martorell 2015; Girlguiding 2018).

While we would not wish for even fewer leading women in the public eye, popular role-model solutions are often based on simplistic ideas of gender-matching, in which the complex relationships that young people have with media figures are reduced to an assumption that exposure will lead to imitation. There has been some ground-breaking work investigating the ways in which engagement with celebrities helps shape the formation of youth aspirations (Mendick et al. 2018) and some exploration of girls' discursive construction of leadership in educational contexts (Shinew and Jones 2005; Baxter 2006). However, there remains a need to interrogate popular claims that 'inspirational' role models offered to girls have a transformative, enabling effect on leadership aspirations.

Our analysis here disrupts some assumptions inherent in claims about the impact of role models by exploring the complexity of girls' engagements with women in the public eye. We demonstrate ways in which role models may be both 'sites of struggle' (Mendick et al. 2018, 13) and sites of 'visual media governmentality' that Angela McRobbie identifies as regulatory spaces where 'the benchmarks and boundaries of female success are established' (2013, 122). We offer an analysis which attends to the meanings girls attach to the women leaders they admire and to how these meanings are shaped both by wider gendered discourses and by the inequalities that girls experience along intersectional axes. We begin by arguing for the problematic nature of role model solutions in terms of their reliance on representation, their conservative and simplistic assumptions of media effects, and their mobilisation of neoliberal tenets. We then turn to data from our 'Girls, Leadership, and Women in the Public Eye' project to show how girls themselves respond to role models available to them in media contexts.

## THE REPRESENTATION PROBLEM

The under-representation of women in decision-making roles is identified globally as an issue of pressing significance (European Commission 2018; European Women's Lobby 2018; World Economic Forum 2023). There exists a range of high-profile initiatives and data-gathering organisations across political and corporate sectors with a focus on the proportion of women leaders. Example initiatives in the United Kingdom include 50:50 Parliament (https://5050parliament.co.uk/) and the Forbes 30 per cent Club (https://30percentclub.org/). Internationally, bodies such as the World Economic Forum (20233) and United Nations Women (2020) collect data on women in roles of local and national decision-making but do not cross-reference this with other data such as demographics of class and race. Gender pay gap reports, compulsory since 2017 in the United Kingdom (Cabinet Office 2022), again focus on gender inequality as a single axis, while media responses to published reports such as the BBC's (BBC.co.uk 2017) focus on gender and earnings at the top (Nielsen 2019). Media and political attention to this issue have helped bring about what Lorna Finlayson (2018, 793) describes as a fetishisation of representation, whereby a concern with the presence of women in leading roles is elevated to be the most prominent of concerns about gender inequalities. There is a case that a combination of scarcity plus power would make roles of influence those that women should seek to occupy first, and nobody wishes to align themselves with 'defenders of the sexist establishment by attacking efforts to combat the status quo' (777). However, as Finlayson argues, a focus on representation in terms of numbers alone is problematic in three ways: First, it is often based on an assumption that having more women represented in the most powerful and high-profile roles is indicative of greater equality more generally in an organisation or society. Further, it can be assumed that representation is productive of such equality, via what has been termed 'trickle-down' feminism (Jaffe 2013), as women with the most powerful roles are assumed to create conditions in which more women will flourish. Finally, representation-based solutions are often presented as constitutive of equality in themselves.

Such simple counting of women neglects other key relations of domination and exclusion, such as class and race. Encouraging more already-privileged women to 'lean in' to top leadership roles could lead to a scenario of improved representation in percentage terms that does little to improve the general status of women, while at the same time providing statistics that suggest progress – what Anne-Marie Enderstein (2018, 2) describes as 'an equality mirage'. Further, implicit in concerns regarding the persistent under-representation of women in top professions is an approval of the competition and individualism required to achieve such roles (Cawston 2016). Catherine

Rottenberg (2018) sees the corporate feminism of popular campaigns such as Sheryl Sandberg's *Lean In* (2013) as the birthplace of neoliberal feminist subjectivity, in which a woman recognises gendered inequality but commits to her own individual economic advancement in response rather than to collective action and social reform.

Inherent in the popular calls for more women leaders is an uncritical reproduction of leadership itself in its most androcentric political and corporate forms. Despite a growth in business fields of post-heroic models that emphasise relational and collaborative leadership skills (Storberg-Walker and Haber-Curran 2017; Enderstein 2018), leadership in the popular imaginary is based on values of masculinity (Koenig et al. 2011), including masculine definitions of femininity (Calás and Smircich 1991; Bierema 2017). We can see these values in discourses of the heroic, strong individual and the complementary empathic communicator (Ford 2016; Adamson 2017; Enderstein 2018). As we argue in chapter 4, popular girls' leadership initiatives, while couched in terms of empowerment, work to stabilise the masculinist and corporate values and structures that subjugate and disempower women.

Rather than focus on the existence and number of role models, here we offer a consideration of the *conditions of visibility* for women in the public eye and what their presence might mean for girls. We are not only interested in interrogating the assumptions underpinning role model solutions themselves; by examining the nature of girls' engagements with highly visible women, our findings illuminate how girls themselves intuit the limits of representation as a measure of equality within these contexts.

## THE ROLE MODEL SOLUTION

The idea of the inspiring role model and the focus on women in leadership roles are closely entwined, as both assume that increased visibility of women in top positions will encourage others to follow suit (Finlayson 2018). This assumption is not without evidence; the functions of role models in the formation of youth identities and aspirations have been explored in audience and educational domains (Jung 1986; Nauta and Kokaly 2001; Gauntlett 2002; Read 2011; Allen and Mendick 2012; Jackson and Vares 2016), while the idea of the importance of leadership role models for women has gained traction both in corporate arenas (see, for example: Fraser 2014; Pereira 2012; Taylor et al. 2011) and in organisational and management studies (Singh et al. 2006; Hoyt and Simon 2011; Simon and Hoyt 2013; Adamson and Kelan 2018; Latu et al. 2013, 2019). A range of media, institutional, and academic texts thus contribute to the production of social knowledge about the value of leadership role models to girls and women and the ways in which they may operate. Given its popularity, it is surprising that as a concept the role model remains somewhat ambiguous beyond being 'someone to look up to' (Gauntlett 2002, 211). Its operations become yet more indistinct when role models are 'distant' media figures that may form part of a public pedagogy (Giroux 2004; Gibson 2003; Stead and Elliot 2019). While the idea's roots lie in, and are often conflated with, the psychological concept of modelling (Bandura 1965), this cannot stretch to explain how such influence might occur in wider mediated and discursive contexts.

As well as concerns surrounding the lack of definition, issues inherent in role model assumptions mirror some key concerns identified in media effects claims. These include an agenda led by wider cultural anxieties, an assumption of fixed meanings in media texts/objects, and a presumption of inadequacy in audiences/subjects (Gauntlett 2002). In both, there is a tendency to assume a particular influence of media on children and youth (Jung 1986) – the 'third person effect' (Davison 1983), which describes how people tend to see others rather than themselves as vulnerable to mass media, the assumed influence increasing with the social distance of such others. This 'third person effect' is evident throughout a well-established history of anxieties over girls as especially vulnerable to media content, stretching back to the Payne-funded studies of 1926–1935 and extending into contemporary concerns over girls' media and online engagements (Blumer and Hauser 1933, 205; Perloff 2014; Antonopoulos et al. 2015; Jackson and Vares 2016). However, an important difference exists between role model assumptions and media effects claims in one regard: in the latter, 'third parties' are typically held to be vulnerable to negative media messages, but not to positive content (McLeod and Eveland 1999) whereas in girl-empowerment initiatives, role models are assumed to work in benign, socially desirable ways. This, we suggest, is because role model solutions are a manifestation of the discourses of both optimism and anxiety that coalesce around girlhood (Gonick 2006). In such solutions, girls are simultaneously at risk in terms of their vulnerability to undesirable media messages (Mendick et al. 2018) – here in the form of non-endorsed role models – and the locus of hope as potential entrepreneurs of the self and of the future (Banet-Weiser 2015).

## ROLE MODELS, NEOLIBERALISM, AND EMPOWERMENT

In their attempts to shape individual subjectivities via materials that are, in principle, freely available for any girl to access, popular role-model campaigns align with neoliberal thinking that ignores material inequalities beyond gender and promotes instead 'equality of opportunity' (Rose 1999; Littler 20188, 153). Thus, in the same way that they fail to change masculinist models of leadership, they also fail to challenge the 'intensified inequality' that is a key consequence of neoliberal policy (Brown 2015: 30).

These campaigns belong to the genre of girl-empowerment initiatives that centre aspiration as the desirable, necessary force behind individuated social mobility, and in this case, potential leadership (Harris 2004; Banet-Weiser 2015; Biressi 2018). For example, Sandberg's 'Ban Bossy' (2014) exhorts girls to take responsibility for their perceived ambition deficit, while 'The Female Lead's (2019) '5 Key Messages' place the onus for success squarely on the individual girl.[1] Such campaigns thus reproduce the central tenets of neoliberal feminisms: they acknowledge the existence of inequalities but elide the social relations that produce them (Rottenberg 2014). They characterise barriers to girls' personal ambition as surmountable through the development of self-sufficiency and leadership skills (Harris 2004; Banet-Weiser 2015) and the kind of self-promotion that Julie Wilson (2017) describes as the 'hustle' element of neoliberal subjectivity. In this way, role-model campaigns model the internalisation of responsibility and the surmountability of adverse contexts through self-regulation that are fundamental to neoliberal subjectivity (Foucault 2008, 226) and to the myth of meritocracy (Littler 2018).

A reliance on self-sufficiency as the chief means by which girls might navigate routes to power is of particular concern in current economic contexts of austerity. In their assumption that exposure to remote figures via mass media is sufficient to address the diverse, entrenched barriers and exclusions that exist, role model solutions obscure the extent to which support structures for young people have been eroded (Mirowski, 2014; Clack and Paule, 2019), and the particular impact of this on women and girls (De Henau and Reid 2013; Negra and Tasker 2014; Allen 2016). In these contexts, as we detail in chapter 1, spaces for young women to engage with communities and develop civic attachments to explore gendered restrictions and organise resistance have diminished or been reconfigured (Harris 2004: 151). This reveals the underpinning political economy of role model solutions: the need to fund youth clubs and school programmes for girls, for example, is obviated if the same impact can be achieved simply through exposure to media figures. The obvious shortcomings of this model are identified by Finlayson (2018, 781), who sensibly observes that there is little use in displaying inspirational posters in schools of sports champions, if all the local pools and playing fields have been closed and sold off. Like global girl-empowerment campaigns (Calkin 2015, 10), the cross-spectrum popularity of such solutions may well lie in their failure to articulate policy or economic measures designed to address structural inequalities.

## ROLE MODELS AND THE BLURRED CATEGORIES OF LEADER AND CELEBRITY

Even if one were to accept the premise that exposure to an increased number of female role models will fuel girls' leadership aspirations and result in their achieving positions of power later in life, the nature of the role models themselves as sites of contestation raises further issues in terms of sanctioned forms of visibility. 'The Female Lead'(2019), for example, aims to provide 'alternative role models to those ever-present in popular culture' and warns against 'celebrities and actresses' as role models; at the same time, its book of 'sixty inspirational women, from many walks of life' frames these alternatives in glossy, upbeat, celebrity-style (Dunn 2017; ) thus deploying the blandishments of celebritisation in order to counter the perceived allure of celebrity.

'Ban Bossy' (2014) and 'Lean In Girls' (2023), however, feature a range of celebrities and public figures in their materials, offering inspirational posters, personal narratives, and videos with messages from music and teen TV stars, as well as women politicians and executives. That role models for girls should be drawn from celebrity and media, as well as political and corporate fields is unsurprising, given the gendered, raced, and classed complexities of celebrity culture (Yelin 2020) and the superior representation of women in numbers alone in celebrity arenas (Finlayson 2018). Neither is the public anxiety this can provoke. The blurring of celebrity and leadership is reflective of a wider cultural shift, which sees the increasing involvement of celebrities in political movements and processes and both corporate leaders and politicians constructing celebrity identities (Marshall 2014; Adamson and Kelan 2018). While Mary Beard (2017a, 13) observes that power has always, in a sense, been 'an elite thing, coupled to public prestige, to the individual charisma of so-called leadership, and often, though not always, to a degree of celebrity', Zoonen (2006, 288) notes that 'what distinguishes the current generation (of women leaders) from their predecessors is their ascendance to power in profoundly mediated contexts'.

The blurring is also apparent in the ways in which politicians construct celebrity identities with what Marshall (2014) describes as an 'affective function', attracting support around personality and interests rather than party policy. Such 'celebritisation', with its associations with the ephemeral and the low-brow, provokes cultural anxiety – for example, well before Donald Trump's presidency and Kanye West's declaration of candidacy, West and Orman (2003) caution us that

> if we don't take back the celebrity politician system, citizens might well face a political contest between a basket-ball player versus a football player, or a

comedian versus rock star, or a movie star versus a television situation comedy star. (119)

Anxieties over both the celebritisation of leadership and 'improper' forms of celebrity (Allen and Mendick 2012) inform the restrictive ways in which girls are expected to admire role models; these are heavily policed both in terms of the kinds of role models sanctioned for admiration and within the discursive formations of leadership and celebrity themselves (Kokoli and Winter 2015; Mavin and Grandy 2016; Yelin 2015; Tischner, Malson and Fey 2019).

## Role Models, Cruel Aspirations, and Audiences

In the focus group interviews, we asked girls to nominate or describe any women whom they saw as leaders or as possessing the leadership qualities that are explored in chapter 1. Questions focused on their perceptions of the representation and experiences of women leaders and on factors that enable women to occupy such roles. We deliberately refrained from asking participants specifically who their 'role models' were and avoided the term unless and until participants used it themselves. This was partly due to the lack of clarity in existing attempts to define what role models are and how they work, as described above, and also because questioning participants in this way, we felt, attached an importance to their choices that may not have been intended, especially in the imbalanced power context of the research taking place in a school classroom with adult researchers (Epstein 1993). Asking someone to nominate a role model implies that such a figure influences their aspirations and possibly their life outcomes (Jung 1986; Nauta and Kokaly 2001; Awan 2008). This fails to acknowledge that individuals have unequal access to social and economic resources to improve their conditions and that aspirations can be 'cruel' in their fostering of attachments to unachievable futures (Berlant 2011). Asking girls to name women or describe leadership qualities they admire or the women whom they feel possess such qualities, therefore, is not the same as asking them who their role models are.

## BLURRING THE CELEBRITY/LEADER DIVIDE

The first common assumption around role models that collapsed in discussions with girls was the categorisation of public figures as a 'good' or 'bad' influence along a fault line of celebrity or leader. Girls' responses erased distinctions between these two categories, identifying leadership qualities among female celebrities, and regarding as celebrities some figures more commonly considered to be leaders. Two strong patterns that emerged early in the data analysis were admiration concentrated on a few global figures, and within this, a blurring of the celebrity/leadership divide. The top figures named as favourites and mentioned in constant discussion were US First Lady Michelle Obama; the singer Beyoncé; New Zealand prime minister Jacinda Ardern (post-pandemic); comedian and talk show host Ellen DeGeneres; girls' rights activist Malala Yousafzai; and actor and feminist advocate Emma Watson.

The most sustained positive discussion focused on Michelle Obama and Beyoncé in all participant groups, with Michelle Obama emerging as the figure of greatest interest/admiration. In this chapter, we focus, therefore, particularly on these two women. It is not solely because of their prominence and popularity, but because discussions surrounding them coalesce around neoliberal myths of self-improvement, the policing of women's domains, and the risks of visibility.

While indicating the pervasiveness of celebrity politics in the public sphere, especially for youth, our participants' perceptions of women as leaders at first appear to evade adult categorisations of 'celebrity' and 'leader' (Marsh et al. 2010). While the celebrity aspects of leadership were recognised – for example, Molly remarked that 'Basically leaders are celebrities because everybody knows them . . . as soon as they step into that power, they are automatically a celebrity because they're in the public eye', and Amina observed that as 'a leader you get a lot of attention don't you. Kind of celebrity and things like that' – girls were invariably less concerned with what kind of public role a woman occupied, and more with how far her concerns were seen as representing issues of importance to themselves.

However, their choices are also illustrative of ways in which girls' explorations of such ideas are shaped by the wider discursive context in which they take place; three of the favourite women leaders are also among those identified by Anita Biressi (2018) as exemplifying mainstream politics' attempts to revivify itself through mobilising girls to promote conservative political discourse, a discourse in which both representations of and exhortations to female success are taken as signs that equality has been achieved.

We found a top six consisting of two Black women, a lesbian, a Muslim woman, and self-proclaimed feminist to be politically interesting, but it also played into popular anxieties around the celebritisation of leadership and youth admiration of celebrities. At a public engagement event, where we presented these initial findings, some attendees viewed the dominance of celebrities as a matter of concern. Such concerns reproduce conservative models of the public sphere and of what constitutes appropriate representation (Street 2004; Yelin 2016); they indicate how role model solutions rely on the adoption of endorsed figures for admiration but, as an inevitable adjunct, are accompanied by 'media effects' fears of unwholesome influence.

Such public anxieties over girls' admiration of celebrity role models and the simultaneous mobilisation of the same figures within popular leadership discourse demonstrate taxonomic negotiations in the ongoing construction of the categories of 'role model' and 'women leader' and illustrate the discursive contradictions and strategies inherent in the making of new social knowledge (Foucault 1969).

## INTERSECTIONALITY, PRIVILEGE, AND THE IDEA OF OVERCOMING

A second way the girls' ideas about leadership pose problems for common assumptions about role model solutions is the fact that by focusing on the existence of a female role model as de facto evidence that gender barriers are surmountable, role model discourse inadequately accounts for the way that girls experience the (in)accessibility of positions of leadership through intersecting axes of race, class, and regionality with gender.

Participants' discussions suggested that they did see women's presence in high-profile roles as a sign of wider equality. They saw women overcoming difficult conditions, including gendered restrictions, to achieve status and power as demonstrating that society is working as it should be in terms of providing opportunity and rewarding merit. This was tempered, however, with the ideas of 'austere meritocracy' (Mendick et al. 2018, 9), entrenched forms of classed and masculinised power, and the 'implied whiteness' of ideal forms of femininity, including those implicit in ideals of female leadership (Biressi 2018). Just as celebrity culture is classed, raced, and geographically contingent, and hierarchies of oppression operate along these axes (Skeggs and Wood 2008; Tyler and Bennet 2010; Currid-Halkett 2013; Christiansen and Richey 2015), class, race, and gender were pronounced in the framing of both of girls' admiration of prominent women and of the awareness of their own opportunities. Both Michelle Obama and Beyoncé promote a form of girl empowerment that is centred on personal confidence, self-determination, and individualism (Pomerantz et al. 2013; Mirza and Meetoo 2018); these qualities were exemplified in group discussions and in popular memes of both figures shared by the girls. One of the most popular variants shows images of Michelle Obama with the following extract from a speech given at a London girls' school in 2009: 'Whether you come from a council estate or a country estate, your success will be determined by your own confidence and fortitude'.

This transatlantic meme encapsulates the kind of 'popular parable' described by Littler (2018) as encapsulating the Western narrative of social mobility, a narrative that both obscures social division and promotes an image of the elite as ordinary individuals, 'just like us' (116), who are living a life attainable by us. Michelle Obama was seen as representing the possibility of flourishing in adverse circumstances; for example, Shameem felt that 'it just shows that someone who came from a background or was born as a minority, can have that opportunity to be in the spotlight'. For Shameem, Michelle Obama's Black identity served as a marker of disadvantage – for all her global visibility, participants knew little of her socio-economic background. Similar discussions took place around Beyoncé, who was described by Chloe as having 'had so many, like, difficult situations in her life'. Michelle Obama and Beyoncé were both felt to have earned their influence through a combination of hard work and the 'right' kind of motivation, themes which will be examined in more detail in chapter 3.

Their success and prominence were, however, understood as taking place in contexts of wider inequality that particularly disadvantaged women. Apprehension of these contexts was shaped by participants' own experiences of inequality along intersectional axes. For Black participants, Michelle Obama was read first and foremost through her identity as a Black woman. For these girls, Obama was a figure of pride and possibility in terms of representation, as is shown in this exchange:

*Toya:* Because I watch her and she's like, "I'm a Black woman, I'm here talking to you here, you can make a change." That was quality.

*Tani:* She's proud to be Black. Not a lot of women now are, like, proud to be Black.

The participants in the same group praised Beyoncé for celebrating Black culture and women in the face of public hostility:

*Toya:* You know that Superbowl performance? She did the arrow thing, she did a wonderful formation, she got a lot of, like, hit backs for it.

*Ayana:* She got a lot of remarks for it because she did women things in her performance.

However, neither Michelle Obama nor Beyoncé's Black identity was mentioned by white participants; this is suggestive of the wider erasure of racial specificity inherent in popular white feminisms (Banet-Weiser and Portwood-Stacer 2017). In media coverage of both women, a foregrounding of universalising, feminised factors such as relationships, fashion, and family has been identified (White 2011; Short 2015; Utley 2017), and indeed these factors figured in participants' discussions. Such foregrounding locates both women within traditional patriarchal structures and renders them intelligible in ways that are consistent with Eurocentric ideals of femininity (Block 2017, 163).

**Absent Role Models and Classed Geographies**

Classed geographies came into play for girls from disadvantaged regions around the UK. While admiring the same women, they were less likely to see their presence in the public eye as indicative of wider equalities, but rather as exceptional. They did not see successful women as overcoming similar hurdles as themselves and recognised that many who occupy positions of political or celebrity influence are drawn from already privileged groups. In a school in the post-industrial north-west of England, there was consensus among participants that the apparent opportunity modelled by women leaders was not easily realisable for themselves. Leaders were discussed in ways that reproduced wider framings of classed and elite femininities (Mavin and Grandy 2016; Tischner, Malson and Fey 2019) and of the operations of privilege via institutional and geographical signifiers (Savage, Bagnall, and Longhurst 2001; Currid-Halkett 2013), as indicated by the following exchange:

> *Geri:* If someone came here, like, from somewhere where it don't look like this, they'd be shocked. But, like, I don't think people know that there are places like this in England.
>
> *Maya:* Yeah, like, all the posh country, they'd run a country on their beliefs and how they've been brought up, so with money and everything they've ever needed. Whereas, if you've got people that have nothing, they could possibly be better leaders because they've had to try harder to get why they are. So if you had to, if you took people from places like Bradford, they may be in better control than people from posh places because they can, they've actually had a chance, an opportunity, like, an opportunity to see the rest of the world for what it really was, instead of being in their own little bubble of richness and happiness.

Here, representation of the disadvantaged by the elite was a matter of concern: rather than generating the 'intrigue of difference' (Littler 2018, 135), leaders from privileged backgrounds were seen as remote and elite; rather than inspiring, they emphasised girls' sense of their own disadvantage and disempowerment.

> *Becky:* If you're higher up, people are more likely to listen to you . . . but if one of us was to be like, we want this to happen, I don't, kind of how society works, you wouldn't really get like much recognition for it.
>
> *Serena:* That is it, the higher up you are, the more respect you have and having respect is . . . you have some sort of say in what happens.

While participants reproduced some of the meritocratic narrative of 'earned success' attached to Michelle Obama and Beyoncé, in terms of their own lives, they saw ideas around equality of possibility and self-made success as myths. They struggled to name other leaders as emerging from disadvantage or whom they felt could relate to their own experiences. A sole focus on gender as the indicator of equality means that for these girls, proffered female role models may serve to further normalise structures of power and inequality because those endorsed for their admiration, or achieving positions of power outside of celebrity, are too often drawn from a privileged pool.

## ROLE MODELS' MOTIVES: MAKING A DIFFERENCE VERSUS SEEKING POWER

The third way in which role model discourse falters at the point of its encounter with girls is the failure to take into account the proliferation and strength of cultural narratives that penalise women for seeking power and restrict its exercise to more traditionally feminised domains. Here, we bring into our analysis girls' discussion of Hillary Clinton; because she was frequently evoked as a kind of foil to Michelle Obama's virtues in ways that illuminated girls' sense of the ways in which women can and should achieve and perform leadership.

The curtailment of women's participation in structures of power is not a contemporary problem; Rebecca S. Richards (2015) makes a compelling case for gendered difference as both inherent in the creation of, and appropriated by, the policing of the patriarchal 'nation state' in ways that render women's seeking of power as a destabilising challenge. Mary Beard (2017b) demonstrates that mechanisms that silence women and sever them 'from the centres of power' have been practised for thousands of years in Western cultures. At an organisational level, gendered discourses shape and constrain ways in which leadership might be understood and performed, as well as defining who might occupy positions of power (Iverson, Allan, and Gordon 2017, 510). Although the space allowed to women leaders – be they celebrities, corporate stars, or politicians – in contemporary culture has expanded over the last century in Western democracies, it is still constrained by gender in ways that resonate with the essentialised, feminised leadership traits described above. Further, contemporary conditions of visibility for women add new pressures which compete with older but nonetheless potent gendered mores, adding new tensions and complexities to navigate, and these increase exponentially along intersectional axes. For the girls in our study, these coalesced around issues of authenticity and motive.

As discussed in chapter 1, that women leaders should be seen to work towards creating greater equality was an important criterion for most participants, and both Michelle Obama and Beyoncé were lauded for promoting the interests of girls in particular. Judgement of both women, however, depended largely on perceived authenticity, and this authenticity was linked to perceptions of motive and to claims to struggle. Beyoncé's celebrity status was seen as driven by a kind of ministry to girls, as exemplified in this exchange:

> *Ayana:* I don't even think Beyoncé does it for the money. She just wants to be heard and wants to make a difference.

> *Tani:* It's just like that thing that girls can run the world if you want to, don't give up.

The image in figure 2.1 is one of several of Beyoncé shared by participants across the focus groups and is typical of the memes representing the singer that were popular among the girls, featuring a direct-to-camera head and

**Figure 2.1     Image of American Singer Beyoncé Found Online by a Participant.**

shoulders, straight-faced pose, with an accompanying motivational quotation. The monochrome aesthetic is frequently deployed by the singer, connoting authenticity and establishing Black women's bodies into representational traditions that have previously excluded them (McLarney 2019). The accompanying text locates her power in personal authenticity, evoking a discourse of inner voice and confidence that resonates with popular confidence discourses addressing girls described in the preceding chapter. The final sentence, 'I run my world', evokes her global hit single: 'Run the World (Girls)', from which indeed the title of this work derives.

Michelle Obama's desire to promote girls' interests was seen as her key motivation in seeking power.

*Shameem:* I think she wants to be a leader because she'll be good for young girls like us and she has an impact on us . . . people would know that she's actually in it for that, not just because she's famous.

*Helen:* I think because . . . whilst she was First Lady she didn't take advantage of the fact that she had tons of money now and she . . . she did a lot of stuff to help the environment in the community, not just, like, herself. She donated to a lot of charities and she's kind of, like, I think she was a role model for most girls, I think.

*Tani:* A person who works in the White House shouldn't be like focused on fame and all of that . . . But like for Michelle Obama she's different because she's trying to help people and the only way she can help people is by getting known.

Here, Beyoncé's celebrity and wealth, and Michelle Obama's political celebrity status are seen as inevitable adjuncts of power, as means of doing good rather than as sought for their own sake – fame becomes 'the only way' a woman can help people. This 'doing good' discourse aligns with essentialised models of the caring, ethical woman leader (Prügl 2012; Lewis 2014; Enderstein 2018) and becomes a way of reconciling the individualism of popular leadership models and neoliberal self-advancement with acceptable modes of femininity.

Although both women claimed to want to empower girls, there were notable differences in participants' reception of Michelle Obama and Hillary Clinton in terms of perceived motivation, for example:

*Maya:* She (Hillary) was in it for power as well. Her husband had done it and she was already in politics and she just.. for her it was probably just being sick of being the one in the background, not making the proper decisions.

*Rachel:* I think the difference between Hillary and Michelle, is that I feel like Hillary was a lot more, well she still is, a lot more power hungry than Michelle.

Hillary Clinton's professed desire to inspire girls was called into question, with Helen expressing scepticism over Clinton's (2016) election night tweet (shared by a participant within this group) ) that told 'every little girl who dreams big' that 'tonight is for you' thus:

> I don't think that she was 100% all for girls, I think she might have just tweeted that because, you know, oh hey this could win me the election I guess.

Significant in the way Hillary Clinton and Michelle Obama were discussed was the fact that Clinton had put herself forward for a powerful public role. The girls' judgements reflect a wider cultural disparagement of women who are perceived as staking a claim to patriarchal territory (Beard 2017b; Manne 2018) and the hostile arena created for women by the confluence of celebrity and politics (Zoonen 2006, 299). Studies of press coverage of both women reveal that Michelle Obama's not seeking presidential office for herself while Hillary Clinton had done so shaped the different media treatment of the two women (Rhee and Sigler 2015; Utley 2017); in aiming for the presidential role, Clinton was denigrated for poaching on male preserves (Manne 2018). This was not only the case in the USA: British press coverage gave us such analyses as 'Irrational ambition is Hillary Clinton's flaw' (Applebaum2008). Girls' discussion of fictional characters and celebrities also reflected this wider disparagement of women staking claims to power – Bella admired the Harry Potter character Professor Minerva McGonagall as a leader because she had not sought leadership, saying,

> she never wanted more than she had as a teacher. Like, she was happy with what she had, but then she took the role that somebody gave her, instead of like going around trying to put down other people. And I think that people, even if she wasn't in power, I think people still would have, like, listened to her, respected her and even though she's, like, strict and stuff, people still like her, which shows that they know that she's a good person.

Abuya's admiration of Emma Watson was in part because 'she was just picked on the street, out of a fluke', epitomising Richard Dyer's theorisation of the way that luck is commonly mobilised in discourses of celebrity success to mitigate envy at the rewards of fame (1979, 42).

While participants' preference for Michelle Obama over Hillary Clinton may also be symptomatic of the generational divide between the two women's appeal (Dolan et al. 2018, 87), it indicates how girls' engagements with women in the public eye are shaped by and normalise wider discourses of gender and power and the perceived limits to a woman's domain. Some participants recognised that public opinion of Hillary Clinton, including their own, was shaped by the media treatment she received as a result of seeking power through election – for example, Rachel observed:

> Hillary obviously was going for president, so she was more in the spotlight than Michelle, so people were going to look for her insecurities and look for bad things about her.

This sense of appropriate domains for women in the public eye was also an area where girls made some distinction between different kinds of celebrity and leadership. This is demonstrated in the following exchange, showing awareness that public approval for a woman is contingent on perceptions that she is staying in her lane:

> *Laura:* So if it was Beyoncé, no one really has an opinion unless they don't like her music. But no one really hates her with that passion that they might hate someone in politics.
>
> *Toya:* The people that don't like Beyoncé, the only reason why they all say they don't love her is because people were branding.

Such responses indicate the critical and nuanced readings that girls as experienced consumers bring to media texts and figures, and also the ways in which their views are inevitably shaped by the wider discursive regime in which their meaning-making takes place. This has implications for the aims and claims of role model solutions; while girls are clearly not the passive dupes of media messages, the gendered values and ideologies that participants reproduce in their discussions carry the hegemonic weight of wider culture and are unlikely to be shifted far by individual examples.

Participants' perceptions of motivation were also complicated by those of authenticity, and these align with narratives of self-improvement and overcoming. As Littler (2018, 121) observes, media framings of powerful elites often present them in terms of the meritocratic myth that 'no matter where you start off in life, you can, with passion and effort, compete and rise up'. The idea of authenticity as a media construction around such narratives of struggle and just deserts is inherently self-contradictory and ambivalent (Trilling 1972; Holmes 2005; Banet-Weiser 2013; Yelin 2020), but such 'authenticity' is not only a feature of popular representations; it is central to what Allen and Mendick (2012, 2) describe as 'the moral economies of personhood and processes of class-making.' While such processes might render the too-authentically working class less valued in the eyes of audiences (p.3), when combined with aspiration and upward mobility in narratives surrounding both Michelle Obama and Beyoncé, disadvantage conveys authenticity, as we have seen above. Michelle Obama's perceived political outsider status also made her more relatable and accessible to the girls; participants expressed a sense of her contrast with traditional power holders, with Carly observing that 'she's not like all politicians who just walk around and tell you what to do and try being above everybody else. She can be like a normal person, but then she can also have the politics side as well'. The evocation of 'normal' here is significant in the light of Littler's (2018, 120) identification of 'normcore' as representational strategies via which the elite perform 'ordinariness' (Dyer, 1979) rather than difference, drawing on meritocratic discourse that frames them as hardworking, deserving, and every day.

## GIVING VOICE AND THE RISKS OF VISIBILITY

Lastly and most significantly, fundamental to our issue with role model solutions is that they assume that increased exposure to women in the public eye will show girls what they can achieve and inspire them to want to achieve similar status. This assumption does not take into account the hostile conditions of representation faced by women in the public eye. It ignores ways in which visibility operates as a form of power and control, shaping the representation of women and other subordinated groups along intersecting axes of increased intensity and negativity according to distance from the traditional white, male, privileged identities associated with power. The public eye, therefore, is not a neutral space; access to it and representation within it are intricately linked to power dynamics, reproducing or challenging existing structures and hierarchies. Our discussions with girls reveal that witnessing hostile representations and reception of women in the public eye often operate as a cautionary tale against seeking positions of power which entail visibility, actively discouraging them from aspirations to become the next generation of women leaders.

While the girls in our study reproduced some of the restrictive discourse surrounding women who explicitly seek power, they did express a desire to see more women in powerful roles. However, they saw the experiences of women in the public eye as providing evidence of gendered discrimination rather than as evidence of equality achieved. They saw inequality constituted by the very conditions of visibility for women; across our participating schools, girls identified elements of discrimination, misogyny, and risk inherent in life in the public eye. They recognised the particular dilemma that the polarisation of femininity, visibility, and politics creates for women (Zoonen 2006, 299), with Ayana observing that while fame entails the risks of visibility, 'if they're not famous, no one is going to listen to them'. Women were perceived as having less leeway to make mistakes and as less likely to be praised for their successes than men. Becky felt that 'You're not acknowledged for what you do right, you're acknowledged for what you do wrong', while Molly observed that 'women get judged more'. Serena imagined how it would feel to be a woman leader in the public eye thus: 'Everything you do wrong is enlarged. So it's just like super pressure for being in charge. Because you're on the face of everything, so if you do one wrong then it could go worldwide'. Ruth described how:

> I think it's people who usually don't like being leaders is because you're responsible and, like, everything in your day is sort of, like, seen by people, so that's why people usually cower away from leadership things, so it's like everything in your day is being watched by somebody somewhere. So it's that feeling that you never shake.

Participants' impressions of the risks of visibility are borne out: women leaders face more media abuse and more questioning of their capacity than do men, combined with a relentless focus on appearance (Ross 2002; Campbell and Childs 2010; Gershon 2012; Garcia-Blancoand Wahl-Jorgense 2012; Ross et al. 2013; Tischner, Malson and Fey 2019).

This scrutiny of women's appearance loomed as a deterrent to making oneself visible and was raised as a concern for girls across the groups and regions. Girls in North London were very aware of body shaming and online hate targeting fat women, lamenting inequalities in the treatment of women depending upon their body size, and articulating a cultural mandate of thinness which extends to the women they perceived as the most successful and powerful.

> *Fara:* If a fat person was to wear a two piece swimming costume, social media likes to destroy them. Like, they like to use a lot of hatred words against them. But, like, if a model, if someone who was, like, slim, skinny, was to wear anything like that, they would give them so many kind remarks. But, if it was for someone who was very big, it's just hatred. So why do they do that to destroy? [ . . . ]

> *Toya:* Even Beyoncé, you know? All these celebrities. They all have to lose weight at one point. Even Beyoncé had to lose weight.

> *Fara:* It's like no one can accept you just how you look. You have to be labelled or given a name.

What is at stake is the question of which bodies are 'weighted with authority', as Christina Fisanick argues,

> white, male, able, heterosexual, and middle-class, the 'normal body' persists even though this physical representation is now a demographic minority . . . it is also the body that can seemingly overcome its own embodiment and rise above

the ghettoed locale occupied by those of us (women, people of color, people with disabilities, gays and lesbians, the aged, the fat) who are always already associated with the lived body(2007, 239)

Other girls spoke with admiration about plus-size Latina actress Jessica Garcia and plus-size Canadian comedienne Fatima Dhowre for persevering in the face of public criticism of their weight:

*Kelly:* About body image and how people bring you down about it. [ . . . ] There's this girl on a show called 'On my Block.' [ . . . ]

*Tani:* Jessica. The fat one. Sorry. [ . . . ]

*Kelly:* So then she, she sometimes, but in that show she had to, she was wearing tight things and things that showed her legs. But, she got a lot of hate for that. And she still does good things, apart from being an actor. [ . . . ] But also people dissed on her a lot and yet she still tries to make a change and have an effort to not let those people affect her.

*Interviewer:* So you think women leaders who don't look in a standard way have a harder time?

*All:* Yes.

*Kelly:* Yes they just get dissed on for what they're trying to do.

*Tani:* Yeah like the comedian Fatima. No one knows her name, so I said Fatima.

*Kelly:* Exactly because she said, I remember she said that my name is Fatima because I'd rather you call me that because I know you're going to do it behind my back anyways. So you might as well say to me, to my face. That's my name. Instead of just doing it behind my back, just call me that innit.

*Tani:* Yeah she's not shy to say 'I'm fat'.

*Kelly:* She's great.

*Claire:* And she's funny. She's really great.

*Tani:* Yeah and people love her for that.

*Kelly:* Yeah because she's standing up for herself.

Just to be visible with a fat body, in an otherwise homogenously fatphobic culture, is viewed as social justice work. As well as double standards in the treatment of thin or fat women, the girls identified double standards in terms of the role of appearance in the treatment of men and women in the public eye. They discussed the media as setting and perpetuating norms and benchmarks of women's appearance, norms which the girls saw as policing and proscribing who is and is not viewed as a leader. Fara offered this:

*It's because of media. Because, you know how good leaders, they dress a certain way. It's because they are trying. It's because they've already thought of every area. So, they've already thought of what the media would say. So, they are dressing in a specific way because of the media. [ . . . ] It's because the media, they think a good leader should just, um, everything that we've said leads to the media.*

*Interviewer:* Okay do the media pay attention to what male leaders look like?

*All:* No. No!

Other girls ascribed this normative function to social media, identifying a space in which ideas are formed around what leaders should look like specifically, and what women should look like in general.

*Ada:* I think people have this mentality that leaders are supposed to dress smartly.

*Fara:* It's because of what social media portrays of us women.

*Interviewer:* Go on and what is that?

*Fara:* Basically social media makes it look as if we have to look some type of way as a dressed up publicly. They make it seem that we need to be slim, we need to be this . . .

Their use of 'us women' and 'we' suggests that they felt themselves interpellated by these discourses which set benchmarks for famous women's appearance. Through discussion of celebrities, Ayana identified conventions of appearance as a means of excluding women from leadership for performing the 'wrong' kind of femininity:

Let's say if I dressed up how Miley Cyrus or someone dressed up, but I might have the same mentality as a good leader, they would think that I'm a bad leader because of my appearance.

Molly similarly felt that women's appearance should be irrelevant to leadership and that scrutiny of how women look was a mechanism of distraction making it harder for women's voices to be heard, saying: 'appearance doesn't really matter in leadership, but it is, because that's how people view them. [ . . . ] If they don't look the part, people are going to judge them on the looks and not really focus on what they have to say.' Debates between the girls unfolded in the groups about whether to reproduce or challenge the discourses which police women's appearance:

*Tani:* Rhianna . . . What is she always wearing, man?

*Ayana:* She feels comfortable wearing that, let her have it. [ . . . ]

*Toya:* She put two things on her nipples and she come in there and she just walked around. Her bum was showing. This part was showing. She just walked in naked. At least she covers herself and she feels comfortable doing what she does. But – and the media doesn't portray it like that! They will be like 'she!'. They always worship what she wears. And secondly, lastly, she, just because she – you know how she dresses. Because of how she dresses, people automatically have this bad mentality of her. But she works with children. I remember she went to Africa to help children reading and she donated money.

The unreconciled competing discourses in Toya's response to Rhianna's wardrobe reveals the 'impossible space' of femininity as competing cultural expectations of female modesty, attractiveness and confidence overdetermine womanhood (Tseëlon 1995). Toya's account both outlines the weight of signification as Rhianna is at once celebrated and denigrated, and highlights that media representations of celebrity are a process of public policing of female participation in public life that unfolds with the girls watching, acutely aware of what is praised and censured (often simultaneously). It is significant that Toya reproduced the understanding of leadership demonstrated across the groups in which they are less concerned with what kind of public role a woman occupies, and more with how she supports and furthers progressive social causes. Girls in the Home Counties similarly articulated famous women's sexuality and adherence to feminine beauty norms and their contribution to social justice as if they are in tension:

*Fiona:* I feel like as well as there being, like, really positive ones, I feel like there are quite negatives ones as well. Like those people use their like social media presence to, like, kind of, like Kim Kardashian, like she's positive like she got someone out of prison, who was in there wrongfully. But then she like puts all this stuff kind of degrading women like . . .

*Annabel:* That's the thing isn't it, the reason she has this platform is because of like the way she looks.

*Mina:* There's a sex tape.

*Freya:* But the reason she has this power is because of the way she looks. But the thing is I don't mind if she does that, because she does help people. So she is not a good role model for body image, but I think she's a good role model in morally how she helps people.

This conflicted ambivalence around women's appearance replicates cultural censure around women whose appearance is perceived to court visibility. As Yelin argues, 'femininity has always been decorative and specular. The supposedly unseemly difference in this instance is the invitation to an admiring audience, which one ought to be able to attract with ease' (2020, 144–5). These girls articulated the double bind of post-feminist power in which beauty and sex appeal operate as both a source and containment of women's power (McRobbie 2009). In the process, they demonstrate the failed logic of role model solutions as they seek to identify 'good' role models among high-profile women who are always already bearing the weight of contradictory, irreconcilable censure (Yelin 2020) and as such ultimately operate as cautionary tales.

Part of the cautionary function of the cultural scrutiny of women's appearance lies in girls' recognition of the unlevel playing field in which odds are stacked against women. Discussing Donald Trump's criticism of Hillary Clinton's appearance in political debates, girls in Wiltshire identified the unequal standards of appearance applied to men and women:

*Leah:* I don't think he would have been the same about a male candidate.

*Molly:* No.

*Serena:* I think he would have come up with stronger things because when, I feel like it's the stereotype when women are criticised because of how they look, they sort of get knocked down, because they're being told that they're not, like, you know, the model shape or you know what all this is. I feel like men, they probably have that pressure on inside, but they don't ever get to them on the outside.

*Leah:* I think like Donald Trump is an example of, and as he did against Hilary Clinton, I feel like if he, I don't, he wouldn't do that against a man because they need to show they're more, it's like . . . I've forgotten the word, it's not like prey or something, they're masculine and they've got to show whose better, dominance. And I think the only way you could show dominance is by proving something and so he would have to do it properly, he couldn't pick out somebody's looks, but with a woman he thought you know I've already proved enough by being a man.

Girls in our North London group evoked the presidential debate in which Donald Trump followed Hillary Clinton closely around the stage as she spoke, in behaviour variously described by reporters as 'skulking' and 'prowling' (*The Guardian,* 2016) . This was an instance of their awareness of the theatre of American politics (evoked far more frequently than British politics, pre-COVID). The image in figure 2.2 depicts Clinton speaking with apparent confidence to the camera, microphone in hand, while Trump lurks behind her, eyes so focused on her back that he appears to be squinting, with the camera angle emphasising the height discrepancy, so he appears to loom

**Figure 2.2   Image of Hillary Clinton and Donald Trump during a Presidential Debate Found Online by a Participant.**

over her. Participants, like journalists, recognised this behaviour as a public demonstration of masculinised bullying.

In the girls' understanding, men must compete with other men in terms of dominance, whereas men are perceived as always already starting from a position of dominance over women. The girls identified the focus on women's appearance rather than their leadership competencies as a mechanism by which women are precluded from being considered serious contenders before a competition even begins.

Girls in a Home Counties school described feeling under constant scrutiny of their femininity and saw holding a leadership role as in itself breaking the rules of femininity. They gave examples of having been targeted by adverts which construct leadership in business as exclusively male, which they contrasted with online cultures which interpellate them as women to aspire to roles and lifestyles which are predominantly decorative and specular.

*Charlotte:* Yeah whether we like it or not, women are literally all the time just, every focus is on our etiquette, how we behave, how we, like if we don't fit into the standard, which the normal standard isn't leadership for women. So, like, if we are out then everybody judges us whether we like it or not and whether they like it or not, because it's just implanted into our brains that women can't be leaders, because it's not normal, like, not many women have done it. So I don't know if, like, including more women would change that.

*Alicia:* I mean on Instagram you look at posts and it's girls on boats in bikinis and then you get advertising roles about building a business and it's a guy sitting at a table in a suit.

*Alicia:* There has not been a single ad that I've seen about building a business that has involved a woman, or that hasn't been a man suggesting to a woman
. . .

*Mina:* Patronising.

Further evidence that such scrutiny of women functions to actively deter girls from desiring power that comes with visibility came in the girls' descriptions of ways that their own decisions about their relationship to appearance and visibility were made in consideration of the treatment of women leaders they witnessed.

*Freya:* I think a lot of the mainstream media as well like, like even politicians, like every move is analysed and, like, everything is analysed to an extent whereas, like, it's a lot more pressure, because anything you do or say it can be like recorded. And even in the public eye, appearances play a big role. So, Theresa May there's a lot of, like, the walk that she did, that was advertised more than what she actually said and, as a girl, I'm, like, I don't want to be judged by my appearance because I've been for my appearance. And then going into like a leadership role, I'm concerned about how I look. So when I would go to practice at the boys' school, I would see girls around me who had got so much make-up on suddenly. Around the school they'd wear nothing and suddenly they'd got all this make-up on [...]I think there's an idea that leaders have to look a certain way and I think the masculine and I think there's just been this way that females should look a certain way and that suddenly females think that if they look a certain way, they might get more attention in the media.

*Annabel:* Then they are not taken seriously.

*Charlotte:* And then they are not taken seriously and then our points aren't made. I think that's something that, I know when I do my choir, I don't dress up, because I don't want other people to think oh I need to look really nice going, because I think that's something that I've noticed.

For these girls, the media treatment of women leaders informed their own desire not to be seen as courting visibility through care and consideration of their own appearance. The theatre of punishment in which women cannot both meet the demands of specular femininity and be designated leaders led these girls to understand a cultural imperative that they cannot be both appealing to look at and be taken seriously. That the girls formed their ideas about how they would be treated by society through a process of observing how society treats women in the public eye can be seen in the links girls in Bradford drew between the treatment of female celebrities and the ways they experience being sexualised themselves:

> *Maya:* Yeah but woman do get sexualised a lot. Like Marilyn Monroe she is still a powerful role model but because she was sexualised and she stood up with that, but I think it's done to the extreme and now that's all that you see with other women. It's just an object.

> *Jade:* It's like girls are constantly being told that we can't wear this, we can't do that. It's like now in school, we used to be able to wear skirts, but now we can't.

> *Gerri:* Yeah because of the boys.

> *Jade:* They might be distracted.

The girls understood cultural currents in which women's appearance distracts from their voices and their being taken seriously as contenders for power, while reporting that the institutions around them are more concerned about the ways that girls' own appearance might distract from male achievement than girls' barriers to power. In Glasgow, girls expressed disappointment that the women offered to them as fictional representations of powerful women were not spared the cultural mandate of sex appeal for women in the public eye:

> *Ruth:* The only thing that puts me off about female superheroes, like more recently is that they are overly sexualised.

> *Charlie:* They sexualise them a lot. [ . . . ] They always have like skin tight costumes and sit on the table . . . .

> *Tamsin:* Their boobs are shown. [ . . . ]

> *Charlie:* But then that could be women in real life though. They are always sexualised.

While girls across all of the groups spoke around a subtext of the dangers of conforming to the benchmarks of feminine attractiveness, which would expose them to the risks of appearing to court an admiring gaze, girls in Glasgow made explicit the rape culture at the heart of this logic. With disappointment, they identified that women are required to be sexy and also punished for being sexy by threat of rape. They linked the models of power and visibility available to them in the media to their own imminent risk of rape in a victim-blaming culture that would identify their appearance as the cause of rape, rather than male actions. They also articulated the weary knowledge that *not* dressing a certain way also will not save them, 'it just happens'.

> *Ruth:* I know. I know it's a tiny bit off topic but . . . rape, men are always like women are asking for it, they wear short skirts. I should be allowed to walk about my house nude and not asking if .. or raped or anything like that.
>
> *Charlie:* I feel like if a lassie was raped and like she's sitting there in like leggings in a t-shirt, guys will still say she's asking for it [ . . . ]
>
> *Gen:* They could even be wearing the most baggiest clothing and still be saying
>
> *Ruth:* Or the activists, this is what I wore when I got raped [ . . . ]
>
> *Charlie:* Nobody has ever asked for that to happen, it just happens.

Such are the high costs of visibility and female power in the minds of the girls we spoke to and the 'impossible space' of womanhood in the public eye. Girls were all too aware of the competing demands placed upon visible women and their irreconcilability. In these conditions, they are cautioned rather than inspired by the female 'role models' they view in terms of the risks of visibility. In each group of participants, there was a consensus that, far from encouraging aspiration, the experiences of women in the public eye operated as a deterrent. Chloe summarised how 'that women can be less ambitious because of these limitations and how they see how other women leaders get scrutinised'.

The perception of the degree of risk was a key area in which girls' views on representation as constitutive of equality differed along intersectional lines. For Black participants in a London school in a disadvantaged borough, the need for representation was felt more acutely, while the risks were seen as far more intense. For these participants, Michelle Obama and Beyoncé's status as women leaders was not seen as evidence of a more equal rebalancing of power; rather, the girls identified the intersecting pressures and disadvantages created by gender and race and the negative attention that campaigning on equality issues draws down upon women (figures 2.2 and 2.3). They viewed the exceptionality of influential Black women as highlighting the barriers to power and the risks faced by BAME women more widely:

> *Avril:* Michelle Obama for example, all the people who don't like her are kind of, like, obvious about it and upsettingly, partially it's because of her race and because she's a woman I guess.

*Kelly:* I think that that's and every time she does her speeches I think she does try to make that point across, not by directly saying it, but by sort of saying that she just wants to help even if she either gets dissed, or not really recognised as much, she is at least making the change which is what's important to her.

*Ada:* She (Beyoncé) is letting her voice be heard.

*Judith:* Beyoncé is a good leader because she's speaking up for other women that can't be heard.

**Figure 2.3   Banner Created by Our Research Participants in a North London School Site.**

The idea of representation as giving voice to the disenfranchised was a key theme with this group; some of the girls made a poster for the session with the logo 'Just because you don't know my story don't mean I have no voice', conveying their awareness that the barriers to 'voice' for girls lie outside the girls themselves – they speak but do not fit into the dominant frameworks of cultural intelligibility (fig. 2.3). The non-standard use of the second 'don't' underscores the link between privileged modes of expression and the valuing of voice.

Formal representation in politics was seen as ineffective in promoting their interests; for example, Toya maintained that 'in this world that we're in, government is out of the door'.

## VISIBILITY AND RISK

Visibility is often a requisite for power, and for the already marginalised, visibility means risk (Yelin and Clancy 2024). When considering leaders they admired, members of the North London group listed Black leaders who had been arrested, assaulted, or assassinated, and Toya summed up starkly: 'Every Black person that's done something good got shot in the head'. She described women, especially Black women, as living with a hyper-awareness of risk and of the surveillance that accompanies those in the public eye most intensely, observing that, 'Black women are smart, they know how to get around, because they will know, they can sense when someone is looking at them. Not only Black, women in general. Because we're more scared'. Girls' own awareness of the threats confronting women who seek to enter traditionally male spheres of power was consistently demonstrated to us. Similar lessons were drawn from Malala Yousafzai – while Yousafzai is highly prominent in role model discourses pitched at women and girls, our participants saw the combination of her age, gender, and determination to make changes as leading to the precise outcome described by Toya. We started conversations about women leaders and ended up in conversations about the risk of physical harm, murder, and rape. Ruth observed that 'rape, men are always, like, women are asking for it'. Elsewhere, Fara felt that the reason we need more women leaders is that, 'I feel like they should know how it feels. But then, like, anyone that's got raped, they should know how it feels like.' In response to the question 'Do you see yourself as a leader in the future?' Toya's response was 'I don't want to get shot in the head and I don't want to be, like, oh she's a woman, she can't do it. This world that you're in, you can't do it, it's a man's world'. Toya's perception of scrutiny and hostility is borne out by analysis of media representations of Black and Brown women politicians. They may receive more press attention than white female candidates due to exceptionality but that press coverage is 'exceptionally negative and narrowly focused on their ethnicity and gender' (Ward 2017, 43), and they receive by far the greatest amount of online abuse (Demos 2016; Amnesty International 2018). This came into sharp relief in the UK press early in 2024 when details of an influential Conservative Party donor Frank Hester was recorded in a meeting saying, 'It's like trying not to be racist but you see Diane Abbott on the TV, and you're just like I hate, you just want to hate all Black women because she's there, and I don't hate all Black women at all, but I think she should be shot" (Mason2024)

Rather than imagining themselves as future decision-makers, Black participants in this group saw the level of risk confronting Black women leaders in the public eye as too great to contemplate for themselves.

## CONCLUSION

If the properly aspiring, empowered girl who will grow up to close the gender leadership gap is a new kind of subject necessitating a new regulatory mediascape (Kokoli and Winter 2015), the campaigns promoting leadership role models for girls can be viewed as a part of that new mediascape in their attempts to tap into celebrity youth cultures and to shape discourses surrounding women and power. Our findings indicate that popular role model initiatives are, however, problematic in several ways: In their focus on representation alone and their single-issue axis of gender, role model solutions are difficult to reconcile with intersectional feminisms and wider equalities agendas. Further, their uncritical adoption of media effects assumptions means that they fail to take into account the situated realities of girls' engagement with public figures, nor the conditions of visibility for women in the public eye. In our study, rather than simply accepting and wishing to emulate women leaders, participants' views reflected feminist concerns that having more women represented in positions of power is not necessarily indicative of wider equalities nor likely to promote their own access to decision-making roles. The meanings the girls attached to the women leaders they discussed were shaped by their own contexts in terms of gender, class, and race. Within these contexts, however, girls drew on and reproduced global media discourses surrounding women and the 'proper' pursuit of influence. Such discursive regulation further limits the possibilities of girls imagining future power for themselves.

In contrast with the claims of role model solutions, our findings suggest that being exposed to more leading women in the public eye, however popular such women may be, is not enough in itself for girls to view their own conditions as surmountable nor to imagine themselves in decision-making roles in the future. Participants' engagements with figures that might be described as 'role models' were shaped not only by their own experiences but by their awareness of the increasing hostility directed at women in the public eye, and of the particular targeting of Black and Brown women within this (Demos 2016). Conditions of public visibility are so hostile to women that exposure to coverage of influential women may deter girls from leadership rather than encourage them. These findings further illustrate the limits of contemporary exhortations to voice and to visibility for girls identified in chapter 1: the incitement to discourse is outweighed by the risks of speaking up. This was succinctly summarised by Serena, to whom we leave the final word: 'These things don't make me think I wouldn't want to be in charge, they make me think I don't want to be known for it'.

## NOTE

1. We offer a more detailed analysis of the neoliberal feminist address of popular girls' leadership campaigns in chapter 4.

## Chapter 3

# Girls on Meritocracy, Monarchy, and Hardworking Celebrity Black 'Queens'

In their consideration of power, who gets to wield it, and how it is obtained, girls in our study expressed both a desire for and scepticism of the promises of meritocracy. In their recognition, both that society does not consider them to be candidates for leadership and that the cost of visible positions of power for women is higher than they themselves wish to pay, girls identified the reproduction of social power through inheritance as an affront to their tendency towards systems which foster justice, equality, and fairness. In this chapter, we consider girls' discussions of meritocracy, hard work, overcoming hardship, inheritance, and the tensions between these concepts.

We examine how participants responded to Meghan Markle as a public figure whose star image intersects these contradicting themes and to institutional royalty as a concept. Having grown up in a context of neoliberal austerity, we found the girls to be politically aware, sceptical of hereditary principles, and concerned about inequality and the cost of the monarchy. The study that we draw upon here not only addresses a dearth of empirical analyses of public perceptions of royal celebrity, and the relationship between royal visibility and celebrity culture, but also interrogates the mediation and reception of the broader interpenetrations of race, gender, power, and royalty that Markle's star image (Dyer 1979) represents. We reveal the ways that British school-age girls respond to, and internalise, ideas about power, privilege, royalty, work, and meritocracy. More broadly, we demonstrate their negotiations with the concept of inheritance through imagined racial and royal 'bloodlines'. We examine how the myths of meritocracy that underpin celebrity culture and a trend towards celebrity support for social justice issues shape the girls' expectations of the role of a cultural figurehead. We also explore girls' navigation of the tensions between the monarchy's stated role in supporting social causes and their role in upholding a regressive status quo.

First, we will examine the girls' framings of royal celebrity and how these relate to their understanding of inherited privilege, their belief in meritocracy, and their sense of social justice. Then we examine how participants discussed inherited privilege in terms comparable to common narratives around state welfare benefits, the undeserving poor, and the question of what might constitute 'deserving' royalty – a question which directly challenges the hereditary principle. We then consider Markle's royal celebrity alongside other Black women whom the girls discussed using a rhetoric of queendom: singer Beyoncé Carter-Knowles, rapper Nicki Minaj, rapper and actress Queen Latifah, and TV personality Oprah Winfrey. Lastly, we explore how the girls understand both royalty and race through the concept of 'bloodlines'. These discussions reveal the girls' capacity to disrupt traditional ideas of hereditary power, as they question upon whom it is conferred and find the status quo lacking.

## MEGHAN MARKLE AND ROYAL PUBLIC IMAGE MANAGEMENT

'The hereditary principle hangs by such a precarious thread', warns the Queen Mother in Netflix drama *The Crown* (2020). The warning, issued to Princess Margaret, is that the monarchy must work to manage its public image to secure the confidence of its subjects and, thus, the institution's continuance (in the episode this is done by hiding royal cousins with supposed genetic 'faults' to protect the appearance of an impeccable bloodline). While the episode and dialogue are fictional, the fate of the royal cousins is not, and we shall show how ideas of bloodline and inheritance permeate 'real life' everyday engagements with the concept of monarchy and its reproduction in the public imaginary. Since this episode aired, the monarchy has undergone succession with the death of Queen Elizabeth II and the passing of the crown to King Charles III. This follows a period of crisis in its public image management, for example, allegations of sex trafficking against Prince Andrew and accusations of racism against the royal family made by the Duke and Duchess of Sussex, Prince Harry and Meghan Markle, after their departure. At the heart of this royal PR crisis is the question of who deserves power. This has tested the precarious thread imagined by *The Crown,* with debate centring around polling data that suggests a decline in popularity of the British monarchy among young people (Royston 2024). However, surprisingly little is known about the attitudes of the young people upon whom the monarchy's future popularity depends. This chapter goes some way to address this lack, examining the attitudes of girls from the time of the wedding between Prince Harry and Meghan Markle to the present, through media events in which discourses surrounding both inherited privilege and race intensified in popular culture.

Markle's entry into the British royal family has been understood as part of the effort in image management alluded to by the (fictional) Queen Mother of *The Crown,* as her feminism and status as a successful, Black female celebrity were co-opted by the monarchy to project the appearance of modernisation (Clancy and Yelin 2018). This narrative of progress afforded the monarchy support in traditionally Republican sections of society (Bradby 2020; Freeman 2018), but was later jeopardised as Harry and Markle moved to North America and resigned as senior royals and gave a controversial interview with Oprah Winfrey explaining that institutional monarchy was not, in fact, a hospitable environment for Markle as a biracial, Black woman, and/or her proclaimed progressive goals.

Media representations of Markle demonstrated a sudden pivot from adulation to censure (Yelin and Clancy 2021), demonstrating explicit and implicit racism, sexism, and ageism (Willson 2021; McLennan 2021). Positive coverage centred around a misguided celebration of the 'postracial' Britain Markle is held to represent (Andrews 2021) and her efforts to position herself as politically progressive after leaving the royal family (Clancy and Yelin 2021). Another set of narratives that surrounded Markle, which has not been discussed elsewhere and offers a backdrop to the celebrity values of hardworking meritocracy that concern this chapter, are those about Markle's relationship with work: for example, the characterisation of her as the early-rising, hardworking, demanding 'Duchess Difficult' (Hussein 2018), and stories that focus on her early career history, especially periods of struggle or sexualisation (Allen 2018). The subtext to these stories is a culture clash with the habitus of the upper classes, signaling classed scepticism around her appropriateness as a royal bride. We will argue how characterisations of Markle's work history and work ethic jar with existing frameworks of royalty and inherited power, and as such were a key foundation for what the girls we spoke to saw as Markle's appeal.

## THE ROYAL FAMILY, FANDOM, AND GIRLS

This chapter is positioned to address the lack of empirical work on royalty and celebrity, especially young people's attitudes towards the monarchy, as this offers the closest indication we have of whether the popularity that secures the continuation of the royal family persists into the next generation. As such, we turn to girls themselves as a larger societal debate rages about why support for the monarchy among young people might be in decline (Royston 2024).

It has been three decades since the last comprehensive scholarly study into attitudes towards the British royal family. Michael Billig's *Talking of the Royal Family* shares interviews with British families, as 'to talk about royalty is to talk of many other things. . . . To study talk of royalty is to investigate the tones and patterns of contemporary consciousness' (Billig 1992, vii). Much of the other scholarship that does exist focuses on more fan-like audiences who are already fervently invested in the royals, through interviews with those who have travelled to witness royal public appearances (Rowbottom 1998; Otnes and Maclaran 2015; Widholm and Becker 2015). As a result, royal audiences have been frequently framed as uncritical of the monarchy and the inequality it represents, using the royals to construct their sense of national identity (Nairn 1988; Rowbottom 1998) and smoothing over envy and class differences (Rowbottom 1998; Billig 1992; Mendick et al. 2018).

The lack of empirical audience work in the study of celebrity has been frequently lamented (Holmes 2004; Couldry 2004; Turner 2010; Barnes et al. 2015). As Mendick et al. ask, why do 'researchers focus on fan cultures, and neglect more everyday, ambivalent and even hostile engagements with contemporary celebrity?' (2015, 374). In their conversations with teens about aspiration, Mendick et al. identify 'celebrity as a site of struggle that is put to work by young people, informed by their own experiences and by their class, gender and race' (2018, 13), and find that the younger generation of royals in particular are deployed in the job of 'defusing resentment at the growing inequalities' under Conservative austerity (138). Headlines claiming the 'Duke and Duchess of Sussex are single-handedly modernising the monarchy' (Furness 2019) 'co-opted' Markle's feminism and the celebration of racial 'diversity' she represents to defuse resentment against the royals (Clancy and Yelin 2018). As a Black working woman entering the seat of British hereditary power, Markle represents an intervention into a 'princess culture' that is repressively classed, gendered, and racialised (Yelin and Clancy 2021; Gregory 2010; Faulkner 1997; Shome 2001). As the targets of this 'princess culture', the attitudes of girls in particular to such 'shifting collective imaginaries of racialised nobility' (Yelin and Clancy 2021) illuminate how such ideas are engaged with by the people most implicated by them, especially in relation to their own gendered, classed, and racialised identities.

Fandom is frequently constructed as feminised irrationality (Williamson 2005; Williams 2011) and combines with assumptions about girl audiences particularly understood as 'at risk' (Harris 2004; Projansky 2007), overly invested in parasocial relationships (Horton and Wohl, 1956; Ferchaud et al. 2018) or prone to acts of collective hysteria (Duffet 2013). Scholars of girlhood and the media have worked to redress these problematic assumptions, showing instead, for example, that girls' engagements with celebrities reveal complex acts of wider meaning-making (Duits and van Romondt 2009) and criticality in relation to gendered inequities (Keller and Ringrose 2015). And yet, such constructions persist in media discourses of, for example, Markle inspiring 'TOO MUCH HYSTERIA' (Chan 2018), a heavily gendered choice of words locating emotional excess specifically in the female body (Devereux 2014). It is in this context of gendered constructions of fandom and princess culture, and also understandings of royal audiences as particularly uncritically invested, that we turn to girls themselves to better understand their negotiations of privilege, inequality, race, and celebrity in their discussions of Markle's entry into the royal family. The racial politics of girls' fandom demand attention given the fact that mainstream representations of Black femininity frequently fail to represent the complex experiences of Black girl audiences (Lewis 2019), audiences who use fan practices to challenge, negotiate, and actively work against racist ideologies (McPherson 2019; Connor 2019; Kalterfleiter and Alexander 2019) and who are less likely to see themselves positively reflected in positions of power (Smooth and Richardson 2019). While the girls we spoke to occupy a range of ethnic and racial identities, the discussions revealed the centrality of the ways in which gender and race intersect in their engagements with women in the public eye.

## GIRLS' FAVOURITE ROYALS ARE ANTI-MONARCHY FIGURES

When girls were asked to think of examples of positive female leaders, some drew upon female royals. For example, one girl in Glasgow chose Mary, Queen of Scots, because 'she always persevered and fought for her country'. Meanwhile, in a conversation about who the girls would trust to lead them to safety in an emergency, two girls in Glasgow concurred on the sixteenth-century monarch:

*Ruth:* Mary Queen of Scots.

*Tamsin:* I was about to say that.

However, rather than an example of monarchical sentiment, this choice can be read in light of contemporary feminist retellings such as the 2018 Josie Rourke film *Mary Queen of Scots*, which casts Mary Stuart as a woman caught in struggles with patriarchal systems. Moreover, given that the girls who chose Mary Queen of Scots were based in Glasgow, this choice must primarily be understood as an assertion of their Scottish identity and as such can be interpreted as an example of the girls positioning themselves as oppositional to the Windsors and the contemporary King *of England* in the choice of a historical figure associated with plots to overthrow and murder Queen Elizabeth I, then queen of England.

One girl pulled up an image of Mary Queen of Scots on her phone and offered this as her chosen image of a female leader she admired. Whereas girls usually chose contemporary memes and photographs, this portrait of Mary Queen of Scots was the only painted artwork among the images found online and selected by the girls. The severe gaze of the unsmiling, formal portrait emphasises the queen's dignity in a manner common to royal portraits of the era designed to convey the sitter's suitability to their leadership role. Featuring the queen in sumptuous sixteenth-century fashion with pearls decorating her hair, ears, and embroidered, stiff, high-necked, puffed-shouldered doublet of glowing coral silk, narrow, corseted waist, and artificially wide, panniered hips, the portrait may appear to be anomalous in the sample of images and remote from the girls' experiences given the historical distance of nearly 500 years. However, the historic watercolour by François Clouet is thought to be painted in 1558, placing the queen at 16 years old and therefore within the age range of our participants. The choice of someone who was famously crowned at 6 days old and ruled Scotland in person from the age of 18 could therefore represent these girls' desire that their youth should not impede their opportunities to hold power and responsibility (figure 3.1).

Another example of girls choosing a historic royal figure as a good female leader precisely because they represent anti-royal sentiment was Princess Diana, who they explained was admirable precisely because she contravened royal protocol and existed in contention with institutional monarchy. In Wiltshire, Molly chose Diana because 'she broke all, like, the royal rules really. Like, when AIDS was a big thing, people wouldn't go near people with it, they thought "oh I'm going to catch it, oh I shouldn't go near gay people". But, she went to a charity, she hugged them.' Whereas for Molly, this break in royal protocol and homophobic cultural discourses around AIDS signified Diana was a rule breaker, Lynn in Cardiff understood the same historic moment as a sign of the non-hierarchical approaches that we will examine in chapter 4: 'like, she just seems, like, very like down to earth. Not like taking the power that she had as a princess to her head, but like, I remember like, correct me if I'm wrong, but I think she went to, like, this hospital and, like, didn't she have, like, gloves and she took them off [...] I feel like a leader has to have that, like, openness and so you can feel like you can talk to them'.

One girl searched for and selected an image of Princess Diana in a hospital holding a patient's hand (figure 3.2). The photo was taken at the Shaukat Khanum Memorial Hospital in Lahore in 1997 in what turned out to be her last visit to Pakistan. Wearing a simple Pakistani Shalwar kameez in vibrant

**Figure 3.1     Image of Mary, Queen of Scots, Found Online by a Participant.**

blue, Diana stands out against the gleaming white bedsheets, doctors' coats, and hospital walls. Her height, blonde hair, and white skin further mark her as the visitor in this space. Eyes locked on each other, the warm smiles of Diana standing looking down and the patient prone in her hospital bed looking up override the abjection of illness (Kristeva 1982) and the spectre that it may be terminal, signified by IV drips that loom behind them and the scarf that covers the cancer patient's hair. In the centre of the photograph is their hand-shake. As participant Lynn observed in relation to other similar famous photo opportunities, neither wears gloves and the suggestion is of a warm intimacy unconcerned with anxieties of germ transfer. The image sits within the way

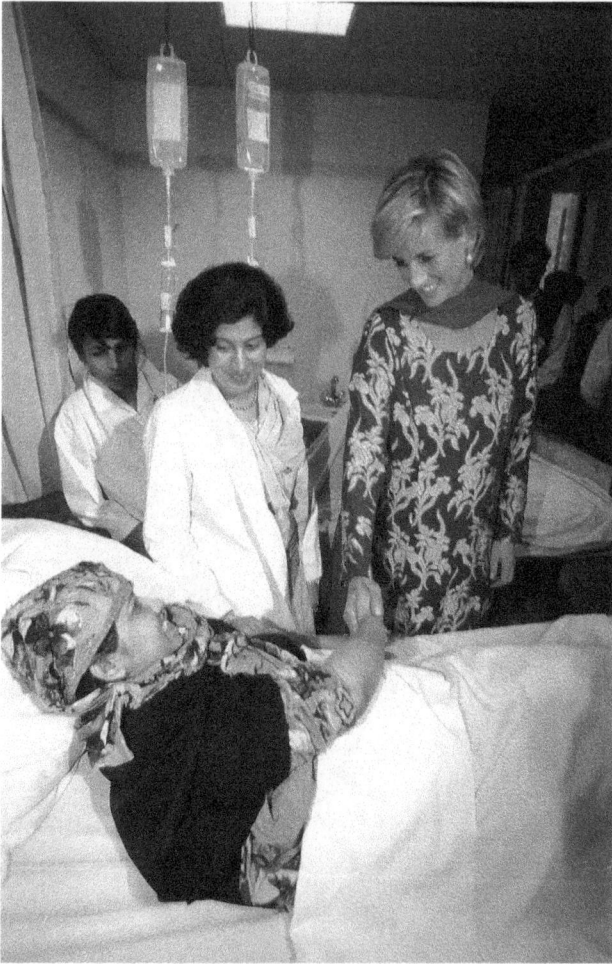

**Figure 3.2   Image of Diana, Princess of Wales, Found Online by a Participant.**

they discussed Diana with admiration in relation to leadership characteristics of being 'down to earth', open, approachable, progressive, and in contrast to institutional monarchy, its regressive protocol and 'taking the power that she had as a princess to her head'.

The girls in Glasgow who chose historic rebel Mary Queen of Scots also raised Princess Diana as an example of positive representations of female leadership:

*Ruth:* I mean, Princess Diana was quite good as well.

*Tamsin:* She didn't care about the royal . . .

*Ruth:* Like those royal guidelines that she had to follow as a member of the royal family and she didn't. I mean you know what the 'revenge dress' is don't you? The black dress that she wore with the necklace, that's against . . .

*Tamsin:* The royal stuff.

*Ruth:* Because she showed off quite a lot of skin and all that with it.

The girls' chosen royals were both aligned with and at odds with royal power. The state of being a royal figurehead was not, in itself, read as leadership, rather the mutinous disobedience required to go against the 'rules', 'guidelines', and 'stuff' of structural monarchy was the admired quality. Rebellion against the British monarchy as an institution was a key criterion for viewing a royal individual as a good leader. That they connected this to the policing of female sexuality and the double bind of attention on feminine appearance, discussed in chapter 2, suggests that their choice of women they see as ungovernable is tied to the hostile landscape girls perceive with which women with power must continually negotiate. That is, their choices implicitly speak to debates of structure versus agency and women's capacity to act upon and within a misogynist environment. The 'revenge dress' in particular, an off-the-shoulder velvet mini dress worn in smiling photographs after Diana's separation from her husband, is an icon of escape from maltreatment by (at the time of the Glasgow conversation, newly minted King) Charles III. That is, it locates Diana's power within her sexuality and attractiveness (McRobbie) but situates that power within the wider, limiting structure of patriarchal harm at individual and institutional levels.

In their discussion of royal figures, the girls frequently collapsed categories, revealing the instability of distinctions between roles such as royal, leader, and celebrity, and of fact and fiction. Discussing Wonder Woman, Asian girls from the East Midlands focused on the signification of princesshood, a trope deeply rooted in British folklore that is firmly associated with repressive ideas of femininity, perfection, and whiteness (Gregory 2010), which the girls saw as a tension with the dynamic vigour and aggression of superheroineism:

*Zainab:* She was able to fight and she was strong, but she was also a princess. So, it shows, like, us women: she was a woman, she was a princess, and she was a fighter [ . . . ]

*Maryam:* So, when she mentioned that Wonder Woman is a Princess and that she, like, fought. And her idea of brave. But, I feel like she was a bit, like, too much.

*Interviewer:* Tell me more about that?

*Maryam:* Yes. Murder.

*Interviewer:* Yes murder is probably a bit too far isn't it.

*Maryam:* So, like, she was a princess as well. But, she didn't want to be the typical princess. She wanted to, like, be different to the others. So, yeah.

*Zainab:* Talking about princesses, Princess Diana.

The rapidity with which the girls segue between fictional representations and historic figures shows that leadership, in the minds of the girls we spoke to, hinges upon the causes and characteristics that a woman stands for, rather than the specific role or job she holds. The prospect of murder and the threat of physical harm is fundamental to the girls' consideration of what they perceive to be the risks of visibility and is founded upon concrete recent examples such as the shooting of Malala Yousafzai. As shown in chapter 2, this is not the only point in our fieldwork that the conversation turned to discussions of media representations of murder and another of these examples will be discussed in detail in chapter 5. For now, this exchange shows that Princess Diana comes to mind as a positive example alongside ideas that are anti 'the typical princess'. We will now examine how this criterion of atypicality emerges in conversations about Markle, as does this flexible approach to the concept of royalness, which sees the girls segue instantly between historic royal women and fictional superheroines.

## UNSTABLE TAXONOMIES OF ROYAL CELEBRITY AND GIRLS' DESIRE FOR POSITIVE SOCIAL CHANGE

Hostile media reactions to Markle can be understood as illustrating wider currents of racism in contemporary British society (Hirsch 2020; Malik 2020; Yelin and Clancy 2021), and this Otherness (Said 1978; Ahmed 2010) to the royals was perceived by girls we spoke to in North London and understood to be implicitly racialised: 'Not going to lie, when Meghan Markle came inside the Prince's life, everything started to change. [ . . . ] She's actually helping people outside. She's not really with them [the royal family], she is more the person outside the family'. Nonetheless, it was clear that the girls we interviewed saw this as a positive quality that signaled a moment of progressive change with far-reaching ramifications.

Girls in the Home Counties similarly expressed a belief that Markle's entry into the royal family was significant and unexpected: 'When she was first announced that he was marrying her, I was just like, "no way!"' They readily listed examples of her support of social causes: 'I think a lot of people do like her, and she supports a lot of charities. Like, she went, like, she does all of these charity works. When she went to Australia and stuff. And what she wrote on bananas for people.' The reference to bananas is to a photo opportunity in which Markle visited a charity named One25, which provides 'food bags' to sex workers. Markle wrote messages on bananas, including 'you are strong', 'you are special', and 'you are brave', typifying the kind of neoliberal, celebrity feminism and its confidence cult(ure) discussed in chapter 1, in which women are 'hailed as enterprising and self-managing subjects' (Gill and Orgad 2016, 332) and encouraged towards individual responsibility through positive thinking in ways which elide structural inequalities that might, for example, lead to reliance on private charity.

As a Black woman in the British monarchy, Markle was subject to relentless criticism in the British media. As we have demonstrated throughout this book, the girls we interviewed were highly alert to the ferocious scrutiny of women in the public eye and could recount the more outlandish charges levelled at Markle:

*Samira:* Like, women have to take responsibility for their actions a lot more than men. Like, men can go around saying – I don't want to say whatever – but they can say a lot more and get away. Compared to a woman, where they are very much, like, brought down and like pinned on that. Almost targeted on that one point they've made.

*Nola:* So, for example, you know Meghan Markle? When she was still here she had avocado on toast and they made this huge big deal about it as though it was something terrible and like . . .

*Sarika:* Yeah, and you see so many people having it now.

*Nola:* If like anyone else had it, it wouldn't really matter.

*Sarika:* Literally.

*Interviewer:* So criticised for tiny things?

*Sarika:* Yeah .

*Nicki:* Avocado on toast is good, it tastes so good! But it's only her what's she been, like, it's put in a bad way. Everyone else it's okay to do, but not her.

*Interviewer:* And why do you think that was?

*Nicki:* It's different for certain people, but because she's already been put in a bad light already. So, they just wanted to put her more into that light I guess.

*Sarika:* I feel like even if you haven't done something necessarily, they will find a way to criticise you. Like you could do like the smallest thing, it might not even be a big thing at all, it might not even be a thing, but people will find a way to criticise you and find a way to, like, bring you down I guess.

The reference is to a *Daily Mail* headline asking, 'Is Meghan's favourite snack fuelling drought and murder?', an inventive reframing of a farming story in which the author found a way to tie human rights abuses in avocado farming to Markle because she was known to eat the fruit (Leonard 2019). This demonstrates how 'Markle is a figure who has sparked such a proliferation of discourse around her that she has proved a useful tool for those wishing to attract audiences and generate media views' (Yelin and Clancy 2021). The story is one of a number of news stories revolving around the harsh censure of Markle for 'crimes' remarkable only for their insignificance, especially when compared to Prince Andrew whose alleged sex trafficking was a concurrent media story (Clancy and Yelin 2021) and whose name never arose in the girls' discussions of monarchy, despite their concluding that Markle was an example showing that men can 'get away' with shirking responsibility for their crimes in ways that women cannot. Markle is another case from which the girls conclude that visibility for women comes with the likelihood that punitive gendered media cultures will 'find a way to criticise you [and] bring you down'.

As interviewers, we did not mention any specific public figures; the celebrities discussed in this chapter were all raised in conversation by the girls themselves. Indeed, Markle and the royal family arose in conversation following a discussion of Beyoncé, which drew upon the vocabulary of royalty to construct her global pop-stardom: 'Beyoncé, she is known more for her singing, because she's known as, like, the queen of music'. The girls' discussions of Markle demonstrated the complexities of royal and celebrity status within wider neoliberal contexts where success and privilege are accounted for through myths of meritocracy. Straddling celebrity and royalty, Markle brings the myths of meritocracy that underpin celebrity culture (Littler 2004, Dyer 1979) into contact with the institution which most enshrines inherited power and wealth. The girls were acutely aware of Markle's special status as both celebrity and royal. Markle's celebrity power was seen to have been newly cemented by her royal status, with one girl marveling that 'people have slept on the floor for this girl!' The royal family were not seen as celebrities: 'I wouldn't say they are celebrities – they are just well-known'. They felt that the royal family needed their own distinct categorisation: 'I think the royal family is a different category altogether, isn't it?' Even when not discussing the royals, questions of what was earned, what was deserved, and what was worked for percolated throughout conversations with the girls, revealing an investment in myths of meritocracy where hard work promises reward, and inherited power is an affront to their understanding of fairness:

*Interviewer:* So what's the difference between a leader and a celebrity?

*Cadence:* Um most leaders have, like, worked hard to become what they are now. And a lot of celebrities, a lot of them have also worked hard, but also a lot of them have been born into celebrity.

*Interviewer:* So it's a question of whether they've earned it or not?

*Cadence:* Yeah.

The girls' taxonomisation of royalty and celebrity chimes with Chris Rojek's three categories of celebrity: *achieved* celebrity such as actors, based on talent and accomplishment; *attributed* celebrity such as reality TV stars, manufactured by the media; and *ascribed* celebrity which, as in cases of royal fame, is a product of bloodline (2001). As Yelin has argued (2016), such distinctions regressively reproduce cultural assumptions about who *deserves* fame and its rewards, with value judgements which do more to police than to describe the boundaries of celebrity (often along gendered, classed, and racialised lines). Markle's royal celebrity demonstrates the inadequacy of such neat categories in a star image where royalty, acting talent, and the gossiped-about private life comfortably fuse all three. Despite their identification of the distinct peculiarity of royal celebrity, the girls understood such categories to be collapsable. When asked, 'Can you think of anyone who you think has inherited their leadership role?' they answered thus:

Lois: The royal family. Phoebe: Yeah, definitely royal family. Esther: And Miley CyrusThrough humour, the girls' responses demonstrate the instability of these categories (via reference to pop star Miley Cyrus' country-singer father, Billy Ray Cyrus) and an awareness that social advantages based upon bloodline and inheritance involve both economic and symbolic capital. Scholarly debates about what distinguishes royalty versus celebrity are longstanding, often centring around Princess Diana's opening up of a more media-friendly, celebrity-informed way of conducting her royal visibility (Richards et al. 1999; Rojek 2001; Shome 2014). By contrast, the girls understood Markle as having earned her celebrity in her own right before she became a royal. In a discussion of the differences between 'leaders' and 'celebrities', Markle was either decisively labelled a celebrity by our participants or occupied both categories, something which was seen to afford greater opportunity for positive influence and change-making in society. For girls in Wiltshire, royalty was seen to compound and increase the influence of Markle's celebrity status, and the likelihood that she would create positive social change.

*Molly:* Both [ . . . ]

*Isabel:* I'd say celebrity. She was, like, mainly a celebrity before.

*Molly:* She was a celebrity before she. . .

*Cess:* [ . . . ] I just knew her because I watched her TV shows.

*Zora:* People would see her as a celebrity mainly, but now she kind of, she can do more.

*Molly:* She has more influence on people now.

*Zora:* Like, as a member of the royal family now, she will have to go to, like, events and do this, that, and the other. When she was a celebrity, she kind of didn't have to do it. So, like, as a member of the royal family, she can get into it and really, like, push.

*Molly:* She can take on the role of a leader.

*Zora:* Yeah. She could take it on, but as a celebrity she has that choice.

Joining the royal family was seen as affording Markle greater opportunity to change society, despite debates over whether royals have meaningful power or adequately deploy their wealth and privilege for the benefit of others. This showed an understanding of how celebrity brands are built through expansion across categories and the contradictions that arise as a result. This tension is exemplified by Harry and Markle's departure from the royal family, which was announced with the trademark and website, Sussex Royal. Media debate ensued over whether they could be considered 'financially independent' while trading on royal credentials, culminating in the queen banning use of their HRH titles or the Sussex Royal brand. The creation of the Sussex Royal brand, in tandem with their departure from the royal family, exemplifies the tensions arising from royalty being both enabling and disabling: the royal *brand* is enabling (evidenced in Harry and Markle's fight to maintain association), while the royal *structure* is disabling (as shown by their need to exit). In line with this, the girls were simultaneously aware that becoming royal might give Markle a platform to 'do more' and were highly cynical about the institutional monarchy's commitment to social progress:

*Donna:* Royalty are power, know better than you. Yeah, if they had power.

*Carly:* Because, do you know, royalty people, all they do is they go like this [gives a comic royal wave]

*Bella:* And they drink teas.

*Mel:* I think the queen is overrated though.

*Bella:* Yeah.

*Alesha:* Sometimes, she doesn't really make a change.

*[ . . . ]*

*Donna:* Yeah, because, like, the royal family are just, they don't even do anything. Having the royal family, everybody goes there and goes "oh hi, hi, hi" [another comic wave]

*[ . . . ]*

*Etta:* Okay so the royal family they don't do anything because the Houses of Parliament, like the Prime Minister, that basically make all the decisions. Because, if the queen wants to do something, then she has to ask the Prime Minister if they can do it or not.

Despite their understanding of parliament as the true seat of decision-making, the girls we spoke to understood royalty as indexical to power. 'Royalty *are* power' [emphasis added], even if that power is perceived to be symbolic. As our participants occupied multiple intersections of denied agency – being young, female, in all but one case state school educated, and, in some cases, girls of colour, queer, or disabled – their discussion of the monarchy as symbolic of the very concept of power was imbued with their awareness that they were commenting upon power that they lacked. Rejecting this hierarchy and reclaiming their status through the right to judge, they mocked and punctured these symbols, consoling themselves with comically condescending royal waves and the idea that they are condescended to by those who are merely impotently ceremonial. In their cheerful irreverence, the girls joked that such pointless gesturing is 'all they do', along with drinking tea, an icon of colonialism invoked by the girls as a symbol of the British class system. This image of a family who 'don't even do anything' but drink tea evokes a charge of laziness. In deeming the queen to be 'overrated' for not 'really mak[ing] a change', our participants recognised that, even if royal power is partially symbolic, royals certainly have the means to change society and condemn them for not doing more.

## 'DO YOU KNOW WHO SHOULD HAVE THE CROWN?' DESERVING ROYALS VERSUS THOSE 'JUST SITTING THERE'

The girls constructed institutional monarchy as *un*deserving while at the same time identifying Meghan and Harry as exceptions by which they prove this rule. Meritocratic discourses of labour function to construct elites as if they 'deserve their wealth and status through [depictions] of their hard work' (Mendick et al. 2018, 53). Through ideas of exceptionality, which in part drew upon Markle's outsider status as a working actress, as a Black woman, and as hailing from the supposed 'Land of Opportunity', the girls were able to evade the irreconcilability of their investments in ideas of meritocracy and their enthusiasm for individual celebrity royals. Like Markle, Harry is positioned as a positive contrast to his impotently ceremonial, lazy family. Harry's association with Markle cements his popularity; the perception of Markle as a dynamic outsider reciprocally builds upon perceptions of Harry, whose 'ordinariness is deemed to be *out of the ordinary* and thus praiseworthy' and whose popularity draws upon charity work and army service (Mendick et al. 2018, 66). Just as the girls we interviewed in north London believed becoming royal increased Markle's potential to change society, Harry was discussed as someone who 'helps people', in contrast to their understanding of royal contributions to society more generally:

*Claire:* It is a failure, but Harry has helped as well, because he's helped loads of charities, he's been in the army. He had a really bad childhood because his mum died so he had a bad life, so it's not fair, because he still helps people. [ . . . ]

*Donna:* Do you know who should have the crown, Harry, not Prince Charles or whoever he is, he don't deserve it.

*Judith:* Prince Charles has taken . . .

*Claire:* It's William.

*Donna:* But William doesn't deserve.

*Alesha:* Because he didn't really *do* anything, all he did was go the army.

*Judith:* [ . . . ] It's Prince William that don't do nothing.

*Donna:* Prince William is just sitting there with his wife and . . . (waves) Like this!

*Claire:* Harry deserves it.

*Mel:* But Harry is younger than William so he's not going to get it.

*[All talking together.]*

*Donna:* All William did was sit with his wife and get his wife pregnant and have more children.

Here, we see discourses of 'deserving' royals versus those that 'don't do nothing', and an inversion of charges commonly levied against people on benefits – sitting around having too many children. This discourse usually hinges on cultural anxieties of a multiplying underclass, squandering collective resources through dependence upon state handouts (Tyler and Jensen 2015;

Jones 2012), and is here upturned to question what level of social contribution represents 'doing' enough to 'deserve' the state handout of a royal stipend. It is worth noting that producing an heir is literally William and Kate's 'job', such as any royal has one. The royal 'work' of tours, photo opportunities, and site visits is highly performative, manufacturing consent for their own continuation ('go[ing] to, like, events and do[ing] this, that, and the other'). Harry receives empathy for the loss of his mother, Princess Diana, as a child, and his military role and charity work effectively shield him from charges of doing nothing. William's storminay contains these same elements of loss and performed labour, but he is comparatively disliked: deemed sedentary, insufficiently active, and, therefore, undeserving. This exchange is the only mention of Charles, then Prince of Wales at the time of the interview, not yet having succeeded his mother, Queen Elizabeth II. He appears in discussion only to be rejected as undeserving: 'Who should have the crown? Harry, not Prince Charles or whoever he is, he don't deserve it'. It is worth noting also that this interview was undertaken before Harry's memoir *Spare* was published, shifting the focus of his star image towards a more confessional model of celebrity intimacy based upon personal revelations. The girls constructed economies of work as they discussed which kinds of work are valuable, with William and Charles deemed to be taking state money for nothing. We don't know how Judith's sentence would have ended, but in a conversation about social contribution or lack thereof, Prince Charles is understood as someone who takes. This discourse continued across geographical locations and time periods, echoed closely by girls in Cardiff in a discussion about whether Queen Elizabeth II could be seen as a leader in the summer after the Platinum Jubilee and before her death:

*Susan:* Obviously there were, like, huge celebrations for her the other week, but I don't know if she is even really, like, a leader. I don't really know, yeah.

*Sarika:* Like, no offence, but she doesn't actually *do* anything. She has people to do it for her. [ . . . ]

*Susan:* Yeah, I know and that's kind of what I think, like, I'm not a huge, I'm not particularly, like, into following the Queen, or the Royal Family. But, like, I guess she sort of has a role. She kind of, like, represents a bit [ . . . ]. But I think you're right. Today she doesn't really, like, *do* that much.

After Queen Elizabeth II's death, girls in Glasgow repeated the desire for the royal class to work in what they considered to be real jobs:

*Ruth:* She was like one of the first female monarchs who actually went to war and with other people. I think she worked on the cars or something.

*Tamsin:* She did, aye.

*Ruth:* She worked on the cars. So, she was the first one who actually, like, done a job.

For these girls, for whom inherited power is an affront to their idea of fairness, when searching for value in the royal family, they turn to the one point in 1945 during which they consider Queen Elizabeth II, who reigned as monarch for 70 years, to have 'done a job': royal 'duties' do not count as labour for our participants. The girls' conversations were permeated with discourses of meritocracy, which are some of the most 'prevalent social and cultural tropes of our time' (Littler 2018, 1). Littler explicates the relationship between hereditary power and the legitimising potency of meritocratic discourses of hard work: 'The rich will frequently talk about how hard they work, especially when their money comes from unearned income, trying to offset extensive privilege by framing their activity in terms of manual labour . . . a necessary mode of self-presentation for contemporary entitled elites' (2018, 128). The justification of what the girls identify as a leisure class who 'don't do nothing' hinges upon one example of manual labour which occurred almost 80 years ago. While their benchmark for approving of public figures is heavily imbued with a vocabulary of meritocracy that has frequently been used to blame the poor for their poverty, the girls in our workshops pointed to, and took issue with, the limits of meritocracy in a society with hereditary power.

## 'THINK LIKE A QUEEN': BEYONCÉ, NIKI MINAJ, OPRAH, HARDWORKING CHOSEN QUEENS, AND QUEENDOM AS EXCELLENCE

The views of the girls on celebrities they believe to exemplify hard work offer a counterpoint, illuminating how they use discourses of meritocracy to problematise the hereditary celebrity of royalty. In contrast to the characterisation of monarchy as sedentarily undeserving of their privilege, the girls discussed stars they view as passionate about their work, positively changing society, and not in it 'for the money' (despite also being very rich).

Throughout their discussions, the girls offered examples of women they saw as having positive leadership qualities. Beyoncé, Michelle Obama, Malala Yousufzai, and Oprah Winfrey were discussed in terms of the girls feeling that they were better represented by those who they felt had overcome discrimination. This logic extended to Ellen DeGeneres and the homophobic discrimination they saw her as overcoming to become a powerful queer woman.[1] As such, among the top answers to our question asking which female leaders they admired, three women of colour and one lesbian consistently appeared: Obama, Beyoncé, Yousufzai, and DeGeneres.

The girls' preferences for women they perceived as overcoming discrimination and hardship were not a straightforward question of seeing themselves represented; rather, such narratives interact with their appetite for a meritocratic society. This is not merely the common, if simplifying, exhortation that representation matters, as these preferences remained regardless of our participants' own racial or sexual identities. Rather, the girls saw the upliftment of marginalised groups as beneficial to all and identified that marginalised women are forced to work harder than their White, hetero-counterparts.

Discourses of 'hard work' frequently uphold and legitimate inequality under capitalism (Littler 2017). However, hard work was integral to the girls' vocabulary of admiration and achievement, underpinning both their criticism of monarchy and their praise of certain celebrities. American singer Beyoncé is one star whom the girls we spoke to viewed as a good leader according to these criteria of hard work and social change. The girls construct contrasting economies of work around Beyoncé and the British monarchy, which hinge upon benchmarks of effort and social contribution, and find the British royal family lacking on both counts: an institution that 'don't do nothing' 'doesn't deserve'. Beyoncé, with her apparent well-deserved high status and commitment to social change, is especially pertinent for royal comparison, as the girls we interviewed constructed her through a conceptual framing of nobility, (which then became the spur to discussions of the British royal family):

*Mel:* I don't even think Beyoncé does it for the money. She just wants to be heard and wants to make a difference.

*Carly:* She wants women to be seen and heard, that's why everybody loves her [ . . . ]

*Toya:* The people that don't like Beyoncé, the only reason [ . . . ] is because people were branding. You know how people were calling her the queen? That's the only reason why they get – why is she being called the queen, why are you putting tags on her? Number one, she is royalty, there is royalty in her blood.

*Judith:* That's true.

*Bella:* Yes, there is, I watched snapchat. And number two, she didn't choose the name, people gave it to her but because that's what people call her, they try and use that. That's the only thing they have on her.

In her cultural output, Beyoncé performs extreme hard work according to the demands of neoliberalism. The lyrics to *Formation* (2016) assert 'I work hard, I grind 'til I own it'. As bell hooks observes, 'black women are spotlighted, poised as though they are royalty', but for hooks this is 'capitalist money making' and therefore 'certainly not radical' (2016). By contrast, Emily Lordi argues that lyrics like 'Okay ladies, now let's get in formation' mobilise discourses of collective action challenging systems requiring 'people of color (especially women) hustle so hard to survive in the first place' (2017, 131). Beyoncé's combination of problematic discourses of 'meritocratic' hard work with articulated goals of collective progress offers a neat rendering of the girls' existence within and use of discourses of neoliberalism to express desires for another kind of society. This reveals the tensions of progressive girlhood under neoliberalism as they express their desire for social justice alongside rearticulations of the frequent exhortations upon them to 'lean in' as discussed in other chapters.

Any discussions of royalty, race, and hard work must account for the fact that aristocratic wealth was produced by the dehumanising labour of enslaved Black bodies. For Black women in particular, the myth of the Black superwoman derives from slave owners' characterisations of enslaved Black women's capacity to perform physical labour like men (Wallace 1990). Following a neoliberal turn in hip-hop 'hustle' discourse since the 1980s (Spence 2015 ), there is a 'thin line' between this particular slave-era stereotype and Beyoncé's performance of post-feminist grind culture (Chatman 2017).

In the invocation of Beyoncé's royalty, she is constructed as a *chosen* queen, crowned by her fans in the giving of the name 'Queen Bey'. Beyoncé has worked 'to solidify this monarchical identification' (Holtzman 2017, 183), styling herself with crowns, robes, tiaras, and halos and making specific references to historic queens of Europe and Africa such as Queen Elizabeth, Marie Antoinette, and Nefertiti. Most recently and explicitly, she released the 2020 visual album *Black is King*, which offers an allegory of diasporic reclamation of culture, ancestry, selfhood, and pride through the story of an exiled African prince. Through a panoply of aesthetics of Black majesty in costume, hair, set design, and performance, the film asserts Black pride and exhibits the richness, magnificence, and grandeur of Black identities and histories. Such aesthetics of Black majesty, like Markle's presence in the palace, have the potential to 'combat the ideological violence of a colonialist world that is determined to deny the conceptual possibility, let alone the real existence, of Black royalty' (Willson 2021).

That these performances of Beyoncé's are conditional upon her global superstardom means that they cannot be truly understood as democratic. Nonetheless, the girls' idea of a royal status conferred by the people and cemented through performance again destabilises principles of hereditary power. In her elevation to queendom, the girls we interviewed observed that Beyoncé is granted licence where other Black women receive censure:

[Beyoncé] came to accept the award [only] wearing jewellery and nobody said anything. . . . When Rihanna did it everyone was like, 'She's dressing like a prostitute!' [Beyoncé] wore jewellery, literally just jewellery, gold chains and nobody said anything. Everyone worshipped her for that, 'The queen! The queen!' If someone else does it, she's being a prostitute . . . a bad example.

The girls we spoke to showed awareness of unequally distributed risks of visibility, especially for women of colour such as Beyoncé and Markle, who must undertake the additional labour of navigating punitive respectability politics (Harris 2003) and their hyper-sexualisation at the hands of the press if they are to be seen as deserving.

There is ambivalence around the meaning the girls attributed to royalty or queendom. At points, 'queen' appeared as something negative that people 'have on' Beyoncé: a pejorative 'label' with (sometimes racialised) connotations of a difficult 'diva' temperament (Wiedhase 2015) – ideas invoked in the characterisation of Markle as 'Duchess Difficult' in stories about her grueling work ethic and timetable (Hussein 2018). 'The queen! The queen!' is invoked as the repetitive chant of mindless, collective worship by loyal subjects – defaulting to the dominant characterisation of fandom as pathologically excessive (Williamson 2005; Williams 2011; Duffet 2013). Such pathologisation of the masses who coronate their chosen, deserving queens depends upon the anti-democratic, monarchic logic of inheritance wherein 'the people' cannot be trusted to elect their own leaders.

Where Beyoncé was considered the 'queen of music', for other girls Nicki Minaj was the 'queen of rap'. Asked for examples of positive representations of female leaders, two girls responded:

*Susanna:* I have one, Nicki Minaj.

*Lubna:* Yes, me and you.

*Interviewer:* Tell me about how she is represented as a positive leader.

*Susanna:* She is presented as a queen in my eyes because she came up, like, from pretty much nothing. And people were trying to put her down all the time. And people were trying to influence her to do bad stuff, but she didn't do that bad stuff. She carried on and believed in what she believed in, and became the Queen of rap.

Where the young people Mendick et al. spoke to aligned Minaj with the 'illegitimate goals of austere meritocracy: gratuitous wealth and talentless fame' (2018, 114), for these 'care-experienced' girls in Essex, Minaj's trajectory fits with the meritocratic fantasy narrative of overcoming hardship to succeed.

Oprah Winfrey was another Black female celebrity who was both viewed as a good leader because she had overcome discrimination and was discussed through a lens of queendom. One girl remarked upon all that 'Oprah had to go through. . . . She was raped and then kicked out of show business and now she's one of the richest, most powerful Black women in America'. One girl found and shared an inspirational meme featuring a photograph of Oprah Winfrey with towering, glossy natural curls, a fashionable black dress and jewellery, and a beaming smile as if caught mid-laughter, all project the image of Black, female success (figure 3.3). Such online sharing of Black Joy in an era beset with footage of racist police murders has been theorised by Steele and Lu as a resistant act (2018), an understanding consistent with the girls' attitude to Black upliftment and rejection of the institutional White power that the British monarchy represents. Winfrey's hands are open before her as if caught mid-applause, suggesting her role as a TV personality who motivates and celebrates the 'real' people in her studio audiences. Superimposed text in a casual sans serif font offers the motivational, 'meritocratic' exhortation to 'Think like a queen. A queen is not afraid to fail'. Of course, the queen is heavily insulated from the possibility or consequences of failure

**Figure 3.3    Image of American TV Personality Oprah Winfrey Found Online by a Participant.**

because her power is inherited and shored up by systems designed to maintain it. The exhortation then is less to think as if one is unafraid to fail but to think as if one were surrounded by robust safety nets that prevent failure – a reality which royal systems of enshrined inequality ensure are only available to the few. Thus, the girls' attraction to discourses of self-coronation accorded with their wider desire to disrupt monarchic structures of inherited power with something they perceive to be more meritocratic, but again their attempts at disruption remain structured by potent underlying logics of inherited power.

Another example of a Black, female celebrity raised in response to being asked for positive examples of leaders is American rapper and actress Queen Latifah, whose royal, Afrocentric stage name and her album title *All Hail the Queen* have been understood as an expression of commitment to 'a specific racialised, gendered identity [that] challenges Eurocentric ideals', in terms of both white supremacy and fatphobic, Eurocentric beauty norms (Cochran, 2021:16).

*Tani:* Queen Latifah.

*Tell us about her, why do you raise her?*

*Tani:* Oh I just really like her style.

*Fara:* She's so beautiful

*Tani:* She's a loud person, she's beautiful.

*Ayana:* She can sing [ . . . ]

*Tani:* She is out there you know. She doesn't always put too much make-up on because she is the way she is.

For the girls we spoke to in North London, Queen Latifah was valued for resisting the strictures and scrutiny of feminine appearance we discussed in chapter 2, and for taking up space as a 'loud' person. In contrast to 'Duchess' and 'Princess' which have the aforementioned associations of a difficult, pet-ulant, or demanding girl or woman, the rhetoric of 'Queendom' has its own vectors of signification. The contemporary, popular usage was coined by the queer Black and Latinx communities of 1980s New York ballroom culture. Writing about the queer, underground language of Polari, Paul Baker charts how 'queen' originated as a slur rooted in misogynist, homophobic ideas about effeminacy but was reclaimed by the LGBT+ community as a term of endearment and affection (2004, 49) before its adoption into hip hop cultures by figures such as Queen Latifah as 'rap artists empower themselves with a title that speaks to their uniqueness' (Cochran 2021, 16). Etymologically, queen comes from the Old English word for woman and has since travelled both up and down our social scale: 'One form became used to denote those at the top . . . (royalty, those who were best at something, etc.) while the other experienced downward mobility', first being associated with 'ill-behaved' women – 'a hussy, a harlot, or strumpet' – and then 'eventually connected to homosexuality' (ibid.). Through contemporary representations like *RuPaul's Drag Race,* the superlative phrase 'Yasss Queen!' has entered the mainstream cultural lexicon as a form of encouragement and enthusiastic and celebratory support. If the cultural turn to Black majesty (Willson 2021), typified by Beyoncé's creative motifs and reactions to Markle's literal existence as a Black woman in the British monarchy, is an expression of Black Excellence (Hilliard 1995), then 'Yasss Queen!' is an expression of (Black and Latinx) Queer Excellence, which informs the girls' usage of rhetorics of queendom and through a process of mainstreaming has come around to coronate powerful cis-women like 'Queen Bey'.

## 'THERE IS ROYALTY IN HER BLOOD': ROYAL AND RACIAL BLOODLINES

Attending to the ways in which discourses of bloodline surface in the girls' discussions of royalty, celebrity, inheritance, and social change is instructive in understanding the role that public figures play in shaping their understanding of social and economic structures. Lineage and pedigree are concepts which are imbricated in our understandings of both royalty and race and, through both, have perpetuated social division and inequality (and to a lesser extent, myths of meritocracy owing to ideas of inherited ability).

Returning to the girls' discussion of Beyoncé's apocryphal royal blood, they imply that it cements her divine right to global superstardom. The concept of royal blood 'maps the circuit of aristocratic inheritance, predictably directing the flow of blood from generation to generation' (Smith 1999, 29). The crown Beyoncé inherits is that of unassailably iconic fame, democratic in its bestowal from below rather than by dynastic forebears. The discourses of royal blood as evidence of what Beyoncé deserves, however, offer further concession to hereditary logic. If Beyoncé has royal blood, her coronation by fans is more justified within, and less challenging to, structures of hereditary monarchy. *Formation*'s lyrics construct Beyoncé's daughter, Blue Ivy, as her 'baby heir with baby hair and Afros', again reasserting, while making space for Blackness within existing structures of inherited privilege, especially given Beyoncé's billionaire status (O'Malley Greenburg 2020). As Kenan Malik argued regarding Markle's entry into the British monarchy, 'making inherited privilege more "diverse"' (Malik 2019) is hardly the most urgent form of anti-racism while our government pursues 'one of the most overtly racist policy agendas the nation has experienced in decades' (Andrews 2021).

Where Beyoncé is celebrated for her royal blood outside of institutional monarchy, Markle is celebrated for bringing her 'unroyal' blood into it. The girls discuss Markle's lineage in explicitly racialised terms:

> *Donna:* The best thing about having Meghan join the royal family is that she actually has Black in her.
>
> *Toya:* A quarter.
>
> *Donna:* Yeah, a quarter okay, a quarter Black.

The imagined bloodlines of Markle and Beyoncé were discussed as if they offered a source of authenticity for the narratives which circulate in each woman's star image: for Beyoncé, 'royal blood' authenticates her superstar status and perceived regal demeanour; for Markle, its absence makes her a refreshing, more 'authentic' addition to the British royal family, again hinging upon her perceived unroyal, outsider status with Blackness as the desired, needed quality. The girls instinctively understood the monarchy to be what Andrews terms 'one of the premier symbols of Whiteness' (2021) and responded with glee to the destabilisation of monarchy as a racialised category. As such, Harry and Meghan's marriage is cast in the narrative tradition of '"healthy" mixing of blood across class lines [to] regenerate bloodlines that have gone stagnant [through] aristocratic obsession' (Smith 1999, 29). However, the idea of 'mixing' blood presupposes offspring, reproducing the dominant ideas surrounding a royal bride whose purpose is to give birth (Mantel 2013; Clancy and Yelin 2021). Presupposition of an heir, again, reproduces the centrality of inheritance to ideas of royalty.

While the enthusiasm for Markle's representational power as a Black woman was palpable in this conversation, among all of the girls we spoke to, and especially the girls of colour, the language through which they expressed this sentiment – a qualification of exactly *how* Black Markle is – reveals internalised cultural discourses which depict race as an objectified, quantifiable, biological fact of difference rather than an oppressive social construct. Such ways of talking about race run deep in our society, with a history in racist discourses of miscegenation. Since the nineteenth century, fascination with 'conceits of blood purity, heredity, and inherited character' as categories of 'race' are dangerously intertwined with white-supremacist ideas about 'innate, permanent, heritable differences in both the physical and the moral and intellectual capacities of races' (Smith 1999, 29). The invention and policing of such boundaries have upheld white-supremacist hierarchies which persist today. However, despite conceiving of racialised identities in this way, in contrast to racist ideas which police against 'interracial reproduction as a threat to the supremacy of the white race' (ibid., 30), the girls' position was unequivocally pro-Black. Markle represents deserving royalty precisely because, being pleasingly unroyal, they believe she will 'push' and 'do more'. The discursive constructions of the (un)royal blood of both Beyoncé and Markle reveal that the logic of inherited power is so potent in contemporary thought that it persistently structures and undermines discursive efforts to disrupt it.

## MARKLE AND WORK: ARISTOCRATIC EASE VERSUS THE EMBARRASSMENT OF CELEBRITY HUSTLE

Markle's departure from the royal family has been widely discussed in terms of her incompatibility as a Black woman in a racist institution and nation (Hirsch 2020; Malik 2020). The girls' approving discourses of meritocracy and hard work reveal additional incompatibilities in terms of the contrasting economies of labour she and the royal family represent. Returning to the aforementioned popular characterisations of Markle, which hinge upon her relationship with work, as well as the early-rising 'Duchess Difficult' (Hussein 2018), and the embarrassment of sexualised self-promotion from her early career stages (Allen 2018), there is her Hollywood glamour conflicting with William and Kate's strategic performance of normcore,[2] 'Bodenesque' middle classness (Littler 2017), and the racist inflexion of tall poppy syndrome after she 'made it' (Hirsch 2020; Malik 2020). These examples all mobilise discourses of meritocracy which falter at the palace door. While rags to riches stories have always been fabricated around royal brides (Clancy 2015, np), there is a public record of Markle's past labour – from her role as 'Briefcase Model #24' on *Deal or No Deal*, to aspirational lifestyle blogging, to acting in *Suits* – and the continued visibility of this 'hustle' (Spence 2015) is embarrassing to a class system which values 'ease' above all (Bourdieu 1984). The girls liked Markle because she sits within a framework of hardworking, Black, female celebrity success, and this is precisely why she is incompatible with royal structures in which (what the girls identify as little more than) smiling and waving is considered 'work'.

Markle's prior career and existing celebrity capital – her existence across unstable taxonomies of royal celebrity – are also what enable her to leave. Celebrity gives Markle a different power base, not dependent on royal structures of power, as shown when high-profile connections like Elton John and George Clooney came to her support (Furness 2019). Markle's acting career enables Harry to pitch her voiceover services (Ritschel 2020), sign a lucrative programming contract with Netflix (Royston 2020), and produce monetised podcast *Archewell Audio* featuring celebrity guests (Vincent 2020). Thus, her work history facilitates forms of money-making that trade in celebrity rather than royal contacts (the latter being a strategy for which Sarah Ferguson has been shamed (Bates 2010)). This is why the Sussex Royal brand has been a site of such a power struggle. When the Queen barred Harry and Meghan from using the word 'royal' in their 'branding' after their departure from the royal family, the Sussex Royal team responded by leaking to the *Daily Mail* that there was nothing 'legally stopping' them from using the name, its use being justified because 'Harry and Archie have royal blood and no one can take that away' and reassuring that 'it's not like they want to be in the business of selling T-shirts and pencils' (Roundtree 2010). Thus, Harry and Meghan take recourse to inherited power authenticated by bloodline and take pains to distance themselves from the unroyal grubbiness of having to work for income, at the very moment of claiming financial independence.

## CONCLUSION

In contrast to scholarship that positions royal and/or girl audiences as uncritically admiring, the girls we spoke to in turns expressed ambivalence, alienation, and outrage at the royals and the inequality they represent, undertaking complex negotiations that blended their own positionality with their often shrewd and analytical understandings of our highly stratified society. In doing so, they pose complex questions for the enactment of royal celebrity and the continued power and popularity of the royal family. This presents complex challenges for the monarchy, which is under increasing pressure as young people appear to be driving rising support for a democratically elected head of state. Some have sought to blame Prince Harry and Meghan, the Duke and Duchess of Sussex, for this trend. Our data, however, reveal that deeper problems exist in the relationship between the royal family and young people who view them as undeserving of power, lacking in social contribution, and, ultimately, 'lazy scroungers'.

At the same time, as a Black female celebrity who performs meritocratic discourses of hard work and social contribution, Markle squarely fulfils their criteria for those who deserve high status and for whom they mobilise queer rhetorics of queendom as excellence. The vocabulary of meritocracy formed the basis of their critique of the royal family as not deserving their wealth and power. Discussions of celebrity and royalty reveal contrasting economies of work, which hinge upon benchmarks of effort, social contribution, and overcoming disadvantages of which the royal family falls short on all counts: an institution that 'don't do nothing' 'doesn't deserve'. Markle's relationship with work, her representation of Black female success, and her cross-fertilisation of royalty and celebrity (with its discourses of meritocracy) offer a means by which these girls can construct an idea of what deserving royalty might look like. This idea is extended to Harry but no other 'blood royals' who they condemn for sitting around, drinking tea, and having babies – charges commonly levied against people on benefits but which are here upturned to question what level of social contribution represents 'doing' enough to 'deserve' the state handout of a royal stipend. However, with their departure from the royal family, their recourse to the language of 'royal blood' and the ideas of inherited power that underpin it and their repugnance for commercial labour ('selling T-shirts'), Harry and Meghan have framed their new status more within the framework of inherited power than within their meritocratic claims to be seeking financial independence.

Tensions arise as the discourses of hard work commonly used to justify inequality are used by the girls to articulate their intense desire for positive social change to bring about a more equal and fair society. What emerges are the challenges as the girls work to make sense of the many irreconcilable exhortations upon them in a society which encourages their investment in narratives about hard work as their path to success and power, while they are capable of identifying power structures that provide evidence to the contrary. It is in this context that Markle provides a particularly valuable means of understanding how girls make meaning around her racialised, gendered representation and the relative role and value (or lack thereof) of monarchy and celebrity. Through the analysis of their understandings of concepts such as bloodline and queendom, we have shed light on the ways that girls respond to, and internalise, and seek to reconcile contradictory ideas about power, privilege, inheritance, work, and merit.

Ultimately, the girls we spoke to wished to divest the royal family of any public funding. If media discourses surrounding Markle's entry to the royal family deployed her popularity, racial identity, and performance of progressive politics to imply that the institution was modernising (Clancy and Yelin 2018), these girls' responses suggest that rebranding the royal institution fails to manufacture consent for its continuation. Their indignant fury that a 'falling down' institution that belongs to the past should continue to receive public funding, and their outrage at the systematic inequality enshrined in structures of hereditary power deserve the last word:

*Toya:* Two things, number one, no three things, number one Buckingham Palace is falling down, the royal family should fall down as well. Number two . . .

*Alesha:* Oh, Miss why are they taking our money?

*Toya:* Yes!

*Etta:* They take 20p out of every pound we spend.

*Carly:* What for?

*Toya:* Every penny counts, trust me. That 20p that could buy 20 sweets.

*Mel:* Why do they get our money? That's what I can't understand?

## NOTES

1. It is worth noting that this was before the July 2020 *BuzzFeed News* expose of employee allegations of harassment, racism, and workplace toxicity on the set of her eponymous TV show. Yandoli, Krystie Lee (2020a). 'Former Employees Say Ellen's "Be Kind" Talk Show Mantra Masks a Toxic Work Culture'. *BuzzFeed News*. Yandoli, Krystie Lee (2020b). 'Dozens of Former 'Ellen Show'' Employees Say Executive Producers Engaged in Rampant Sexual Misconduct and Harassment'.

2. A style of dress characterised by the deliberate choice of bland, unremarkable, casual clothing.

*Chapter 4*

# Hope and Aspiration

## *Individualism and Collaboration*

The instrumentalisation of feminist ideals in corporate and government agendas and the location of cultural optimism in the figure of the girl coalesce in popular campaigns that encourage girls to aspire to become the leaders of the future. The call to girls as future leaders is a call to imagine themselves assuming power not just over their own lives but in terms of bringing about broader economic benefit and gender equality through their personal advancement. This imaginative journey is to be accomplished by the individual girl, fuelled by the promises of popular feminisms and navigated via the inspiration of high-profile role models. The affective, individualist address of girl leadership campaigns focuses on encouraging girls to *feel* like leaders, rather than on strategies to overcome the entrenched, intersectional barriers to self-determination and decision-making that exist for them.

In this chapter, we use a framework suggested by Janet Newman's (2015) distinction between 'aspiration' and 'hope' within political contexts of austerity to examine discourses of feminism and leadership in campaigns addressing girls and in our participants' discussions of leadership. Newman's (2015) casting of 'aspiration' as individualised but 'hope' as collective provides a hermeneutic which not only resonates with some key patterns in our data but one that allows for interrogation of the discursive premises of high-profile girl leadership initiatives in terms of their alignment with corporate and patriarchal modes of producing subjectivities.

## HOPE AND ASPIRATION

The terms 'hope' and 'aspiration' are often conflated (see, e.g., Rose and Baird 2013; Flechtner 2014; Grant 2017; Lybbert and Wydick 2019). There have, however, been attempts to define and theorise 'hope' in its various manifestations beyond the common imaginary. Notably, Darren Webb (2007) provides a historical overview of the concept as deployed in Western thought; what the kinds of hope populating his taxonomy have in common (with the exception of 'utopian hope', to which we return later) is their locus within the individual. Webb nonetheless recognises hope as essential to social cohesion and particularly to capitalism, which 'requires that individuals study, sell their labour power, consume, save and invest' and 'therefore requires that individuals possess both future-oriented significant desires and a perception that these can be attained' (76). This reliance is, under neoliberalism, manifested in the pervasive discourse of a particular form of hope: aspiration.

Aspiration is central to neoliberal capitalist regimes in their offer of 'a form of social hope' which, rather than seeking to improve the common good, is centred on improving the individual's economic status (Bishop and Willis 2014, 779). Webb (2007, 76) notes that fostering such hope in the face of contradictory evidence of attainability is a means by which capitalist society is stabilised. This stabilising form of hope is the 'cruel optimism' of Lauren Berlant (2007) – cruel because it sustains attachment to the unattainable even when such attachment threatens wellbeing. Berlant accounts for its pervasiveness and persistence because 'the continuity of the form of it provides something of the continuity of the subject's sense of what it means to keep on living on and to look forward to being in the world' (32). Neoliberal aspiration thus works to stabilise both capitalism and the individual within it through a particular and cohesive form of subjectivity that is shaped around unmet desires. Capitalism is also intrinsic to the birth of feminism as a collective movement, as through the workings of industrialisation, women were brought together in conditions that both enabled the exploitation of their labour and fostered organised activism against such exploitation (Faludi 2013, np). It is under specifically neoliberal forms of capitalism, however, that we see feminism itself appropriated and redefined as an individualist project that ultimately works to sustain patriarchal relations of domination (Rottenberg 2018).

A key discursive strategy of neoliberal governance has been to set aspiration against collectivism (Littler 2018), with such success that Sarah Amsler (2008, 2) sees the latter, in the form of utopian hope, as in danger of extinction within public culture. Newman's (2015) 'hope' is both intrinsic to and a product of collectivism. It is associated with community and collaboration and is 'central to narratives that inspire political action' such as the formation of political parties, public institutions, and movements that seek to improve life at wider social levels (n.p).

Newman also identifies hope in newer forms of resistant activism and campaigns that may 'appear defensive' but nonetheless 'offer new social and political possibilities' (n.p.). Such a model of hope is suggested by contemporary youth activism of which girls are at the forefront; recent examples include the growth of school feminist groups (Jackson 2021) and the international school climate strikes (see, e.g., Roy 2019). Set against the individualism of aspiration, Newman's model of hope bears some resemblance to Webb's (2007, 77) 'utopian hope' in its attachment to imagined, possibly unattainable futures; this does not, however, render it merely wishful. This is important when considering collective hope as it appears in youth activism, which is often dismissed as utopian and thus immature and fanciful by adults (Taft 2011, 161). As Richard Rorty observes, the task of politics is 'replacing shared knowledge of what is already real with social hope for what might become real' (Rorty 1998, 18–19).

Hope and aspiration, then, cast respectively as collective and individualist modes of conjuring a better future, represent 'specific forms of existential politics' (Raco 2009, 436) that shape and are embedded in governance and in individual subjectivity. It is these 'specific forms' that we identify and explore in girl-focused leadership initiatives and in our participants' discussions. Our exploration reveals tensions between the dominant aspirational models of public leadership discourse propagated by popular leadership initiatives and the ways in which these are taken up, adapted, or rejected by girls as they form ideas about how they might wish to change the world. It adds to the body of feminist scholarship that Jessica Taft (2014, 15) describes as providing 'an important counterpoint to the popular discourses that celebrate girls primarily as privatised neoliberal citizens who pursue their own upward mobility'.

## ASPIRATION, LEADERSHIP, AND FEMINISM

The deployment of discourses of aspiration as part of a broader educational and cultural address to youth and their shaping of youth subjectivities has been extensively investigated (Francis and Skelton 2005; Allen and Hollingworth 2013; Berrington et al. 2016; Spohrer et al. 2018; Mendick et al. 2018; Ansell et al. 2022). The pervasiveness and intensification of such discourses are especially concerning in contexts of austerity that increasingly limit the opportunities and support available to young people (Bradford and Cullen 2014; Mendick et al. 2018; Reed 2020). While it is girls who bear the brunt of austerity policies (Harris 2004; Allen 2016; Hall 2022), girl empowerment initiatives nonetheless address girls as self-responsible subjects capable of transforming their lives and prospects through a confident mind-set (Banet-Weiser 2015).

The model of leadership proffered to girls in popular campaigns is centred on individual aspiration rather than collective hope. There is, as discussed earlier, a well-established relationship between leadership and individualism via the lone, heroic, androcentric authority figure (Muir 2000; Ford 2016; Adamson 2017; Ford and Morgan 2023). This mythological figure is perpetuated in contemporary organisational and populist contexts (Eksi and Wood 2019; Knowles and Little 2019), in regimes of neoliberal austerity (Sinclair 2014; ) and in post-feminist assumptions of meritocracy (Nash and Moore 2019). As we discuss in chapter 1, the 'lone hero' model exists in oppositional tension with alternative, post-heroic, feminised leadership variants posited as the solution to the increasingly visible failings of late capitalism (Kelan and Wratil 2018; Pullen and Vachhani 2021; de Jong 2021) and as better suited to the digitised and service-orientated economies of the post-industrial West (Enderstein 2018, 3). This binary tension was particularly visible during the COVID-19 pandemic, which exposed the limits of neoliberalism and individualism (Flynn 2022; Liu et al. 2023, Card and Hepburn 2023) and during which public discourse surrounding leadership was increasingly gendered (Aldrich and Lotito 2020; Garikipati and Kambhampati 2021). Women's leadership is popularly gendered as ethical, collaborative, and connected, indeed as more 'human' than men's (Wilson and Newstead 2022), leading to calls for more women's involvement in powerful corporations to curb the potentially damaging excesses of unbridled capitalism (Prügl 2012; van Staveren 2014) and in government to ensure wellbeing and survival in times of crisis (Huang 2021). Here, while reinforcing hierarchised gendered binaries (Debray et al. 2024), essentialist ideas of 'women's qualities' combine with a mandate to work outside of these in masculinised leadership modes to create an 'impossible space' (Tseëlon 1995) of conflicting gendered demands, which simultaneously require and rule out women's suitability for leadership.

It is possible to trace these diverse strands of leadership discourse in high-profile campaigns that address girls, as popular and corporate attention turns to them as the potential leaders who can deliver equality in the service of a more secure future for capitalism. This is at odds with the aims of specifically *feminist* leadership in which inclusivity is fostered as an ethical rather than an economic imperative (Chin 2004, 2). Feminist leadership emphasises collaboration – but such collaboration is foregrounded in the interests of ensuring equal voice, not because it is an innate property of women (Hoyt and Kennedy 2008, 204). Indeed, Becky Francis and Valerie Hey point out that it is the duty of feminists to 'challenge the discursive premise' of individualist aspiration and redirect focus to structural causes of inequality (2009, 225). We align our analysis here with that of feminist duty and call for a recalibration of popular understanding of leadership that might enable girls to recognise and realise their collective power. Such a recalibration would not necessarily entail a sea-change in terms of how decision-making has been observed to actually work in organisations, which is often less individualistic and ego-driven than popularly supposed (; Gronn 2008); rather it would mean a deliberate re-shaping of how leadership is perceived and constructed in the public imaginary, through greater attention paid to distributed and shared models of decision-making, and less to the hero/figurehead leader.

## GIRL EMPOWERMENT AND POPULAR
## LEADERSHIP CAMPAIGNS

Popular girls' leadership campaigns are a part of the wider 'market of empowerment' described by Sarah Banet-Weiser (2015) which gains its purchase via a perceived crisis in girls' confidence and self-esteem, while also positioning girls as privileged consumers and potential entrepreneurs. In this market, it is empowerment itself that is the commodity, as the imagined girl is in need of intervention to realise her potential as a future economic contributor, and increasingly saviour (Masciandaro et al. 2016; van Staveren 2014; Prügl 2012). Like Banet-Weiser (2015, 185), we do not dispute the necessity for the empowerment of girls nor are we denying their subordinate position within wider patriarchal cultures that socialise them as submissive and insecure. Rather, we argue that popular girl-focused leadership initiatives, while appearing to promote change in terms of equality, work to sustain the very structures and masculinist models of governance that limit girls' opportunities and produce them as inadequate. The strategies of such campaigns focus girls' energies inward and elevate individual aspiration but are silent on both the need for, and potential of, collective activism to challenge inequalities for the wider social good.

Girls' leadership campaigns proliferate across the internet and in non-virtual realms, offering everything from inspirational quotes – see, for example, girls-build.org (no date), a Los Angeles organisation that runs the #girlsbuild hashtag campaign on Instagram, to downloadable training materials – for example the National Literacy Trust/Lancôme partnership's 'Words for Work: Women in Leadership' initiative – to running national and international events for girls. Some offer all of the above: for example, 'Girl Up' (www.girlup.org no date) runs social media campaigns such as #Girl-Hero, supplies free resources and virtual guidance for organisers, and offers the opportunity for girls to take part in international summits. The examples we focus in this chapter are among the most high-profile initiatives: Sheryl Sandberg's 'Ban Bossy' and 'Lean In Girls' from the USA, and Edwina Dunn's UK-based 'The Female Lead'. These campaigns are the brainchildren of women who are themselves successful corporate leaders – Sandberg was the chief operating officer (COO) of the global behemoth Facebook and founder of Leanin.org, while Dunn is CEO of a high-profile global data and consumer insights company, and has received an OBE for data services. Their girl-focused campaigns have achieved global penetration, as indicated by geographical analysis via NVivo of the location of responses to their Twitter feeds (@Banbossy, @LeanInGirls, and @the_female_lead), by their recognition at government levels, and by endorsement from established girls' organisations such as the Girl Guiding and Girl Scouts movements.

'Ban Bossy' (banbossy.org, no date) is the original girl-orientated spin-off campaign from Sandberg's international bestseller *Lean In* (Sandberg 2013) and the precursor of her more recent 'Lean In Girls' (leaningirls.org no date) leadership development programme aimed at 11–15-year-old girls. *Lean In* (Sandberg 2013) itself is seen by feminists as symptomatic of a wider neoliberal phenomenon in which a reinvigorated discussion of gendered inequalities is couched in terms of the advancement of individual women, while social and collective justice are off the agenda (Rottenberg 2018, 57). If *Lean In* is, as Catherine Rottenberg (2018, 61) argues, 'a site in which the neoliberal feminist is born' as she learns to internalise responsibility for her success rather than locating impediments in structures of male dominance, then the 'Ban Bossy' and 'Lean In Girls' programmes can be seen as an attempt to induce an earlier birth. As does *Lean In,* they proclaim themselves as feminist while shifting focus from external oppression to internal deficit. 'Hope' as the collective endeavour defined by Newman (2015) is reduced to a vague anticipation of 'trickle-down' feminism from which other women will benefit, as Sandberg (2013, 7) claims that 'conditions for all women will improve when there are more women in leadership roles'.

Ten years separate Sandberg's two girl-focused initiatives. There is a difference in detail and organisation of resources they offer – 'Lean In Girls' is a whole curriculum package as opposed to 'Ban Bossy's' leaner booklet of suggestions, *Leadership Tips for Girls* (http://banbossy.com/teacher-tips/ no date)(). The key contrast, however, is in the recognition of conditions of gendered inequalities: while 'Ban Bossy' barely mentions such inequalities, on the 'Lean In Girls' home page, a large headshot of Sandberg is accompanied by the strapline: 'Girl Power is Not Enough.; Girls Deserve Real Talk on Bias' (https://www.leaningirls.org/ no date). This 'real talk' entails inviting girls to identify gendered stereotypes. This focus is entirely absent in the 2014 'Ban Bossy', mirroring the wider generational change discussed in chapter 1, in which popular feminisms have rendered the recognition of gender inequality not merely acceptable, but fashionable, where it was previously proscribed. It is interesting, however, that in such recognition, Sandberg chooses to frame structural inequalities as 'bias', a term more suggestive of individual attitudinal preference than social and economic disadvantage. The promised 'real conversations' with girls about stereotypes form a key part of the 'Lean

In Girls' curriculum package; like 'Ban Bossy', they offer solutions that are also attitudinal, and as such lie within the individual girl.

'Lean In Girls' and 'The Female Lead' initiatives draw girls' attention to a range of manifestations of inequality in schools and in adult life, but, like 'Ban Bossy', they cast the individual girl as the agent of change and work on shaping girls' subjectivities in response to wider gendered inequalities. The 'Ban Bossy' campaign's *Leadership Tips for Girls* (2014) offers behavioural and attitudinal adjustment tips that focus on overcoming a supposed confidence deficit; the more comprehensive *Lean In Girls* (2023a; 2023b) curriculum materials provide a range of resources and activities which aim to do the same, while *The Female Lead*'s '5 key messages' briefing (2019b) has a similar focus. As such, these campaigns can be seen as part of the wider gendered discourse in which confidence emerges as the central technology for girls' self-monitoring and self-improvement (Gill and Orgad 2017, 21). The attitudinal adjustment of these campaigns constitutes the key focus and strategy of a form of feminism that is individualised and corporate rather than collective and social. Both Sandberg's and Dunn's girl-oriented initiatives provide frameworks for mobilising the self-surveillance and demeanour management central to confidence technologies discussed in chapter 1.

## READING THE MATERIALS: SELF-IMPROVEMENT, RISK-TAKING, AND RESOURCE

Sandberg's 'Ban Bossy' campaign and her 'Lean In Girls' programme, in common with many girl empowerment organisations, offer free, downloadable materials. The 'Ban Bossy' resource, *Leadership Tips for Girls* (http://banbossy.com/teacher-tips/ no date) is characterised by individual aspiration and self-responsibility, with overtones of the 'heroic' leadership model described above. The idea of 'risk' appears repeatedly in this short document as girls are encouraged to develop the courage necessary to adopt behaviours not typically endorsed as feminine. This will, it alleges, give girls 'the exhilaration of overcoming an obstacle', while risk avoidance, they are warned, may result in them 'paying the price later'. Similarly, risk-taking is central to the address of 'Lean In Girls'; it is the focus of one of the five curriculum sessions in the *Challenging stereotypes & inspiring girls to go for it* (2023a) curriculum pack. The sessions provide detailed, staged activities to be undertaken with girls. These stages involve identifying gender stereotypes and a subsequent range of activities in response to the inequalities represented in those stereotypes. The activities entail work on the self to boost confidence (1), to encourage disregarding the spectres of personal failure and peer disapproval in decision-making (4), and then suggest risks girls should take in the face of these spectres (12). Choosing something 'scary' is repeatedly advocated.

Risk-taking itself is a behavioural strategy associated with heroic, individualist models of leadership (Illiashenko 2019; Berry 2000), particularly in the contexts of the shrinking state under late capitalism where individual subjects must ensure their own well-being (Adams 1999). In these girls' leadership materials, the advocation of risk-taking brings together the tenets of neoliberalism with those of popular feminism, in recognising inequality but locating its resolution within the individual girl as a bold entrepreneur of the self. Nowhere are possible risks for girls in adopting behaviours described as 'risky' suggested beyond embarrassment or peer disapproval. Yet, as we saw in chapter 1, girls themselves are very aware of the consequences of making claims to voice and space. The exhortation to girls to disregard risk in contexts where women in the public eye are subjected to unprecedented hostility and material harm fails to recognise the real threats that face girls in making themselves visible in arenas of power.

Rather than social and economic justice, 'Ban Bossy,' 'Lean In Girls,' and 'The Female Lead' offer girls leadership as a means of self-actualisation. The 'Lean In Girls' homepage (leaningirls.org/ no date) opening text states that

> It's never been more important that we empower our girls. That's where Lean In Girls comes in. We want to equip girls to be self-assured, resilient, and inclusive everyday leaders and inspire them to lead boldly. And we want the world to remove the obstacles in girls' way and encourage them to lead on their own terms.

and exhorts the reader to 'Clear a path for girls', but to what end remains unclear. The aim of producing 'inclusive leaders' through 'real conversations' and 'rejecting limiting stereotypes' is not tied to any particular kind of inclusivity, but rather to fostering the self-confidence of individual girls. Similarly, the homepage of 'The Female Lead' states that.

> . . . we aim to challenge stereotypes, break barriers, and foster a more inclusive society where every woman feels empowered to pursue her dreams. (https://www.thefemalelead.com/)

The inclusivity here lies in enabling diverse but individual aspirations to success. These girl-orientated campaigns constitute part of a wider 'fetishization' of representation (Finlayson 2018, 793) discussed in chapter 2, where having more girls and women in leadership roles is in itself seen as indicative and constitutive of wider equalities, while wider inequalities are elided. The earlier 'Ban Bossy' campaign claimed to empower girls 'with life skills to change their world' (*Leadership Tips for Girls* no date, 3), but neither the nature of such world-changing nor the necessity for it is elaborated in the earlier campaign. Tip number eight, 'Change the World' at first appears it might develop this idea, but the discourse is pulled firmly into line with corporate feminism as the girl reader is told, 'Running a campaign gives you amazing practice for speaking and marketing yourself as a leader'; activism is only advocated in pursuit of self-promotion. The girl leader is thus cast as a self-improvement project in the making: 'The time to start building female leaders is now!' Her effort is described as a form of capital investment that will 'pay off for years to come' in terms of skills that, she is promised, 'you'll use throughout your life'. 'Hope' in Newman's (2015) sense of collective endeavour is absent: while girls are advised to ask for help when necessary from an adult, collaboration only appears when girls are cautioned against doing more than their fair share in group projects or instructed to join with friends in monitoring one another's self-effacing behaviours.

## READING THE MATERIALS: IMAGINATIVE LABOUR

Both The Female Lead's *Classroom Resources* (https://www.thefemalelead .com 2019a) and the Lean In Girls' curriculum package (https://www.lean-ingirls.org/program-curriculum# 2023b) mobilise aspiration as an imaginative exercise, suggesting obstacles to equality and advancement can be overcome through fostering feats of individual envisioning. 'The Female Lead's (https://wsixtyww.thefemalelead.com 2019a) *Classroom Resources* pack starts by encouraging girls to recognise gender inequalities in a range of adult contexts such as pay, occupational exclusion, and media objectification. However, as with 'Lean In Girls', no structural explanations are offered. While girls are invited to consider the prevalence of limiting stereotypes in a range of different contexts such as toy advertising and STEM fields, stereotyping itself is treated as a cause rather than a symptom of inequality. The possibility of a collective feminist response to the inequalities that it encourages girls to identify is sidestepped as girls are then invited to choose for reflection an individual woman's path to 'her own unique kind of success', drawing on examples from *The Female Lead*'s own book (2017b) of 'sixty inspirational women'. The strategy offered for tackling inequality is that of reflection on an endorsed role model, followed by structured tasks that we describe as imaginative labour. These tasks constitute a set of instructions for the formation of individualised aspiration: Girls are told to note down their 'biggest goal for the future' (https://www.thefemalelead.com 2019a) but this goal must be 'something you really want for yourself' rather than a social good. The individualised goal identified, the next stage involves the development of attachment to that goal as girls are invited to conjure the feelings associated with achieving it. Task 3 enjoins girls to 'Think really hard: do you feel confident about your ability to achieve this goal? Can you see any obstacles in your path that worry you? If you do, write them down. Giving voice to your worries can make them less scary!' Thus, the proper response of the girl when she recognises evidence of oppression is to note and alter her attitude towards it, as though the very recognition is sufficient to overcome entrenched forms of oppression. Similarly, in the 'Lean In Girls' *Challenging stereotypes & inspiring girls to go for it (*https://www.leaningirls.org/ program-curriculum#_2023b) curriculum pack, the activities enjoin girls to imagine the possible fears and limitations experienced by successful women offered as affective role models. These limitations include poverty, disability, and minoritised ethnic identity. Girls are invited in each case to 'imagine how (the exemplar successful woman) felt' and then to identify the behaviour that helped the women overcome individual fears, rather than to identify social, cultural, and economic restrictions that poor, disabled, and minoritised women encounter. Individual 'courage' is always the answer, rather than collective effort to address the structural causes of inequality. As in the 'Lean In Girls' (https://www.leaningirls.org/program-curriculum# 2023b) materials, the defining characteristic of The Female Lead's (https://www.thefemalelead .com 2019a) resource is its encouragement of girls to recognise various manifestations of gendered oppression *without*, while at the same time locating the fix *within* the girl. The particular strategy of both is to foster the girl's capacity to develop those individualised, future-oriented desires (Webb 2007; Berlant 2007) that are central to the maintenance and stability of the neoliberal status quo. In shaping the girl as the self-responsible entrepreneur, it focuses her attention on her own feelings and ambitions, rather than on collective strategies for overcoming systemic inequalities.

## PRESCRIBED AUTHENTICITY AND PRIVILEGE

The motive provided for the leadership that girls are exhorted to aspire to is that of authenticity; girls are addressed as unique holders of innate potential – 'leadership superpowers!' (leaningirls.org/, no date) – that can be realised through girls paying attention to their 'inner voice'. This inner 'authentic' self is the same as that characterised by confidence discourses discussed in chapter 1, in their conjuring of an essential self damaged by wider gendered cultures but restorable through appropriate intervention. Like confidence, authenticity emerges as a technology of the self, achieved through (self) disciplinary intervention – what Dawn Currie describes as 'prescribed authenticity'(2015, 5). In girls' leadership initiatives, this authenticity is manifested through 'speaking up' – girls are repeatedly exhorted to 'speak up' and 'speak out' as an expression of their 'inner voice'; failure to do so, girls are warned, may mean missing 'the opportunity to surround yourself with people who know and love the real you' (*Challenging stereotypes & inspiring girls to go for it* 2023, 9).

We discussed in chapter 1, how exhorting girls to 'speak up' implies a privileged as well as a gendered kind of voice while entailing difficulties for girls minoritised along axes of race and class. Exhorting girls to authenticity presents similar problems. Even for girls occupying more privileged identities, such authenticity is problematic. Paule describes elsewhere (2017) how 'successful girl' discourses hold in irresolvable tension the mandate for the girl to both 'be herself' and 'improve herself'. Leadership discourses present the same dilemma in requiring girls to shape themselves, through a constant process of identity work and self-labour, at the same time as enjoining them to demonstrate 'authentic' behaviours and traits hitherto associated with masculinised success. For girls with marginalised identities, the problems are intensified. As Marnina Gonick (2003, 11) argues, the valuing and legitimation of certain behaviours depend not only on the status of those behaviours within but also on the status of the girl expressing them. There is some acknowledgement of this in the 'Lean In Girls' Facilitator Handbook (https://www.leaningirls.org/program-curriculum 2023)' – for example, adults are cautioned that: 'It is especially important to consider the possibility that you are misinterpreting assertive behavior as aggressive or disrespectful. Research shows adults are especially likely to unfairly judge the assertive behavior of Black and Latina girls' (22). There is no similar caution with regard to the potential demonstration of classed and racialised behaviours among more privileged girls. Such warning itself assumes privilege in the facilitator role, as one who is liable to 'misinterpret' the assertiveness of marginalised girls. In fact, as Jessie Daniels (2016, 15) reveals, 'Ban Bossy' itself is based on data that privilege the needs of white girls. The activities designed to build girls' confidence and courage through risk-taking do not recognise cultural difference – for example, girls are invited to challenge grades with teachers, to question curfews with parents, and to police the social behaviour of peers with no acknowledgement of cultural contexts or identities that may render such behaviours differently appropriate or risky for different girls.

## RESOURCES AND NETWORKING

Neither 'Lean In Girls' nor 'The Female Lead' campaign addresses intersectional disadvantage and privilege. Both programmes recommend taking advantage of external resources, but the differing capacity of individual girls to access such resources is elided. For example, *Ban Bossy* (no date) encourages girls to engage in extra-curricular activities in order to develop leadership skills. Such activities have been identified as important in repro-ducing the values and networks of privilege (Gonick 2003; Scardigno 2009; Covay and Carbonaro 2010), while, as discussed in chapter 1, activities avail-able to less advantaged girls have been significantly reduced under neoliberal and austerity regimes as a result of cuts to schools' and youth services fund-ing. *The Female Lead* (2019b) has 'Asking For Help' as one of its five pillars; this 'help', it transpires, is traditional networking – one of the key skills by which the 'future girl' is to be empowered (Harris 2004). Networking appears here as a capacity that can be developed by an individual rather than as a form of cultural capital that relies on familiarity with social genres (Lee and Chen 2017, 7). *The Female Lead* (2019a) elides the role of privilege in networking, suggesting that

> Even if you feel like you don't have a network, we can guarantee that there is at least one person out there rooting for you, or willing to root for you: your net-work can include friends, family, teachers, your Head Teacher, careers advisers, business mentors, youth leaders, religious leaders – or anybody else who helps and supports you, or may be able to do so in the future.

While we do not mean to understate the role that key cultural workers can play in supporting the progress of individuals, the advantage enjoyed by those with adult connections to help access the fields they wish to enter cannot be overlooked nor can the implications of cuts to the public services that should help reduce this deficit for the less advantaged.

This was borne out in our data. The girls who had access to adults in lead-ership roles in their everyday lives were able to identify the nature of the roles in fields to which they aspired and to understand the means of achieving them. For example, participants whose families ran businesses expressed the desire to do so themselves; those who knew lawyers or medicos discussed the work with understanding. Popular girls' leadership initiatives rely on individual aspiration and initiative: a key part of their strategy is advising girls to build and exploit networks of support. However, few participants in our study who expressed ambition to work in a specific field had useful connections with that field, and thus were unsure of how they might enter it and of what the actual work might entail. Molly said, 'It's just really I don't know just what happens in most environments, workplaces and education too', while Isabel summarised the problem as 'I feel that people don't know the way, it's the path you take to get there that people don't understand.' Isabel also saw cer-tain kinds of leadership as only possible if 'you know people that are relatives or friends of people that have already done it or you know they're already up high status' while Maya recognised that 'their support network', including 'a good family that supports them', were central to the fostering of leadership in girls. This indicates girls' own perceptions of the ways in which privilege is reproduced, and of the inadequacies of initiatives that rely on working on the individual girl's subjectivity while eliding the role of advantage.

The discourses of 'Ban Bossy', 'Lean In Girls', and 'The Female Lead' can thus be characterised, in Newman's (2015) terms, as aspirational rather than hopeful; like many aspirational discourses aimed at young women (Allen 2014) the kind of agency they promise is not equally available to all. Nor do the strategies they offer, in turning the focus of activity inward, offer a future in which such inequalities may be addressed as a core aim of feminist endeavour. Rather, they foster the creation of the aspiration described by Berlant (2011, 1) as 'cruel' in invoking desires that may be an obstacle to flourishing. They cast the failure to aspire properly – Sandberg's (2013) 'ambition gap' – as the cause of failure to attain the aspirational status. The ideal girl subject they evoke recognises gender inequalities, but has developed confidence and self-belief in her ability to overcome them. Her goals are individualised and her notion of feminism is fulfilled through the attainment of these personal goals. The data we explore suggests ways in which girls' own visions of leadership reproduce or conflict with the popular discourses represented in these girl-orientated campaigns.

## INDIVIDUALISM AND COLLABORATION

Our data suggest that for girls, 'leadership' is a complex configuration of individual aspiration and social hope. A key finding was that girls saw working collaboratively as offering them more possibilities for effecting change than would developing influence as individuals. Zainab saw collaboration as essential to women's being able to wield power, saying, 'What we all need first, the women, first we need to be a team', while Nicki saw teams as more efficient and responsive, expressing her desire to be involved in decision-making, 'may involve like a few leadership parts like in groups, if I have to be in, like, a team with people and have the thing to come up with ideas quickly to get things done'. Chloe agreed, explaining why she thought collective action might be more effective in achieving goals:

> Because if you have a group of people combined that are believing in the same thing and working well together, you're going to get more things done and you'll all help each other to make the best possible outcome.

This preference for collective action was tied to social hope rather than to personal ambition; for example, Isabel felt that by working together, 'There are so many things that you could change . . . people could, say, like, stop poverty, stop stuff like that'; Daisy identified collective action as the best way to achieve key global goals like peace, and Amina, in common with other participants, saw climate change as an issue that could be tackled by both local groups and international movements. Bea saw collective action as the key to improving conditions for women in particular and cited its historical importance: 'No but not just a single person, but groups like the Suffragettes who fought for things for women'.

The image of suffragettes shared by participants in a Scottish focus group was one of several in the genre that girls across different sites shared (figure 4.1). The colourised, originally monochrome, image shows two young,

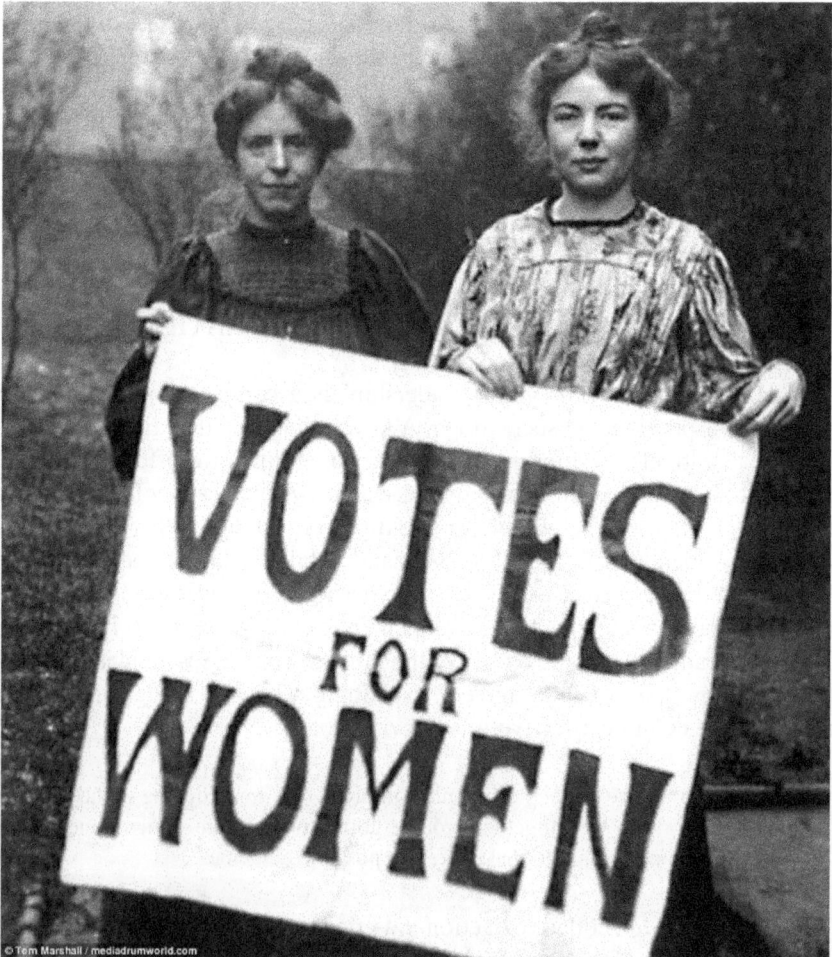

**Figure 4.1  Image of Suffragettes Found Online by a Participant.**

white women in Edwardian dress, looking towards the camera and holding a hand-painted 'Votes for Women' banner. It is an image of collective, female activism and is clearly over a century old. Participants tended to share such historical images of suffragettes, or of American Civil Rights activists, when discussion turned to collaborative action; no more recent examples were offered of images showing girls and women engaged in collective political change-making.

Images of teams and groups of women in other domains were shared between particpants (see Appendix re method) , including sports teams such as the English football 'Lionesses', tennis-playing sisters Serena and Venus Williams (an image in which sisterhood rather than competition was the theme), talent show dance troupe Nu Crew, and acapella singing group from *Pitch Perfect*. Beyond such images associated with sports and entertainment, there were few instances of collaborative achievement by women available to them circulating within public and popular domains. The disappearance of collectivism from popular discourse (Amsler 2008, 2) noted above is both illustrative and constitutive of the predominance of stories of individual girls because such stories are 'more legible . . . than the story of feminist collectivity' (Banet-Weiser 2018, 104).

Participants' preference for collective action was not only because they saw it as effective; it was, for them, an ethical issue – a way of ensuring inclu- sion and representativeness tied to the 'listening' trait discussed in chapter 1. Chloe explained that 'you could make people more comfortable sharing their ideas. . . . You can help other people and direct them in sharing their ideas', while Eva and Chloe saw 'making people feel accepted' as crucial in achiev- ing consensus to bring about change. As noted in chapter 1, such discussion reproduces wider gendered tropes of femininity, and specifically women's leadership, as caring and connected (Prügl 2012; van Staveren 2014); how- ever, the girls politicised these qualities in terms of thinking about how they might bring about change more effectively as well as more ethically. Finally – and importantly – the girls saw collective leadership as providing a buf- fer against the pressure and exposure faced by individual women leaders, a theme which we expanded in chapter 2. Samira, evoking the metaphor of size/taking up space as observed in chapter 1 described how she didn't 'really see (herself) like in big leadership roles in the future' but was comfortable in a collaborative decision-making context: 'so I feel like even though you work in a team, I don't feel like there's any leader there personally, because I guess you all have to work with what you have and one person really can't take the lead to that'. Her anxiety around an individual being in control was not just about personal pressure though; it was about too much power resting in one leader. Samira was not alone in expressing such misgivings. Although participants acknowledged that a good leader could achieve a great deal in providing direction and cohesion, the potential for too much power resting in one person troubled them. They were concerned about how such power might affect a person's ability to make good decisions, and the potential for an individual to serve only a small group of interests. While Diana, Princess of Wales, was admired by Lynn in Cardiff for ' not, like, taking the power that she had as a princess to her head', Donald Trump was seen as an example of the individual having too much power; Rachel described him as 'more thinking about changes for himself and his type of people . . . he's only representing the interests of a particular group, not of everybody'. As Daisy summed up: 'There might be a problem trying to get one person to try and bring about world peace because they'd be in control of the world'.

The promotional image from *Pitch Perfect* shared by girls in a Home Counties comprehensive school setting shows the cast arrayed on a low yellow wall in various poses evoking confidence (figure 4.2). The ensemble cast includes Black actor Ester Renay Dean and Korean-American Hana Mae Lee. They are dressed similarly but not uniformly, suggesting individuality within a team. The costumes are all black, including leather jackets, high heels and thigh boots, jeans, and mini-skirts. Despite the diversity of casting, the image hints at its deployment of cultural stereotypes: Rebel Wilson, who plays a fat, working-class character, has a raised hand making a gesture that could be a pistol; her mouth is open as if mid-yell. The other cast members are posed in more traditionally feminine ways; the Black actor is the only other cast member not smiling, reproducing in her role both the 'sassy' and the 'angry black woman' stereotypes (Mizejewski 2014) and suggesting that these are the two characters, the Black girl and the fat girl, who are marked as transgressive. The film  was popular among participants in several groups, as were other

Figure 4.2    Image of the Acapella Choir Cast of the Film *Pitch Perfect* (dir. Jason Moore 2012) Found Online by a Participant.

films and TV shows featuring show choirs, cheerleaders, and dance troupes. *Pitch Perfect* was particularly praised by girls for what they saw as its inclusive casting and its showcasing of comic actor Rebel Wilson in a leading role. They saw her as body-positive and enjoyed her outspokenness (the character introduces herself as 'Fat Amy'). The *Pitch Perfect* franchise is seen as part of the growth of female-led films in mainstream Hollywood cinema (Scott and Dargis 2015), and as allowing new potential for female comic performances.

Despite their concerns around the potential for power to be exploited by individuals, there was also some evidence of what Sneja Gunew describes as the hailing into being of the fleeting 'what if' subject (2008, 11), where girls imaginatively 'tried on' leadership subjectivities for size. Inhabiting these positions, however vicariously and temporarily, troubled some participants who tried it. They thought about how they themselves might be tempted into cronyism if placed in a position of individual power: for example, Toya felt that if she were prime minister, 'my friends will try and take advantage of it . . . you're my friend and you say let's do this, I'd be like let's do this!' This concern was reflected in an image shared by the girls on the closed Facebook groups featuring a quote by the British singer Adele: 'I define power by having the confidence to make your own decisions and not be swayed by other people'. It is interesting that this pattern did not appear in the post-COVID-era interviews, but rather, in the 2022 research sites, girls were more likely to recognise the dangers of individualist leadership and cronyism. Girls' leadership initiatives function as a part of a wider discursive address that interpellates girls as the leaders of the future in ways that align with neoliberal, late capitalist agendas. While such 'hailing' should work to affirm that subjectivity, we have seen that for our participants, their responses were often ambivalent.

Individual aspiration was nonetheless expressed by many participants – they wished to become lawyers, doctors, sporting champions, to head up charities, lead schools, and run businesses. For some girls, the idea of occupying a leadership role was attractive in itself: For example, Molly said, 'I'd like to think I'd be like a leader of a company or of a business or something'. She saw this as 'something everyone aims for . . . they want to climb high up the ladder, to earn more respect and stuff like that', while Isabel thought that 'the higher up you are, the more respect you have and having respect is, it's not empowering, it just makes you feel like people respect you, you have some sort of say in what happens'. While this exchange initially appeared to reproduce aspirational tropes of individualised, neoliberal self-advancement, Becky moved the discussion of desire for power into a consideration of social good, saying:

> If you're higher up, people are more likely to listen to you. So like Michelle Obama she can speak her word and something will happen about it, but if one

of us was to be like, we want this to happen, I don't, kind of how society works, you wouldn't really get, like, much recognition for it.

The motive here – the seeking of power to advance community benefit – was one that characterised the discussion of favourite leaders/celebrities in every group and in the online forums; as we saw earlier, the women most admired were consistently those that were seen to advance equalities and social justice. Tani summed up the motives of such leaders as 'they actually want to do something good and actually once they are in power'.

It is important to note here that girls and women are socialised to be selfless, that wanting to do good is a sanctioned reason to want power as a woman, while wanting power for its own sake is not. As we discuss in chapter 2, participants reproduced wider cultural judgements of women who were perceived as making claims to patriarchal territory and favoured women whom they perceived as 'accidental' leaders. 'Doing good' was also an endorsed motive for leadership for women. As Taft (2014, 262) points out, 'the gendered expectation of community care work [is] part of the shift from a citizenship model that emphasises individuals as rights-bearing subjects to a more neoliberal approach that focuses on the responsibility of each individual subject to provide for herself and for others'.

Among our participants, these socially sanctioned forms of desire were energised by their consciousness of social inequalities and oppression, and can thus be seen both as an expression of the age and gender-specific kind of call to active citizenship under neoliberalism identified by Taft (2014), and a critique of conditions that render such citizenship necessary. However, the association of women with particular kinds of caring, ethical citizenship did not emerge with neoliberalism – in the United Kingdom, it has been central to historic arguments for women's civic engagement. For example, Barbara Bodichon, writing in 1869, argues thus:

among all the reasons for giving women votes, the one which appears to me the strongest is that of the influence it might be expected to have in increasing public spirit. Patriotism, a healthy, lively, intelligent interest in everything which concerns the nation to which we belong, and an unselfish devotedness to the public service – these are the qualities which make a people great and happy; these are the virtues which ought to be most sedulously cultivated in all classes of the community. And I know no better means at this present time, of counteracting the tendency to prefer narrow private ends to the public good, than this of giving to all women, duly qualified, a direct and conscious participation in political affairs. (5–6)

This not only demonstrates how civic engagement itself is historically gendered but also indicates the facility of neoliberalism to adopt existing discursive truths and fold them into the subjectivities that it creates.

In describing their own aspirations, Tani, Kelly, Judith, and Isabel expressed a mix of personal ambition and desire to implement wider good. Tani said, 'I want to be a lawyer because the system is unfair', and while Isabel thought that becoming any kind of leader would bring personal satisfaction, it was as Minister for Education she felt she could address social inequalities to 'give every kid the same opportunity to get the job they want'. Judith saw herself as 'something important in, like, the music industry . . . using music to inspire other people and just help them and then from that just do sort of like charity stuff'. She wanted to 'make people's voices be heard, because nowadays there's a lot of people that don't speak up'. Kelly agreed that this was 'the whole point of speaking up'. She elaborated this in terms that link gender to powerlessness and recognised patriarchal oppression, stating that, 'Men believe we don't have a voice at all, men believe that we are just quiet and that we don't have no power to take over the country'. Kelly's motive for such speaking, in contrast with that offered in girls' leadership initiatives discussed earlier, is connected with social reform rather than personal authenticity.

These exchanges offer an interesting perspective on popular discourses of leadership: while individual aspiration was present, for these participants, a social justice agenda was seen as distinct from 'leadership'. They reproduced the lexicon of popular feminist 'empowerment' discourse that exhorted them to voice in their discussion, but its individualism was inadequate to convey their motives for aspiring to exert influence.

## CRUEL ATTACHMENTS AND INADEQUATE IMAGININGS

Berlant (2007, 32) suggests that neoliberal aspiration is a process of sustaining attachment to an imagined future status. We discussed above how leadership initiatives such as *The Female Lead* work to school this process of attachment as a form of imaginative labour necessary to overcome identified gender barriers, implying that affective commitment is necessary for women's success; they must experience the desire for leadership as a passion, as 'something you really want for yourself' (*The Female Lead* 2019a). Our participants offered perspectives that suggest that the foregrounding of emotional investment through discourses of imagination and passion – rather than, for example, fairness or ethics – in a leadership role means that a lack of such emotion itself can become a deterrent. Participating girls saw the experience of sufficient 'passion' as a key (dis)qualifier: For example, Laura said: 'I don't know, it seems like I wouldn't be passionate enough about, well I would be passionate, but I don't think I would be able to put the ideas across as well as some people who would really want to be there'.

Samantha had similar misgivings with regard to political leadership: 'It just doesn't really (work) if you're not really passionate about being in the Government'. Despite the perceived necessity of 'passion', however, there was suspicion of a strong desire for leadership for its own sake, which tied to the necessity for management of 'confidence' that girls described in chapter 1: Bella feared that 'if you really want to be in charge then you'll just be too confident and you'll end up losing people'. While these suspicions align with technologies of demeanour management, and with cultural suspicion and negative media coverage of women who seek power in traditional male preserves (Rhee and Sigler 2015; Manne 2018),[1] they also reveal the affective politics of aspiration as inadequate for the articulation of motive beyond individual fulfilment.

Where girls do envision themselves holding roles of influence, their imaginings may act as a deterrent rather than a spur as they reflect on the conditions in which women experience leadership. For our participants, this entailed a vivid imagining of the hazards that leadership may entail for women – the very kinds of risk-taking and imaginative labour that are enjoined in the 'Ban Bossy', 'Lean In Girls', and 'The Female Lead' campaigns. While we consider the risks of visibility for girls, and participants' perceptions thereof in chapters 1 and 2, here we explore further risks associated with individualised leadership models. The girls saw exposure to risk as going beyond that of being in the public eye in terms of feminised visibility and misogyny; they feared the exposure of isolation in highly pressurised environments. Maya feared that, 'you'd always have to constantly be up to everybody's standards and you won't be able to ever do anything wrong'; Isabel associated negative exposure explicitly with risk-taking: 'You don't want to be associated with a huge disaster because you took a risk', while Sarika felt that the potential dangers were disproportionate to the actions women leaders might take, saying: 'you could do like the smallest thing, it might not even be a big thing at all, it might not even be a thing, but people will find a way to criticise you and find a way to, like, bring you down I guess'.

Toya summed up her imagining of the individual leadership experience as 'Pressure. Peer pressure, judgement pressure, people pressure. Stress.' Ruth felt it would make her 'cower away from leadership things'. Becky concluded, 'So all of these things would make you think, I wouldn't want to be in charge'. Rather than fostering the courage touted in girls' leadership campaigns, the imaginative labour of projecting themselves into leadership positions results in a 'cowering away' from the perils and pressures they envision; the mitigating comforts of collective responsibility and solidarity do not appear within the affective toolkits of 'Lean In Girls' and 'The Female Lead'.

Risk-aversion runs counter to the central message of the highly individuated nature of girls' leadership campaigns and the culturally masculinised behaviours they promote to girls. Those we examine above offer little in the way of risk amelioration, nor of addressing the reasons why such risk exists; rather, they encourage girls to embrace risk as valuable in itself, as a performance of authenticity. Even where risks beyond peer disapproval or internal anxiety are recognised, there are no strategies for addressing them beyond individual responses. Research conducted for The Female Lead (2017a) identifies hostile social media climates for women as a deterrent to leadership, but places responsibility for resolving this onto individual girls to manage their social media feeds, rather than suggesting ways in which girls might access and contribute to collective campaigns to address online misogyny.

Risk-aversion is not only a leadership trait discursively associated with women, but it is particularly prominent at times of national and global crisis (Aldrich and Lotito 2020; Kabengele, Keller, and Gollwitzer 2023). This was illustrated early in the COVID-19 lockdown when a member of SAGE (the UK government's Scientific Advisory Group for Emergencies) and Oxford University Professor of Public Health Trisha Greenhalgh tweeted the following:

'Covid 19 is everywhere but countries with heads of state managing the crisis better seem to have something in common . . .' above a collage of six images of women leaders (Germany's Angela Merkel, New Zealand's Jacinda Ardern, Belgium's Sophie Wilmes, Finland's Sanna Marin, Iceland's Katrín Jakobsdóttir, and Denmark's Mette Frederiksen).

The tweet carried 17,000 'likes', 4800 retweets, and prompted discussion among 520 users. Responders offered views drawing in apocrypha from a range of contexts, such as 'Investment funds managed by women are more careful, more risk averse' (@CookeLouise 2020); 'That's a well proven trait. Men take more risks than women. Look to data on young car drivers' (@rider45 2020), and 'Is there an "empathy" angle to this too? Are women leaders perhaps more empathetic, prioritising "protecting lives" above anything else?' (@CazzyRNF 2020).

@IanSpindley (2020) linked masculine risk-taking to other forms of privilege, asking, 'Are more male leaders privately educated than women and so believe they are more entitled to be decision-makers?' (@IanSpindley 2020), and (@OsloMatt 2020) suggested that 'Perhaps the women have had to work to the top instead having privilege to ease their promotion. Suffering and caring may bring better understanding than an expensive education. Elitism has little to offer when you discover you are human and fallible'. Risk-taking was specifically linked to individualist, macho forms of leadership; for example, @bigboithebard (2020) tweeted, 'World would be a better place with woman *(sic)* in charge absolutely zero doubt about that in my mind. Ego is the bane of humanity and guys excel at being egotistical,' while @UK_Engineer_Mat (2020) offered: 'I believe Singapore's response is also headed by a woman epidemiologist (not some useless male ego-driven politician)'.

While of course not all commenters concurred – some objected to such gender differentiation, and others just disagreed – in this example of leadership discourse emerging into popular realms, we see a privileging of behaviours that are discursively gendered. The same gendered tropes, however, work to the opposite effect in the individualist leadership models promoted in the popular girls' leadership campaigns described in this chapter, as girls are exhorted to take more risks.

This is not to suggest that in times of crisis, risk aversion is universally endorsed as a political strategy by governments, popular wisdom, or mainstream media: in fact, as we discuss in the next chapter, during the COVID-19 pandemic, risk-taking tended to follow political ideology, with the right/conservatives embracing risk and the left, caution (Chu, Yang, and Liu 2021; Weil and Wolfe 2022). Discussion among participants in Scotland reflected gender and ideological discursive patterns around risk when comparing Scotland's First Minister Nicola Sturgeon's more cautious approach to lockdown during the COVID-19 pandemic with that of Prime Minister Boris Johnson in England:

*Ruth:* Boris Johnson was obviously the Prime Minister at the time, and he was opening the UK back up, but she was like no, we're staying in lockdown.

*Tamsin:* She was trying to protect. . . . She was trying to prevent us trying to get more sick.

As we discuss in chapter 5, girls were more likely to recognise specifically feminised, caring, and inclusive forms of leadership as represented in, for example, Jacinda Ardern and Nicola Sturgeon, as both safe and productive of wider social good, and to see individualist, masculinised models as potentially dangerous, self-serving, and productive of cronyism.

## CONCLUSION

Our findings indicate that popular initiatives, in their focus on individual aspiration, fail to recognise the concerns and priorities in girls' ideas of leadership. First, in assuming girls will aspire to leadership solely for personal status, they ignore the social justice agenda that may motivate them. Second, in their focus on 'fixing' the girl instead of addressing the causes of inequality – indeed, the girl *becomes* the problem through failure to address her own lack of confidence and ambition – they neglect the complex and various forms of subordination that shape girls' lives outside of gender. Finally, in their focus on individual affective and imaginative labour as their key tactics, they fail to offer meaningful strategies that could enable girls to improve their own conditions and those of others, and thus work to sustain the inequalities that they purport to address. Girl leadership initiatives work on encouraging girls to *feel* like leaders, while girls themselves focus on what they would like to *do* as leaders. This distinction is central to the ideology of popular campaigns. In working on altering subjectivities, such campaigns pose no real threat to existing structures; the wider representational politics they embrace allows for the assumption of trickle-down feminism as the key to broader cultural change, while offering no challenge to organisations nor commitment to funding for programmes and activities that might equip girls to bring about the kinds of change they wish to see.

Our deployment of Newman's (2015) distinction has allowed us to demonstrate how popular empowerment initiatives fail to understand the form and focus of girls' hope as collectively orientated. This collective hope is easy for the adult world to dismiss as utopian, but for young people, as well as adults, its political formation emerges and is shaped by real concerns and objectives (Graeber 2011). Imagination among our participants is, as Kyriakides (2014) describes, 'related to desire for change, is the result of socio-material arrangements, and also carries potency of acting on and changing such arrangements'. That potency can only be realised if girls are provided with the tools to address those socio-material arrangements – the structures and conditions – that they intuit as damaging at the community level and not just in terms of the hurdles they may present to individual women. Girls' imaginings of 'leadership' then are characterised by hope but must be sustained through practical strategy. We are not alone in calling for a better way of working with girls than is offered by popular campaigns: Jessica Taft (2011) identifies the need to support such activism through collaboration with us as adults, as well as through encouraging girls' solidarity with one another, while Batsleer and McMahon (2017) urge those working with girls to be alert to the potential for intergenerational alliances. This we see as central to the project of challenging neoliberalisation's appropriation and remaking of feminism as a self-help guide rather than a collectivist project with social justice at its heart. Further, it is crucial in enabling girls to begin to recognise and understand how they might start to dismantle patriarchal conditions that, while encouraging them to 'lean in' and purportedly realise their individual power, work to silence collective voices, and to sustain oppression.

## NOTE

1. Media and participant attitudes to women identified as seeking power is a theme we explored in chapter 2.

*Chapter 5*

# TikTok Ven*troll*oquism, 'Leadership Theatre', and Girls on the Gendering of Power

## INTRODUCTION: 'BORIS JOHNSON MORON FUCK OFF YOU CUNT'

In November 2021, the *Daily Mirror* revealed that the UK Conservative government held office parties, breaking their own coronavirus social distancing rules. Investigations by the Cabinet Office and the Metropolitan Police led to Prime Minister Boris Johnson's resignation after revealing 'Wine time Fridays', karaoke, drinking to the point of vomiting, and leaving via the back door to evade detection (Grey 2022). While popular discourse around Johnson focused on public fury about 'Partygate', a viral TikTok emerged featuring a young Welsh girl asking her Amazon Alexa voice assistant how to say '"Boris Johnson carrots coffee bean 100' in Welsh' – a plausibly deniable, innocent request as befits her youthful voice. The robot's response in stilted, yet upper-middle-class, received pronunciation is 'Boris Johnson moron fuck off you cunt' (@football_ben 2022). In this act of ventriloquism, making the robot say what she may not, the girl finds a creative way to troll the government, 'fuck the patriarchy' and express the collective moment of 'irreverent rage', as Helen Wood puts it (2019), circumventing the systems that position her as remote from power due to her age, gender, and geography. This chapter considers these themes of girls' ventriloquistic creativity in the face of voicelessness in a landscape where rising right-wing populism is served by, and reinforces, performatively masculine power in ways which came into sharp relief during the global COVID-19 pandemic.

When the pandemic began, we were halfway through our fieldwork examining girls' engagements with media discourses surrounding gender and leadership. Those discourses underwent a significant generic mutation during lockdown, both in mainstream broadcast media and in girls' and young women's appropriation of such texts to create their own content on social media. We examine the models of leadership circulating in mainstream news formats and explore ways in which girls' and young women's responses develop new, resistant media genres that resonate with the frustration described by our field-work participants in relation to voice, power, and gendered inequalities.

COVID-19 burst upon the world, shutting down schools and removing our access to participants for more than two years. When schools re-opened, the extraordinary pressures on them precluded participation in projects such as this. During this time of suspension, we remained attuned to cultural phenomena relating to girls, representations of leadership, and instances of girls making meaning around leadership. During lockdown, we consumed daily COVID-19 briefings and, like our participants, we spent time on TikTok. Here, we found material that resonated both with our focus on media representations of gender and interest in girls' engagements with them: content repurposing and recreating recordings of male leaders in state COVID-19 briefings through ventriloquism, lip-synching, and female-to-male drag impersonation. Historically, scholarship on girlhood cultures has 'neglected the queer potential and practices of girls' (Brickman 2016, 444). We attend to the specifically queer character of lip-synching and drag as cultural forms underpinning girls' elected genre of resistance to heteropatriarchal power as a counter to 'the white, heterosexual, middle-class, Western, and presentist framework that continues to dominate girls' media studies and thus public perceptions of girls' media culture' (Kearney 2011, 11). As Kathryn Bond Stockton argues, there are 'queer temporalities haunting all children', who can only be 'not-yet-straight' within a presumed innocence 'merely approaching while crucially delaying . . . the official designation of straight sexuality' (2009, 7). We, therefore, work within Barbara Jane Brickman's framework of 'a foundational interrelation between these two concepts – queerness and girlhood' understanding that '"queerness" has circled around "girlhood" and resided at the margins or even foundations of its very definition all along' (Brickman 2019).

We analysed both the gendered performances of masculine leadership in COVID-era news and this emerging genre of girl-made media they inspired. We analyse one TikTok video each from the many in this genre produced by each of the makers who were key originators of the genre, as indicated by 'views', 'likes', and 'shares'. We consider their context within the particular conditions of COVID-19 broadcasts and their generic conventions as produced and understood within communities of resistance. We place these side-by-side for analysis as a means of interrogating news representations, creating the 'reading effects' of juxtaposition (Calás and Smircich 1991) to displace taken-for-granted meanings about gender and leadership in a particular historical moment. This employs multiple analytic strategies, including reading visual language and identifying resonances, contradictions, and subversion of signifying tropes. Our work on TikTok videos has enabled us to approach both our existing data and that collected post-lockdown with a new sensitivity to girls' relationship to voice and voicelessness, and the ways they attach this to gender and leadership.

Two formats emerged to epitomise lockdown media. In the United Kingdom, the 5pm daily briefing informed citizens of the spread of the virus and the changing parameters of lockdown. These government briefings had a particular visual lexicon we theorise as *leadership theatre*: imposing buildings, formal lecterns, gilded crests, national flags, and men in suits with sombre faces. As production halted on professional programme-making, people turned to TikTok, a social media app where users film themselves pranking, dancing, and lip-syncing. In 2020, one in three British people – over 23 million – had the TikTok app installed on their devices (Kale 2020). The week of 23 March 2020, when lockdown began, UK installations surged by 34 per cent (ibid.). As TikTok was booming, government briefings were punctuating people's days.

Leaders accumulate a specific kind of public authority in times of crisis (Klein 2007), using mass media platforms such as the daily briefing to command synchronous audience attention. Meanwhile, digital textual dispersal and 'produsage' practices (Bruns, 2008) can diminish public authority through audience command over when and where media is consumed. This is possible through the flattening of traditional hierarchies, enabling anyone to comment, and through the potential to reshape and recirculate texts originating from powerful figures, encouraging creative forms of critique from otherwise excluded voices.

In legacy news media, public discourse gendering leadership came to the forefront and was increasingly polarised during the global pandemic and the period of the UK's departure from the EU. While women leaders remain rare, the pandemic also provided a flashpoint celebrating the stateswomanship of leaders like New Zealand prime minister Jacinda Ardern and German chancellor Angela Merkel. Meanwhile, other leaders' performances of masculinity were exaggerated, for example, Boris Johnson's attempt to persuade the public he was 'fit as a butcher's dog' by doing press-ups. This heightened discursive milieu is one in which girls, already under the spotlight as the potential solution to the gender leadership gap, form ideas about power: what it is, whether they want it, and how they might ever wield it. As we have set out in previous chapters, girls are the enduring subjects of 'confidence' discourse (Banet-Weiser 2018), and the global activists and 'girl bosses' of the popular press (Biressi 2018), girls are also the focus of a plethora of leadership initiatives exhorting them to imagine themselves as the leaders of the future. Popular tropes and programmes, however, elide ways in which girls are debarred from decision-making along axes of age and gender that further intersect with factors including race, class, region, and disability. They also fail to recognise both how celebrity is enmeshed with girls' ideas surrounding public roles for women and girls' understanding of the hostile cultural environment that such women in the public eye endure.

In this chapter, we explore media constructs of gendered leadership in the conjuncture of the pandemic; we ask how power is performed, appropriated, and subverted, as well as whose voice can be heard on which stage. Through focus group discussions with teenage girls in the United Kingdom and social media tropes of young women lip-synching male politicians, we highlight their rejection of polarised gender roles, awareness of cultural misogyny, subversion of politicians' performative masculinity, interrogation of the dangers of incompetence, and creative resistance to voicelessness. As empirical researchers working with girls, we are inviting them to share their understandings of how power and gender operate in the world. The researcher, inevitably, transforms such sharing into 'texts' for analysis. During lockdown, when we could not talk to girls, we turned to the spaces where they were producing other 'texts' that engaged with gender, leadership, power, and voice in particular. In this chapter, we consider these two kinds of 'texts' as examples of how girls negotiate and make sense of narratives that circulate in their media worlds. Such an approach enables us to identify a continuity between the heightened anxiety around women's visibility and masculinised power in the COVID-19 era, and the pre- and post-pandemic normality for girls who are subjects of prevailing discourses that exhort them to visibility and voice in a world they know would punish them for that visibility.

## THE POLITICS OF VOICE: GENDER, AGENCY, AND DISRUPTIVE VENTRILOQUISM

Understanding the contemporary politics of voice requires recognition of the systems by which women are silenced, trivialised, and thus severed from the centres of power and how these are historically entrenched in Western culture (Beard 2017b, 2). Mary Beard begins this history 3000 years ago with 'the first recorded example of a man telling a woman to "shut up"' (ibid., 3). Jilly B. Kay continues this history of 'communicative injustice' at the site of the ducking stool, a ritual of public humiliation prevalent from the sixteenth to nineteenth centuries for women who spoke in ways deemed too rebellious or transgressive for their gender (2020a, 1). These histories demonstrate that incursions on women's voices – through punishment, discrediting, and diffuse mechanisms of overt and covert silencing – are fundamental in dislodging women from power. In histories of visual culture, women have predominantly been made visible only where it reinforces a secondary status to men (Rozsika and Pollock 1981). Such representations are 'both structured in and structuring of gender power relations' (Pollock 1993, 55). That is, representations of women as voiceless, invisible, secondary, and removed from power, work to reproduce these conditions for women. With this in mind, we turn to girls to ask how contemporary representations of high-profile women interact with their sense of their own potential power.

Maurice Merleau-Ponty argues that language 'presents or rather it *is* the subject's taking up of a position in the world' (1965, 84), articulating the multiple dimensions of voice as both physical utterance and maker of symbolic meaning, which construct our status in both physical and symbolic space. Voice 'always requires and requisitions space' (Connor 2000, 5) and does so in ways inherently tied up with agency and identity:

> [Voice] simultaneously produces articulate sound, and produces myself, as a self-producing being. . . . When I speak I seem, to you, and to myself, as well, to be more intimately and uninterruptedly *there*. . ., producing myself as a vocal agent. (ibid., 3)

Voice constructs personhood and agency. This is what gives the ancient and peculiar practice of 'making voices appear to issue from elsewhere than their source' (ibid., 14) such potential to destabilise the status quo of identities and their power relations.

As such, the 'history of the social production of space' has a parallel history of dissociated voices or ventriloquism (ibid., 12–13). This begins in 1400 BC with the Oracle at Delphi, where Apollo spoke 'through' a priestess to bestow divine wisdom on earth. It continues through various forms of possession, divination, inspiration, conjuring, and illusion, including the vaudeville puppeteer most associated with the term, and into contemporary lip-synching, social media mash-ups, 'deepfakes', and Amazon Alexa. Whether its purpose is to secure power, provoke reverence and awe, inspire religious belief and loyalty, or sustain entertainment industries, ventriloquism is a 'strategic reconfiguration of the relationship between the voice and the human body' that is 'variously *productive*' (Hirsh and Wallace 2023, 1). For Goldblatt, ventriloquism offers a metaphor for the ways we can simultaneously know and not know: 'Ventriloquism is illusion without deception – a truly deceived audience would undermine the nature of the act. [It] parallels one of the more time-honoured philosophical oppositions, appearance and reality, [and] a double-levelled world view' (2006, xi). We bring the concept of ventriloquism into dialogue with the practice of trolling as defined by the Oxford English Dictionary: antagonistic messages that can be both humorous and corrective in intent. Ven*troll*oquism is thus the antagonistic practice of disrupting the relationship between voice and its source in ways which are humorous and corrective in their strategic and productive attention to gendered performances of power.

If power manifests through voice, ventriloquism plays with the power dynamics of voice to challenge conventional wisdom and countermand the evidence of our senses. Attending to the power of unlocated voices to encourage societies to reflect 'upon the powers and meanings of voice' (Connor 2000, 14), we approach social media lip-synching as a strategic, productive reconfiguration of gendered power relations. In its capacity to disrupt which voice emanates from which body, ventriloquism, in particular lip-synching as a means to impersonate other genders, has been a productive form for queer exploration.

## QUEER HISTORIES OF LIP-SYNCHING AND MALE IMPERSONATION

Lip-synching has a long and significant queer history. 'Cross-dressing' performers have been popular for both queer and heterosexual audiences at least since the late nineteenth century (Chauncey 2008), with a move from live song to lip-synching in the 1960s, as the criminalisation of the drag scene forced the art form underground (Newton 1979). The social media videos of young women impersonating male politicians can be understood as both lip-synching and drag and, as such, a contemporary evolution of two longstanding queer forms of performance. Such gender impersonation offers a moment of 'gender trouble', parodying 'the notion of an original or primary gender identity' and revealing that the action of gender requires a performance which is repeated (Butler 1990, 140). The 'ritualized quality' of drag lip-synching – that is, miming to a recorded audio of the opposite sex – in particular serves to 'emphasise the disjuncture' between biological sex and the gender being performed (Kaminski and Taylor 2008, 51). Drag lip-synching represents a 'manifestation of a voice' in ways which build community through collective memory and shared history: lip-synching repertoires serve to 'exchange historical material . . . without recourse to heteronormative structures of heritability' (Farrier 2016, 192). As large, queer social gatherings, live lip-synching events function as important precursors to community organising and overt political action (Kaminski and Taylor 2008). The study of social movements such as the Occupy movement, LGBT rights, and feminism has shown the importance of collective identity formation to successful collective action (Flesher Fominaya 2010; Smith et al. 2015; Valocchi 1999). Kaminski and Taylor identify the social function of lip-synching as 'creation and sustenance of an oppositional consciousness [which] not only defines who "us" is but also acknowledges some injustice done to "us" and attributes it to structural causes' (2008, 49). In contemporary drag, it is specifically 'attention to the disjuncture between visual and sound (or lip synching's non-sound)' that offers ways to continue to see drag as disrupting gendered norms (Cover et al. 2022, 81), despite some arguing that drag has become depoliticised in 'normative drag culture' (Litwiller 2020). As with the cultural history of ventriloquism, the way that drag lip-synching creates 'layers of sound emanating from different corporeal sources (the body, the recording)' subverts cultural demands for seamlessness and authenticity in gendered embodiment (Cover et al. 2022, 81). However, despite this enduring potential for lip-synching to be a disruptive and resistant mode of gendered performance, the global commercial success of the TV show *Ru Paul's Drag Race*, in which contestants famously 'lip-synch for their lives', in tandem with the entrepreneurial self-branding cultures of social media, has led to the celebrification of drag resulting in 'homonormative narratives of the "good queer", [which delimit] the sorts of queer bodies and politics that are acceptable in the mainstream' (Feldman and Hakim 2020).

While lip-synching is most commonly associated with male drag queen performers, there is an important, frequently overlooked history of female-to-male impersonators, some of whom were the most successful and highest-paid performers active in variety and vaudeville from the 1860s up until 1930 for audiences of both men and women (Rodger 2018). These performances were 'eroticised and often (though not inevitably) politicized' (Halberstam 1998, 233). For upper-class women in early twentieth-century Europe, male impersonation was a means to 'assert a specifically female desire, whether sexual or political' (Vicinus 2013, 163). It is because 'masculinity in this society inevitably conjures up notions of power and legitimacy and privilege [and] often symbolically refers to the power of the state' that male impersonation can be viewed as a performance which nods towards the potential to appropriate male power (Halberstam 1998, 2). For Jack Halberstam, performances of masculinity by women, such as those examined here, are 'the kinds of masculinity that seem most informative about gender relations and most generative of social change' (1998, 3) because of the way they counteract 'the idea that masculinity "just is", whereas femininity reeks of the artificial' (ibid.:234) as 'masculinity has to be made visible before it can be performed' (ibid., 235).

Since Halberstam's foundational work on female masculinity, other scholars in the field have shone a light on a trans-inclusive contemporary drag king scene encompassing performances of a wide range of genders (Sennett and Bay-Cheng 2003), with racially diverse casts, in smaller towns and cities extending far beyond the US urban centres of queer culture (Piontek 2003). Such locations and identities can foster the 'power of marginality', allowing performers to push boundaries in ways not seen elsewhere, and such diversity makes it difficult to specify a universal drag king culture (Drysdale 2019). Indeed, scholars have tended to argue for the ways in which drag king cultures are particular to their geographical locations (Baker and Kelly 2016; Korcek 2010). As such, drag king cultures may be better understood as a collection of participatory cultural activities revealing different affects, investments, and intimacies (Drysdale 2019). Drag is diffuse. In the pandemic, these scenes flourished online; drag king social media abounds with creative 'world-building potentiality', for example, the experimental, Caribbean social media drag king, Mandinga (roughly translated as 'the end times') (Meadows 2022, 8). We consider these affordances of lip-synching as a participatory cultural activity to ask whether these will enable girls to build alternative collective narratives and push boundaries from the margins.

## VEN*TROLLO*QUISM: SOCIAL MEDIA VENTRILOQUISM, TIKTOK, AND COVID-19

Social media have been theorised as spaces in which girlhood cultures flourish (Sales 2016). Under COVID-19, new, ventriloquistic social media forms proliferated and, in the process, upset existing hierarchies and power dynamics. For example, celebrities seeking new modes of income as the pandemic halted TV and film production turned to paid digital platforms such as Cameo, where fans pay celebrities to record messages of the fan's choosing. Drenten and Psarras define this as 'digital ventriloquism' and 'paid puppeteering', and argue that 'direct monetization of the fan-celebrity relationship is re-shaping [its] power dynamic' (2021, 3350).

The enforcement of social distancing as a means of slowing the rate of coronavirus infections intensified the need for virtual interaction (Feldkamp 2021), TikTok's 2020 growth was popularly attributed to pandemic boredom (Kale 2020). The emergence of young, female celebrities like then 15-year-old Charli D'Amelio, the first TikTok-er to reach 50 million followers with her dance routines and lip-syncs, represented a celebratory extension of girls' 'bedroom culture', albeit an exclusionary, sanitised ideal of girlhood deliberately promoted by algorithms which suppressed less desirable images of the disastrous impact of the pandemic on girls globally (Kennedy 2020, 1073).

Different social media applications necessarily offer their own specificities of platform design, which determine privileged or proscribed functionality. As such, they 'encourage, discourage, refuse, and allow particular lines of action and social dynamics' (Davis 2020, 11). TikTok in particular is characterised by ventriloquism and lip-synching; its 'network ventriloquism [creates a] web of dissociations and reconfigurations of users' bodies and voices' (Ramati and Abeliovich 2022, 1). These 'principles of mimesis – imitation and replication

– are encouraged' in TikTok's logic and design (Zulli and Zulli 2022, 1872), as 60-second durations invite complex editing, and sound, voice, and visual effects are seamlessly embedded in the app. Just as lip-synching passes on shared LGBTQ+ history (Farrier 2016), the characteristics of mimesis and ventriloquism, and the way TikTok 'mediates between human and nonhuman voices' suit TikTok to acts of community mobilising 'cultural activism' through shared narratives (Ramati and Abeliovich 2022, 6). These enact a politics of collective memory and identity linking younger users in 'networked publics' (boyd 2011) through a combination of entertainment and political expression, albeit alongside fake news content. Despite it prioritising mimetic and imitative behaviours over interpersonal connection, Zulli and Zulli argue that 'due to imitation publics on TikTok, public service or activist messages through this platform could be much more persuasive than in other formats' as 'users may be more inclined to adopt behaviors or participate in civic activities if they are packaged as "challenges" or "checks" that they can replicate' (2022, 1886). For scholars and public health officials, TikTok offered real-time insights into pandemic attitudes, norms, and misinformation. Like Zulli and Zulli, Southwick et al. (2021) argue for the ways these characteristics particularly suit TikTok as a means to inform public health messaging and public health mitigation strategies. In their analysis of 750 TikTok videos tagged #coronavirus posted from January to March 2020, they demonstrate the instrumental role of the app in the pandemic as it was used for COVID-19 discussion and reflection and the dissemination of misleading/misinformative videos. While many videos evoked 'fear" (15 per cent) or 'empathy' (6 per cent) the vast majority (49 per cent) evoked 'humor/parody' (ibid. 234).

This chapter examines a particular strain of humorous TikTok parody videos that emerged during the pandemic: those in which young women impersonated male political leaders. One such TikTok creator, Sarah Cooper, has been considered in Sophia McClennen's examination of satire under the presidency of Donald Trump, an era which 'defied satire' as during the pandemic 'the audience watching Trump handle the crisis knows that the ending won't go well but also knows that they are stuck in the same play. It's ironic, but not funny' (McClennen 2021, 27). McClennen echoes Piontek's (2003) observations about the 'power of marginality', arguing that the most effective parodies of the then US president came from those on the margins, such as queer musical satirist Randy Rainbow, and Black female impersonator Cooper, as TikTok 'bypassed traditional celebrity venues, offering creators of all types a chance to be seen' (ibid.:29). These satirical artists' use of TikTok as a platform is significant both because Trump was the first president to tweet directly himself, seemingly without the editorial guidance of social media managers, and because of his sustained narrative that 'traditional' media outlets discriminated against him with 'fake news':

He simply wanted it banned. The front-facing argument by the Trump team was that TikTok represented a Chinese threat to national security. For those familiar with Trump's efforts to control his media image, that argument fell flat. Rather, what seemed more likely was that Trump wanted to ban TikTok because the platform represented a social-media platform totally out of his control. TikTok had been used, for example, to successfully ruin a major Trump rally. (McClennen 2021, 30)

While TikTok's algorithms deliberately favour the apolitically aesthetic (Biddle 2020) and allow misinformation to circulate (Southwick et al. 2021), the app was nonetheless 'a space not just to mock the president but also to truly affect his image' (McClennen 2021). Trump's efforts to ban the app suggest it had the potential to cause political leaders genuine concern.

Despite the significance of pandemic social media, television news remained the UK public's dominant source of COVID-19 information (Cushion et al. 703). Public susceptibility to misinformation was not solely attributable to social media but also to gaps in press briefings, which tended to obfuscate the British government's mismanagement of the crisis. UK government briefings carefully limited both opportunities for independent criticism and the public's ability to evaluate their failures. For example, they ceased including comparative international figures for infections and deaths in daily briefings, impeding the public's ability to compare their handling of the crisis to governments in other countries (Cushion et al. 2022, 704). They excluded independent experts in favour of scientists in their direct employ, thereby limiting the opportunity for independent criticism (Morani et al. 2022, 2522). The *leadership theatre* of the daily briefing, as a highly controlled narrative of government competence, is therefore a productive contrast to girls' creative and resistant engagements with ideas of COVID-19 leadership.

In its interactive and creative affordances and its function as a platform for youth to gather and communicate, TikTok provides a space for what Axel Bruns (2008) terms 'produsage', a kind of media production in which boundaries between producer and user roles are blurred as content creators borrow from legacy and other media to make new texts and new meanings. Importantly, the creation of such shared content takes place in collaborative environments. The collaborative nature of produsage is crucial in the development of new and resistant genres; if mainstream media genres are those 'through which powerholders attempt to define the common sense of social life' and 'within which they seek to objectivize and naturalize their power-laden definitions and meanings' (Steinberg 1998, 854), TikTok genres represent alternative definitions and sense-making. Further, genres are not stable categories but are defined through collective understanding (Miller 1994, 62), and as such 'belong to discourse communities, not to individuals' (Swales

1990, 9). The development and circulation of the new genre of girls' political lip-synch, therefore, can be examined as a collective response in terms of their offering resistant meanings to hegemonic discourses, representing a population group excluded from voice in traditional spaces of power.

## POLARISED GENDER, PERFORMATIVE COVID MASCULINITIES, AND FEMMEPHOBIA

Public discourse surrounding leadership and gender became heightened during the COVID-19 pandemic (Aldrich and Lotito 2020; Garikipati and Kambhampati 2021). It is a matter of national and international urgency that women leaders remain rare (European Commission; World Economic Forum). The crisis provided a flashpoint celebrating the stateswomanship of leaders such as New Zealand Prime Minister Jacinda Ardern and German Chancellor Angela Merkel (Bell 2020). They were praised as technocratic and consultative yet decisive, valuing expert guidance while exercising their own leadership. However, these discourses perpetuated gendered, essentialist ideas about women as inherently more caring, for example, praising Ardern's combination of 'science and empathy' (BBC.co.uk 2020). Invocations of familial caregiving in the nicknames 'Aunty Cindy' and the longstanding 'Mutti (or Mummy) Merkel' commonly circulated throughout news media of the time are obvious efforts to domesticate and contain the threat of female power. At the same time, this domestication contained the threat of a politics of care, consultation, and collaboration as a political alternative to the trope of the individualist macho hero endemic in political leadership cultures.

As an example of the widespread use of Mutti to refer to Chancellor Merkel, take the advert from a German milk brand with the headline 'Tschüss Mutti' (or 'Bye Mummy') above an image of a pair of hands holding a glass of milk. Merkel is not explicitly shown or named, and yet the reference to her is easily recognisable. This is what makes the advert such a clear example of the semiotics of Angela Merkel: a pensive hand pose, a bright, block-colour suit jacket, and the word Mutti are enough to firmly signify Merkel and her style of stateswomanship. The hand posture, with fingers touching in peaks while the thumbs rest in a diamond, has been called the Triangle of Power in English-speaking media or the Merkel-Raute (Merkel Rhombus) within Germany. It has been used to signify Merkel in communications from both her own campaign team, for example, a 2013 campaign billboard 'Put Germany's future in good hands' (Deutschlands Zukunft in guten Händen), and as a shorthand in ridicule and satirical impersonation of Merkel. The milk advert was timed with the announcement of Merkel's final term in office almost 2 years into the COVID-19 pandemic. The affectionate, iconic advert is a communication of gendered power and its containment in its use of 'Mutti' in combination with milk as a liquid signifying maternity. It is an example of women's power being defanged through its coding as an extension of domestic, familial caregiving (figure 5.1).

During the pandemic, leaders' performances of masculinity became similarly essentialised and exaggerated. The pandemic was framed as an imaginary war: Trump declared himself a 'wartime President' (Oprysko, Caitlin, and Luthi 2020); Johnson as leading a 'wartime government' (Rawlinson); French president Emmanuel Macron announced 'we are at war', and former president of the Philippines, Rodrigo Duterte, threatened to shoot citizens who defied lockdown orders like they were enemy soldiers (Bell 2020). This invocation facilitates macho posturing such as Johnson's Churchillian mimicry, Trump's calls upon his citizens to bear arms and resist state-imposed lockdowns (@ realDonaldTrump), or Brazilian president Jair Bolsonaro's promise, 'We're going to tackle the virus but tackle it like fucking men' (Phillips 2020). This braggadocio frames a crisis of public health as something that can be managed through masculine aggression and violence, rather than, for example, a politics of care which centres the wellbeing of citizens (figure 5.2).

Compared to Merkel and Arden's measured, quietly technocratic approaches, male leaders shouted their emotional irrationality in apoplectic outbursts and caps-lock tweets with exclamation marks. For example, Trump escalated lockdown tensions when he likened lockdown to citizens

Figure 5.1   German Billboard referring to German Chancellor Angela Merkel as 'Mutti'.

**Figure 5.2    Tweets by Donald Trump.**

being 'under siege!' and called for the American public to 'LIBERATE VIRGINIA' using their Second Amendment right to carry guns. In contrast with leadership characterised by consultation, science, and expertise seeking citizens' trust, Trump's populist theatrics deploy a rhetorical turn to histrionic melodrama and hyperbole that gives an appearance of leadership through spontaneous whim and emotional, fearful outburst. Similarly, when confronted with verified facts about UK care-home deaths during Prime Minister's Questions, Johnson had no considered response and resorted to emotional outbursts, yelling 'That's not true!' (Crace 2020). Johnson used his daily briefings to position those exercising caution (as scientists advised) as excessively fearful, shaking hands with COVID-19 patients on ward visits with bravado in a show to appeal to 'British common sense'. Headlines depicted those calling for stricter measures as in the grips of 'COVID Hysteria' (Kavanagh 2020; Jacobs 2020; Quinn 2020; Hitchens 2020) a term which locates an inappropriately excessive and emotional response specifically within the female (or feminised) body. To tackle COVID-19 'like fucking men', called for a coalescence of misogyny, violence, recklessness, nationalism, and the anti-intellectualism of a nation that has 'had enough of experts' (to borrow the phrase used by Brexiteer Michael Gove when challenged for importing Trump's 'post-truth' politics in his misleading Brexit campaign

(Mance 2016). These particular coalescing themes typify the rise of populist authoritarianism (Yelin and Clancy 2021).

Of course, Johnson, despite his performance of masculine invincibility and disavowal of vulnerability, did get ill and was admitted to intensive care in April 2020. And despite extending 'this conception of virility to the national body [and] avoiding the appearance of vulnerability by denying the threat until it became impossible to dismiss' (Parmanand, 2020), the UK's frailty was similarly exposed. Had lockdown come sooner, the UK death toll would have been halved (Johns 2020). A knee-jerk 'militarized approach to foreign policy problems' leaves society ill-equipped to tackle today's most urgent crises: pandemics, climate change, and rising authoritarianism (Shaffner 2020) Despite the fact that men are more likely to die of coronavirus, men are less likely to wear masks, believing it to be a 'sign of weakness' (Capraro and Barcelo, 2020). Ideas about masculinity, therefore, structure actions and safety on national and individual levels.

Three months after his hospitalisation, in a *Mail on Sunday* interview, Johnson attempted to persuade the public he was 'fit as a butcher's dog' after recovering from the virus by doing press-ups in a surreal display of masculine virility as unconvincing as it was camp. For Halberstam, masculinity 'symbolically refers to the power of the state' (1998, 2). Johnson's athletic performance, dressed in a shirt and tie, in the prime minister's oak-paneled office, combines multiple codes of masculine power. If dominant masculinity seeks to present itself as 'a naturalized relation between maleness and power' (, 1998, 2), Johnson's shaky press-ups were a moment that revealed the effort required to maintain this apparent relation. The spectacle of effortful performance can be understood as a moment of 'gender trouble' (Butler 1990, 140). 'Excessive masculinity turns into a parody or exposure of the norm' (Halberstam 1998, 4) when it is men doing the performance. That Johnson hopes his strained, bodily performance of masculine physical, and state power will be conferred upon ideas of nationhood is cemented by his crouched supplication before a large, flaccid Union Jack flag (figure 5.3).

When disparaging other male leaders, Johnson has frequently resorted to femmephobic, misogynist language: in 2019, he called then opposition leader Jeremy Corbyn a 'big girl's blouse' for demanding Johnson publish the government's no-deal Brexit planning documents (Belam 2019), and his predecessor David Cameron a 'girly swot' for having increased MPs' presence over the summer when Johnson planned to close parliament for 5 weeks to squash resistance to his no-deal Brexit plans (Coates 2019). Under COVID, this sexist, homophobic, feminising logic was directed towards then opposition leader Keir Starmer. As Starmer has used his legal background to give Johnson a thorough and fact-led grilling in Prime Minister's Questions, this was reported in the news through the sexist, feminising stock character of the 'girly swot'. In *the*

**Figure 5.3 Boris Johnson Doing Press-ups for News Reporters in Downing Street.**

*Spectator*, journalist Lloyd Evans (2020) reports, 'The swot versus the wag. The smart Alec against the rugger captain. The chemistry nerd who wants to join the cool kids behind the bike-sheds'. Similarly, *Guardian* columnist John Crace reports, 'Preparation is for girly swots. [Johnson] is the macho blagger who has always been able to wing it, fuelled by a few gags and some hasty last-minute revision' (2020). In this framing, masculinity makes a virtue of incompetent leadership, again hinging upon the particular combination of populist, anti-expert misogyny. These forms of misogynist and anti-intellectual rhetoric 'coalesce, demonstrating intersections between misogyny and the far right [which] suggest a gendering of the fascism/progressivism divide in attempting to emasculate people for being progressive. . . . This illustrates how the ideals of masculine power bubble beneath discourses of right-wing polemicists' (Yelin and Clancy 2021, 185). Johnson seeks to feminise and thereby supposedly undermine the leadership qualities of his rivals – shoring up nationalism in images of feminised opposition.

Prime Minister's Questions offers a spectacle of men's entitlement to use their voices. Parliamentary rules and procedures in the House of Commons enshrine misogynist classical templates for deciding 'whose speech is to be given space to be heard' (Beard 2017b, 20). In this space where male leaders demean one another by loudly calling each other girls', women's role in COVID-19 was constructed as one of domestic caregiving. COVID-era chancellor Rishi Sunak genuflected in PMQs: 'We owe mums everywhere an enormous debt of thanks for doing the enormously difficult job of juggling childcare and work' (Newman 2021). Pandemic lockdowns conceal manifold gendered inequalities, including the fact that 'capitalism cannot survive without free care labour – mostly that of women performed within the family unit – which sustains and reproduces the workforce' (Kay 2020b, 885). It is striking that Sunak specifically describes women in this domestic role at a time when everybody, regardless of gender, was constrained to their home due to lockdown. As such, he naturalises and reproduces the gendered asymmetries of lockdown domestic labour in which women are presumed carers despite the presence of men in the home. As with clapping for NHS heroes, thanks is an inadequate stand-in for competent, funded government policies.

## GIRLS' DEFINITION OF LEADERSHIP AS COMPETENCE AND THEIR CONDEMNATION OF JOHNSON AND TRUMP

These exaggerated gendered tropes have emerged within an existing UK context of leadership dominated by white, male elites and in which media treatments of women and minority leaders are largely hostile and/or trivialising. The teenage girls we spoke to across England, Wales, and Scotland were acutely aware of the problematic nature of leadership discourses and the problems these pose for women, recognising that 'women are, like, expected to stay home and stuff' (Samira), but desiring opportunities to develop their own expertise and experience in leadership within their community. They discussed the gendered coaxing of young people towards different roles, which are mirrored in the gendering of women leaders as consultative while male leaders default to dominance; as one girl from Bedfordshire explained: 'there's a pressure on girls to keep the peace and there's a pressure on boys to take control'. Participants across groups consistently showed awareness of cultural misogyny in the representation and media scrutiny of female leaders. Molly from Somerset opined of Trump: 'I watched his debate with him and Hillary and he was just, not even making political points, he was just making points of how she didn't look good'. Ruth from Glasgow bemoaned:

> Hilary Clinton was actually quite good. I would have said that she would have probably done a better job than him. She probably would have. But, because she's a woman. They try to say, 'No, we don't do that no more, you're all accepted'. But there's still these people that still believe in not letting a woman doing a certain job. [There aren't] as many women world leaders as we would like because it's still seen as a man's job. [It could] be the worst man ever who would go for the job. Like, they could probably put Donald Trump back on that again where a woman who actually might be capable and I'd say Donald Trump would still be put in as president, because it's a woman.

As we have argued in chapter 2, popular discourses seeking to encourage girls to follow in the paths of existing female leaders fail to recognise girls' own understanding of the hostile cultural environment that women in the public eye endure and how this acts as a deterrent to girls when it comes to speaking up and making oneself visible. Our participants showed understanding both of the exaggerated masculinity and narcissism of Trump's leadership and how this strategy drew on wider misogynistic tropes when campaigning against Hillary Clinton. In terms of their ideas of good leadership, the girls frequently raised the importance of competence:

> *Maya:* You don't want to be associated with a huge disaster because you took a risk.

> *Cadence:* If you want to have, like, a large impact on, like, the world or something . . . you have to feel it's something you're competent to do.

In contrast to Johnson suggesting preparation is for 'girly swots', and a Tory government proud to have 'had enough of experts', taking decision-making roles and making changes in the world without the necessary expertise and preparation was unthinkable to the girls. In a discussion about world leaders during the pandemic, girls in Glasgow identified Trump and Johnson as reckless compared to then First Minister of Scotland, Nicola Sturgeon:

> *Ruth:* Boris Johnson was obviously the Prime Minister at the time and he was opening the UK back up, but she was like no, we're staying in lockdown.

> *Tamsin:* She was trying to protect

> *Ruth:* Donald Trump wanted to come out here and build a golf course, she told him no, go back to . . .

> *Tamsin:* She was trying to prevent us trying to get more sick.

> *Ruth:* Aye, she said 'I'm not signing off'.

While this characterisation of Sturgeon as protector reproduces common gendered discourses of women's leadership as more caring, this gendered divide was discussed in terms of competence as much as care.

> *Johnson was a figure of ridicule, reducing South London girls to fits of laughter and jokes about his appearance:*

> *Chioma:* We saw how Boris resigned and . . . we see their faces, like, red . . .

> *Jinani:* His face got red when he was . . .

> *(All descend into laughter)*

This focus on a man's appearance inverts the common gendered scrutiny of female leaders' appearance that was a theme arising consistently across the groups of girls we spoke to. That this feminising focus on appearance centres upon the moment of Johnson's departure from power demonstrates that emphasis on appearance is a tool to preclude an individual's fitness for power.

Girls distrusted the Conservative government in terms of both competence and care. Discussing crime in North London, Fara lamented: 'In my opinion, I feel like they don't care about it. I don't think they care about it at all. I feel like they feel like people deserve to die.' In Somerset, Samantha echoed this mistrust: 'sounds like working in the Government might mean that you become a bad person because some Governments have done really bad things to their people'. Serena attributed this lack of care to the fact that the government recruits from the already privileged: 'it's drawing from, you know, people that are relatives or friends of people that have already done it. They're already up high status so they, you know, don't care.' When asked why these leaders get voted in, Fara explained, 'They lie'.

All of the groups were asked why they felt people seek power, and whether good leaders want to *be in charge* or want to *make a change*. The girls consistently demonstrated suspicion of those seeking power for its own sake, and in multiple groups cited Trump as the prime example of a person seeking power for personal gain and not because of motivation in terms of social purpose. When asked 'Why would anybody want to be in charge?', Maya from Bradford said:

Like, respect. Also, the power because it's just another way of people having the upper hand and feeling better than everybody else. Like Donald Trump for instance, he's doing it purely for the power and control of everybody else and not for what's correct in the world and because he sees things that need to be better.

While the girls saw many celebrities as leaders and, as discussed in chapter 3, admired celebrities using their platform for progressive social causes, the pursuit of fame for its own sake received scorn. Trump was, again, seen to typify this. Asked the same question, North London girls responded,

*Kelly:* Either they actually want to do something good . . . or they just want to be famous and they just want to be recognised by everybody they see.

*Ada:* Trump!

Meanwhile, girls from Bradford said of Trump:

*Shameem:* He wants to be like, all the spotlight on him. . .

*Maya:* He wants to be worshipped. . . . He's acting on his own self-interest, instead of the interest of the rest of his country and he's still thinking . . . he can finally do the things like chucking the Mexicans out. No matter how stupid it is to everybody else.

In conversations about desire for power and fame versus desire for social change, girls made this same argument about Trump through juxtapositions which illuminate overlaps between leadership, celebrity, social contribution, and Trumps origins in reality TV:

*Anna:* Donald Trump again because I think he wants to be in power. Although he wants all these wacky changes. But, I think that's for himself in a way and I think he just likes having the power to feel like he can do what he wants.

*Chloe:* Kim Kardashian, there is no change necessarily that she's wanted to make, she's increasing her popularity and doing crazy things that just increase the talk about her.

As well as reality TV star Kim Kardashian, multiple groups discussed Trump in relation to Hitler, invoking the ultimate cultural demon of dangerous leadership. In Newbury, for example, conversation unfolded thus:

*Interviewer:* Do people like Donald Trump or extremist recruiters use different strategies to good leaders, or the same strategies, but just for bad purposes?

*Chloe:* Yeah you have to be strategic. I do history and you learn about Hitler and how he would promote himself and it would either be through fear or propaganda.

This was echoed when girls in North London were asked to expand on their discussions of Trump:

*Interviewer:* Why do you think people vote for very contentious leaders such as Donald Trump?

*Tani:* Because the, for example Hitler told the Germans stuff they wanted to hear, like promised them stuff and they believed anything they wanted, because at that time they were going through a big recession and he said he would make Germany great again.

*Claire:* I think they are very effective on people and they make a strong impact . . . I think that's why they done that for Hitler.

The most vehement response to Trump came from Bradford:

> *Interviewer:* If you could change something in the world, what would it be?
>
> *Maya:* Donald Trump.
>
> *Interviewer:* Donald Trump. (All laughing.) . . .
>
> *Maya:* For the end to Donald Trump thing. It was on there so I'm answering it, okay? Don't give me that look. Um, you'd only need one person, I mean there's enough people in America with guns like who can shoot the president.
>
> *Interviewer:* So, assassination?
>
> *Shameem:* Like JFK. We don't want another JFK.
>
> *Maya:* Yeah we do want another JFK. JFK was alright and Donald Trump is Donald Trump.

Maya's recourse to violence replicates the violent discourse propagated by male leaders inventing wars, from Trump's incitements to gun violence to 'LIBERATE VIRGINIA' from lockdown to Rodrigo Duterte's threats to shoot citizens who break lockdown. Indulging a fantasy of masculine power, she reaches for 'the master's tools' (Lorde 1984, 27) – this can also be viewed as a form of impersonation. However, while the figure of the American, lone gunman typifies a fantasy of masculine, aggressive individualism, he is also a figure of desperation and impotence, and a narrative which is mobilised to avoid tackling structural change. This trope is racialised; the White, male shooter is characterised as a singular, exceptional bad apple as opposed to people of colour who are taken to represent violence within their community through characterisations of 'terrorists and thugs' (Frisby 2017). While Maya's response may seem extreme, and it is at odds with the girls' ambivalence around masculine tropes of the singular, heroic leader in favour of collaborative and consultative political alternatives, it nonetheless accords with the girls' frustration that power is reserved for the already powerful. In her imagination of state leadership and the forms of power available to her, Maya identified with Lee Harvey Oswald rather than the president. Maya simultaneously expresses awareness of Trump's problematic nature, a violent fantasy desiring his power and freedom, awareness that this is wrong, desire for a less unequal society, and impotent frustration at her position of limited personal agency.

## VEN*TROLLO*QUISM: DRAGGING MALE
## POLITICIANS ON TIKTOK

As we have explained, our fieldwork was interrupted by COVID-19 lockdown school closures. However, our work so far sensitised us to similar discourses of gendered leadership circulating in the texts we could access. We found an emerging viral TikTok genre responding to this backdrop of performative masculinity, articulating frustration at harms perpetuated by incompetent male leaders. We read these tropes as a creative response to the extreme gendering of leadership under COVID-19, which creatively circumvented these constraints on girls' and women's power, voices, and political representation.

The closure of professional programme-making saw user-generated content emerge as key lockdown media. The other media of lockdown was the *leadership theatre* of the government briefing. In Britain, record numbers of viewers tuned in daily at 5pm to learn new information about the virus, data on deaths and hospitalisation, and whether they would be allowed to leave the house the following day (Lawson 2020). The TikToks examined here combine these two forms that so typify the pandemic. At a time of limitation, they embrace the 'world-building potentiality' of male impersonation in social media (Meadows 2022, 8), to pose implicit questions about alternative power structures to the grotesquerie of performative toxicity of masculine leadership theatre under COVID. The audio is from recognisable recordings of male leaders' COVID-19 briefings. The video is user-generated, as women deliver precise lip-syncs and uncanny impersonations combining politics and gallows humour to question male politicians' fitness to lead. We call this *ven*troll*oquism: the use of ventriloquistic modes to undertake online trolling and corrective critique (figure 5.4).

Kylie Scott, then a 26-year-old film student from California, lip-syncs over audio of Trump's ruminations on the virus (@kyscottt 2020). Visually, she has replicated the nightclub setting that her lockdown-era viewers are banned from visiting. Despite the colourful flashing disco lighting, and Scott's silver evening wear and jewellery, humour arises from the knowledge that this must have been filmed at home, and very likely alone. Superimposed text dreams of post-lockdown life while explaining the video concept: 'drunk in the club after covid'. Her physical performance replicates drunkenness. She leans; the low-ball tumbler with ice and lime sloshes precariously as her hands gesticulate wildly; the composition is closely, claustrophobically cropped as if this is a one-on-one conversation in the club's dark corner and her drink might spill on you, her interlocutor (or bored date?). Her facial expressions swing rapidly between overconfident, flirting swagger and crumpled, intense difficulty stringing a sentence together. She nods to herself with self-congratulation as she speaks. The audio is a Trump speech originally delivered from the White

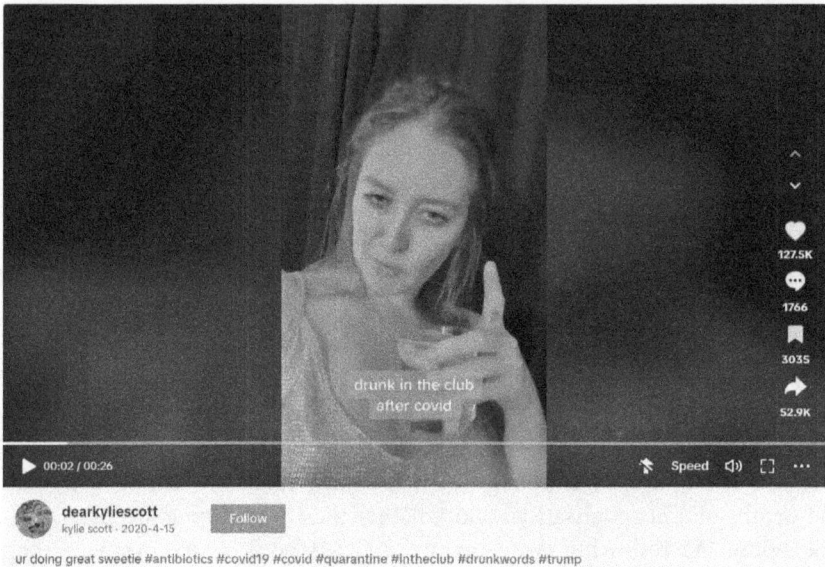

ur doing great sweetie #antibiotics #covid19 #covid #quarantine #intheclub #drunkwords #trump

**Figure 5.4    American TikTokker Kylie Scott Impersonating President Donald Trump.**

House Press Room, replete with wooden podium, US flag, and imposing White House insignia:

> The germ has gotten so brilliant that the antibiotic can't keep up with it. And they're constantly trying to come up with a new. People go to a hospital and they can't. They go for a heart operation but they end up dying from, from problems, you know the problems I'm talking about. Uhhhh . . . (original video at @joshtpm 2020)

Scott's delivery underscores Trump's absurdity, inviting us to focus on how little sense his words make. She highlights his faltering, confused delivery that skips from topic to topic, and his slippery refusal to complete sentences or make explicit statements. Her believability highlights that, divorced from the signifiers of male state power offered by leadership theatre, Trump's words are as useful a contribution to understanding COVID-19 as a local, drunk bore. Her lip-synching serves to 'emphasise the disjuncture' (Kaminski and Taylor 2008, 51) between those at home sharing the joke, who do understand basic facts about germs, and rambling, irresponsible male power failing to manage the crisis. The seedy setting of 'drunk in the club', Scott's flirtatious swagger, and the viewer's cornered point-of-view subtly recall sexual assault allegations against Trump. It is a humorous and effective indictment of his fitness to lead.

British TikTok star Meggie Foster, then aged 27, similarly transposes audio from a Boris Johnson speech from the daily briefing room into a new context: a bedtime story (@meggiefoster 2020) (figure 5.5). The setting casts Johnson as a spinner of comforting fantasies, a critique of the government's refusal to report facts around the poor handling of the virus in the United Kingdom that might lead to critique (Cushion et al. 2022). She reads from George Orwell's *1984,* conjuring a dystopian pandemic with daily briefings of Ministry of Truth doublespeak, another reference to government lies and careful control of the narrative that the state briefings represent, designed as they were to limit space for critique of the government (Morani et al.). She delivers Johnson's speech to a back bench of soft toys and an eager pigtailed child (also played by Foster by means of edited cutaways, as is a common meme trope, the use of which further emphasises Foster's solitude in lockdown). As Johnson, she is dressed in an ill-fitting oversized men's suit and tie, at odds with her youthful face in full make-up. If 'femininity reeks of the artificial' (Halberstam 1998, 234), Foster's exaggerated, youthful femininity performing Johnson's stuffy, exaggerated masculinity deflates his paternalistic authority as he demands, 'you must obey the rules on social distancing and to enforce those rules we will increase the fines'. As with both vaudeville ventriloquism and drag kings, a realistic emulation is not the goal (Goldblatt xi), rather a parodic 'exposure of the theatricality of masculinity' (ibid., 232).

28-year-old Maria DeCotis lip-syncs a press briefing in which New York governor Andrew Cuomo reflected upon the pandemic 'silver lining' of

**Figure 5.5   British TikTokker Meggie Foster Impersonating Prime Minister Boris Johnson.**

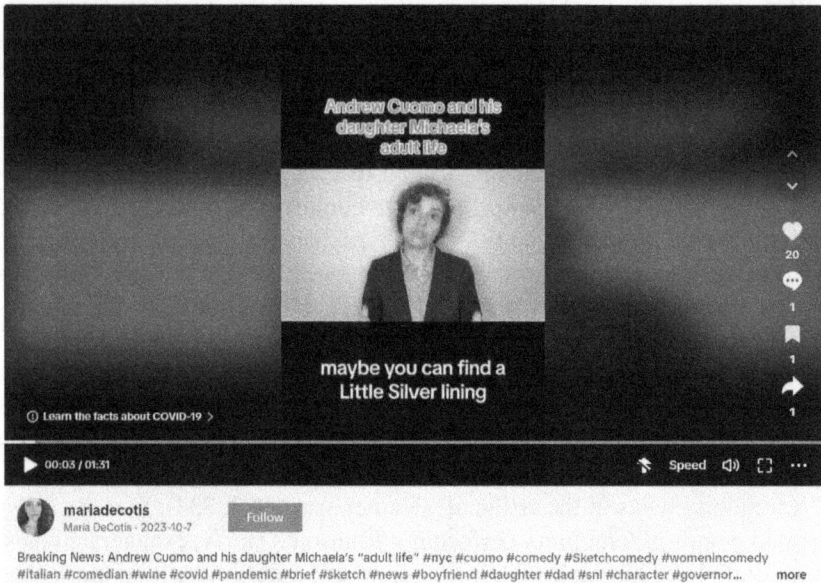

Figure 5.6    American TikTokker Maria DeCotis Impersonating Governor Andrew Cuomo.

spending time with his 22-year-old daughter, a digression DeCotis calls a 'mini breakdown' which had her 'riveted' (Hunt 2020) (figure 5.6). In DeCotis' version, Cuomo neurotically chain-smokes increasing numbers of cigarettes until she has five in each hand and more that she is chewing and swallowing, all while continuing to lip-sync (@mariadecotis 2023). As the trigger for his breakdown is an inability to cope with his daughter's adulthood, DeCotis' Cuomo appears as a haunted man, panicking at loss of control: over women, himself, and the pandemic.

In Sarah Cooper's lip-synch of the now infamous press briefing in which Trump suggested ingesting disinfectant and lighting the body from the inside, her delivery is more deadpan than that of Scott, DeCotis, or Foster (figure 5.7). In a navy blue suit jacket, with understatement, she simply delivers his words: 'We hit the body with a tremendous . . . uhhh . . . whether it's ultraviolet or just very powerful light' (@sarahcpr 2020). For large sections of the video, there is no supplementary conceptual layer, no transposed setting like the club, or a bedtime story. It is simply Cooper delivering Trump's words as if delivering her own press briefing from her home. There is almost no joke. Trump's words are their own punchline, and Cooper's restrained delivery forces the viewer to engage with their dangerous absurdity. She continues: 'aaand I think you said that hasn't been checked, but you're gonna test it'. She cuts to herself playing

**Figure 5.7    American TikTokker Sarah Cooper Impersonating President Donald Trump.**

a blank-faced, browbeaten expert Trump is nominating to test his light theory. 'Me?', they mouth, and later, 'I don't know what you . . .' , conjuring the unhealthy relationship between male leaders and experts evidenced by Trump's untested policy announcement. She lip-syncs 'and then I said supposing you brought the light inside the body which you can do either through the skin or in some other way', miming with her hands the light entering her various orifices, all the while maintaining the serious delivery and tone of the press briefing. The spectacle of a straight-faced woman gesturing up her anus while pretending to be Trump feels subversive in its rejection of sexualisation and the strictures of femininity that Trump has persistently and publicly shamed women for not adhering to (Robson 2020, Scotto di Carlo 2020). Miming ingesting kitchen disinfectant spray, Cooper delivers Trump's words 'it would be interesting to check that. For that you're going to have to use *medical* doctors with, but it, it sounds, it sounds interesting to me'. Her smug emphasis on the word '*medical*'' highlights the risibility of a national press briefing during a global pandemic in which a president speculates on potentially lethal cures while boasting about not having run these ideas past doctors.

As McClennen argues of Trump's effect on comedy more widely, 'one of the particularly challenging components of the Trump presidency for comedians was the way in which he already seemed like an impersonation. Trump's performative style, braggadocio, and basic lack of understanding of the workings of US government all combined to throw challenges to the comedians impersonating him' (2021, 29). In interviews, Cooper has articulated how she responded to this challenge using her own 'power of marginality' in male impersonation (Piontek 2003) articulating the function of what we call 'leadership theatre': 'If a White guy in a suit [is speaking] and people are nodding around him, it's like we've been trained to think, Well, I guess it sounds like it could be true. If you see anybody else, especially me, saying [the same words], I think it highlights just how ridiculous it is' (Robertson 2020). Cuomo has publicly used the N-word in a live radio interview (Duster) and has received a litany of sexual assault allegations (Helmore 2023). Johnson famously compared veiled Muslim women to letterboxes (Elgot 2018). Trump infamously feels entitled to 'grab [women] by the pussy', and his power has consistently depended on exacerbating White supremacist groups, including referring to COVID-19 as the 'Chinese virus' and 'kung flu' at a rally in Oklahoma (Zhou 2020). These women's TikTok videos therefore offer the viewing pleasure of seeing such men bettered by women (and in the case of Cooper, a woman of colour), and imagining their outrage precisely because of their public record of racism and misogyny.

Limited to non-verbal communication, punctuating speeches with mime, reactions, and breaks to the fourth wall, these videos highlight the preposterousness of male leaders' statements just by repeating them. One might call it parody or satire, but there has been no rewriting. In a world where the charge of 'fake news' is used by leaders such as Trump as a defence against critique, this form of undermining impersonation lets the absurdity of masculine *leadership theatre* under COVID-19 speak for itself. The charges are undeniable, the words are on record, and the male leaders incriminate themselves. Through lip-synching, these women harness the potential of dissociated voices to destabilise the status quo of identities and their power relations and humiliate the male leaders they impersonate with devastating precision.

Part of what renders these videos so potent, and the words within them so farcical, is the removal of the signifiers of masculine power and legitimacy that form the visual lexicon of the state briefing – the props, setting, wardrobe, and cast of masculine *leadership theatre*. Gone are the imposing buildings, formal lecterns, and gilded crests for the feminised space of the home. Gone are the solemn aides, for the claustrophobic enclosure of social isolation with a mobile phone app for company. Blazers are borrowed as a shorthand to communicate male state power, or in the case of British TikTokker Meggie Foster, comically oversized, highlighting the borrowed role that poorly fits her youthful femininity – a microcosm of the wider message about who utters these words and holds these positions of power. This removal of the semiotics of masculine state power is used by all four creators and is explained by Cooper thus: 'I look at it as taking off the emperor's clothes. I've basically taken away the podium and the suit and the people behind him nodding. . . . That's why it highlights how ridiculous his words are' (Hunt 2020).

These videos hinge around shared recognition of the male voices that have requisitioned public space. Creative uses of ubiquitous voices offer a silent but effective rebuttal to them and their loud, undeserved, and irresponsibly wielded power. Press briefings watched by record numbers are recontextualised in the recombination of audio-visual elements and playful bricolage that harness the potential of digital spaces for countercultural exploration. These videos continue the longstanding function of lip-synching, exchanging material relating to a key historical moment to build a sense of community around a shared perspective on its injustices, creating and sustaining an oppositional consciousness which defines an us', the injustice done to 'us', and its structural causes (Farrier 2016; Ramati and Abeliovich 2022; Kaminski and Taylor 2008). As they borrow from legacy media and use the creative and collective affordances of 'produsage', these creators make new resistant texts, genres, and meanings at a time when powerholders were defining common sense to naturalise their definitions in ways which threatened citizens' safety (Steinberg 1998). This new genre offered an alternative, subversive collective story of male leadership under the pandemic: one of dangerous idiocy, incompetence, misogyny, confusion, loss of control, and disconnection from reality.

## GIRLS ARTICULATING VOICE/LESSNESS

Reflecting on these themes in our data, the girls raised experiences of voicelessness and not being represented. They recognised the curtailment of women leaders' voices. Asked why there were fewer women leaders in the world than men, participant Chloe stated, 'different voices get heard other than theirs'. They were aware of the silencing of women in public spaces that necessitates the kinds of ventriloquism discussed above. Tani observed, 'you don't see women rising up, speaking their voice up every day, but you see men doing it all the time', while Sarika thought 'that women don't have as much of a voice as men might do. . . . Years ago, I feel like women were kind of looked down on . . . and it's not completely changed yet'. Voice, for them, was essential to representation for the marginalised: Rachel said her definition of a leader was 'Someone who can, like, have a voice for everyone', while Samira explained that under good leadership 'everyone's voice will be heard'. Giving voice was a key criterion for them in defining women in the public eye as good leaders:

> *Judith:* Beyoncé is a good leader because she's speaking up for other women that can't be heard.

> *Ayana:* Oprah Winfrey. . . . Because her voice is heard

Another exchange showed how the girls connected voice to political power and their own desire to wield it, their sense of entitlement to do so, and their belief that they would see and make change within their lifetime:

> *Fara:* Just because you don't know my story, it don't mean I have no voice. I believe because most women don't actually speak out loud about what's happened to them, and they keep to themselves, men believe we don't have a voice at all. Men believe that we are just quiet and that we don't have no power to take over the country.

> *Kelly:* The whole point of speaking up!

> *Toya:* We are the chosen generation.

The girls recognised the role of performative stereotypes of masculinity in determining who is perceived as a leader, and tie these to voice:

> *Annabelle:* You get weak men, people who don't have strong voices and who aren't stereotypically leaders . . . grouped with those women who, because they are all stereotypically weak and such, they don't get to be leaders. So I think when people say men are always leaders, I think just the strong men.

While participants recognised the hostile and undermining ways in which legacy media represent women leaders, they were ambivalent about the possibilities of social media to afford voice. Amanda, whose family immigrated from Ethiopia, recognised the potential of having a 'voice' in contexts of freedoms of speech available in the United Kingdom being used to raise awareness of abuses elsewhere:

> I do want to help, like, people back home . . . I just want to go back there and just help those who are in need, like little children and stuff. Because we have

that advantage, you know, social media and our voices are really, we won't be targeted if we make a certain opinion, like in other countries there is a lack of human rights. So I think that is one thing I want to do is go back there and just help and be a leader.

Others focused on the hostility faced by women visible in online spaces. Jinani described how

your voice is heard like, not on TV or what not, like what you say and what you do can, like, influence people worldwide. But, I feel like it does come with, like, a lot of negatives, . . . you might get a lot of hate and people might like try to put you down for what you do.

When invited to describe the backlash they mentioned further, Susannah and Lubna detailed their witnessing of online harassment and made links to carrying out of 'real'-world violent attacks:

*Susannah:* It's mostly, nowadays it's mostly on Twitter. Like, people, like, let's say for example, like, someone posts a picture. Someone random could, like, randomly attack you for nothing and then they'll say 'oh my gosh you look silly'. Then yeah and then on Twitter everyone can just reply.

*Lubna:* But they say, like, 'you look like lesbian', which she's [*talking about a member of the globally successful Korean girl band Blackpink, Lisa]* not, she's not lesbian. They just say stuff, they make things up and they also, I think they attacked her. They attacked her and everything . . . in person, because they threat her online, 'I'm going to' 'oh you should die blah, blah, blah, and if you don't I'm going to do blah, blah, blah'. And if it's online threat, it's nothing, big deal, but yeah they really did attack her.

While providing platforms for creative and subversive resistance to patriarchal power, such as the lockdown TikToks, social media are also spaces where misogyny proliferates precisely because they afford a voice to women (Barker and Jurasz 2019; Yelin and Clancy 2021), resulting in adaptive misogynistic strategies which 'keep women from full participation on the internet' (Mantilla 2013, 569).

One girl pulled up a photograph of the Thai rapper Lalisa Manobal, stage name Lisa, from K-pop band Blackpink on her phone as an example of a woman leader she admired (figure 5.8). In it, Manobal stands with hunched shoulders and hands clasped before her shyly as if covering her torso with gangly arms. Lisa was 22 when the photograph was taken at Coachella music festival in 2019, but looks much younger. She smiles sweetly and broadly off to stage left to her bandmates out of the frame, as if awkwardly amused by the attention directed to her on stage. Her fringe and long, glossy ponytail suggest

**Figure 5.8    Image of Thai Rapper Lisa from K-pop Band Blackpink Found Online by a Participant.**

a youthful, idealised 1950s femininity. The background glows hot pink against black like their band name, conveying the 'bright lights' and glamour of show business, while also suggestive of the neon aesthetic of late-night clubs and bars. Her layers of thick, chain chokers bring a hard edge to the softness. Her diamante-embellished bra top resembles an armoured breastplate. Her pink microphone is emphasised in its coordination with the accent of pink neon behind her. It is both the symbol of her stadium-filling voice that earns her place centre stage and, as she awkwardly clasps the pink, wireless cylinder before her pelvis, calls to mind an image of castrated phallic power. In its juxtaposition of soft and hard femme, submission and dominance, what appears to be a glamorous image of pop stardom like any other reveals negotiations of youth, femininity, sexuality, modesty, voice, and the reclamation of male power.

## CONCLUSION: 'NUNS PISS', 'MARZIPAN DILDO' AND 'SHITLER'

In January 2024, discourses around gender, leadership, COVID-19, and competence burst into the news again when a fake news report about former Scottish first minister Nicola Sturgeon's leaked WhatsApp messages made real news headlines (Jouker 2024). The viral hoax claimed Sturgeon brandished senior Conservative politicians 'weaker than a nuns piss' [*sic*], 'shitler', and 'as much use as a marzipan dildo' (quoting Scottish spin doctor Malcom Tucker in the political comedy *The Thick of It*): a vivid, chaotic blending of

Tory ineptitude, alcohol, genitalia, messy sex, body fluids, food, faeces, and fascism. In reality, that day, Sturgeon's real WhatsApp messages were read before the UK Covid Inquiry in which she called Johnson 'a fucking clown' in response to his October 2020 COVID-19 briefings (Brooks 2024). She described Johnson's daily briefing as 'awful . . . we're not perfect but we don't get nearly enough credit for how much better than them we are' (ibid.). While not mentioning piss or dildoes, her messages were furious: 'His utter incompetence in every sense is now offending me on behalf of politicians everywhere' (ibid.). Like the TikTok lip-synchs, this hoax combines two more media that typify COVID – this time, viral disinformation and politicians' leaked WhatsApps. The latter entered COVID discourse when *The Telegraph* obtained 100,000 messages from COVID-era Health Secretary, Matt Hancock and continues through the Covid Inquiry as Johnson and others are grilled over their use of WhatsApp to circumvent official government reporting protocol.

The viral hoax tweet is ven*troll*oquism; like the young Welsh girl on Tik-Tok using Alexa to troll Johnson and call him a cunt, the anonymous hoaxer puts words in Sturgeon's mouth to troll the Conservatives. The joke hinges upon voice. It only functions if its audience can imagine these words in Sturgeon's inflection; in this sense, it is an impersonation. While Sturgeon's WhatsApps were less floridly humorous, 'nun's piss', 'a marzipan dildo', and 'shitler' riff off and build upon the clear and explicit fury she expressed at the 'awful', 'offending', 'utter incompetence' of a 'fucking clown', and match an imagined tone of voice plausibly enough for many to believe it was her, or take to social media to express disappointment that it was not. It is not Sturgeon's words, but it is an articulation of women's rage, and it is significant that the expletive language is (imagined to be) uttered by a woman, given the historic punishment of women speaking out of turn (Beard 2017b; Kay 2020a). Ven*troll*oquism claims the innocence of plausible deniability, and the examples here create spaces for the unsayable. It is a reclamation of public discourse in which male voices built a stage with podiums and microphones to broadcast their leadership theatre to a captive audience over whom the pandemic increased their power.

The UK Covid Inquiry found that a 'violent and misogynistic' culture and 'obvious sexism' contributed to the government's significant failures thanks to 'nuclear levels' of overconfidence and disregard for rules (Blewett 2023). One of the UK's highest-ranking female civil servants told the Covid Inquiry that 'the dominant culture was macho and heroic. It was positively unhelpful when the country needed thoughtful and reflective decision-making' (ibid.). As well as failing home-schooling caregivers, policies around domestic abuse and abortion access during the pandemic were overlooked as a result of this macho culture (ibid.). Other failures saw the prime minister choose holidays over Cobra meetings, eugenicist herd immunity policies, the premature end of mass testing, £10bn spent on unusable PPE, and over 200,000 deaths (Gov. uk 2024). In the leadership theatre of state briefings, performative masculinity was a strategy to conceal, deny, or make a virtue of those failures.

The feminisation of caution provided an alibi to place economic interests above human life; the stock identity of the invulnerable brute was used to stigmatise care-based political alternatives that would prioritise public wellbeing. These political alternatives are being imagined by girls around England, Scotland, and Wales. While Sunak's assumptions about 'mums everywhere' and the characterisation of Mutti Merkel and Aunty Cindy seek to domesticate women's power, girls reject this expectation. The girls we spoke to defined good leadership as competent, consultative, and committed to positive social change, something they believed could only be fostered through the inclusion of all voices. To them, leadership is having a voice and speaking for others. They see through the performative masculinity of leadership theatre and its empty signs of authority without competence and name fascism when they see it. The creative work of Cooper, DeCotis, Foster, and Scott strategically reconfigures the voice/human body relationship to puncture and undermine (Hirsh and Wallace 2023, 1). These videos create queer spaces of female masculinity, which highlight the fabrication inherent in our daily gendered codes of power and legitimacy. This resistant new genre reveals the foundational interaction between concepts of queerness and girlhood in which queerness can be found 'haunting if not all girls, then certainly central conceptions of girlhood' (Brickman 2019). In line with the history of male impersonation, they assert female political desire and challenge the notion 'that masculinity "just is"'" (Halberstam 1998, 234), as they expose the hyper-masculine leadership style that emerged under COVID-19 as catastrophically unfit for purpose.

Our fieldwork and analysis of social media tropes reveal girls' and young women's rejection of conventional tropes of leadership as constructed through masculinist, individualist, privileged, and authoritarian norms. Both our fieldwork and analysis of a new social media genre revealed girls' and young women's awareness of cultural misogyny propagated by male leaders they mistrust and castigate as insufficiently competent for the power they wield. Their gendered impersonations emphasise multiple disjunctures of voice/lessness: between women's awareness and critique and the wilfully idiotic wielding of male power, between women's domesticated constraints and the flailing freedom of male leaders commanding public space, and between the seriousness of the crisis and the inadequate male leadership available.

# Conclusion

Despite the burgeoning academic interest in girls as subjects, their engagements with the plethora of texts and initiatives that both claim to empower them and exhort them to claim power remain relatively less well studied. This book goes some way to offer a means of better understanding the concerns of girls as simultaneously the subjects of 'saviour discourses' that interpellate them to rescue the world from the depredations of unbridled neoliberalism, and of 'confidence' discourses that offer a pedagogy of visibility management and appropriate femininity as the cornerstones of women's leadership. Such insights have ramifications for those researching in the fields of feminist media studies, cultural studies, audience studies, celebrity studies, and sociology of leadership, and for scholars and practitioners in education. As such, this is not solely a book about girls' engagements with misogyny in cultures of visibility, crucial though this element may be. Rather, it is an interrogation of ways in which always-evolving forms of capitalism and feminism work to interpellate and recruit girls to their end, and a map of the terrain of girls' desires for, and instances of, resistance. Such an interrogation necessitates new terms, concepts, and tools to examine both the conditions and the emerging responses in girls' dialogic negotiations and experiences, such as 'leadership theatre' and 'ven*troll*oquism'.

The key aim of this work is to contribute to the understanding of ways in which girls engage with public discourses of gender, power and leadership, particularly via the highly visible women they admire. Girls' engagements with such figures are central to popular role model initiatives that argue that such engagements will foster leadership aspirations and claim to enable girls to envision overcoming obstacles in ways that will make such overcoming manifest.

One of the first assumptions of role model initiatives we sought to trouble was that of a mutually understood concept of leadership between girls and the authoritative voices that exhort them to aspire to it. The dominance of 'confidence' discourses in participants' framing of leadership to some extent endorsed this assumption; the leadership initiatives that we interrogate are constructed around activities designed to boost 'self-esteem' and address the 'ambition gap'. This is indicative of an ongoing cultural focus on 'fixing' girls' subjectivities, rather than on the structural barriers that work against their thriving. Even while they invite girls to identify such barriers in terms of sexism and stereotyping, for example through 'real conversations' (Lean In Girls 2023), the suggested action is work on the self. The selective address of 'confidence' to a white, privileged ideal, however, emerged through girls' situated experiences of speaking and being heard: girls from marginalised groups attempting to claim the power that they are assured is there if they are only 'bold' and willing to 'take a risky' experience get cautioned from peers and shut down by authority figures. The concept of 'confidence' itself, however, changes in translation from girl-orientated texts to girls' lives and experiences: it gets stretched to include confidence-as-trust, confidence-as-listening, confidence-as-peer support, and confidence-as-experience. Through their own situated experiences, girls gave reasons why it matters if those who do have power neither represent nor listen to them and therefore do not understand them. The importance of listening as an ethical obligation of leaders emerged strongly in their naming of leadership traits; their experiences of not being listened to themselves make this a priority in their own envisionings of both the leaders they wanted and the leaders they might like to become.

In terms of girls' experience – both actual and desired – our data revealed a depressing picture. The long winter of austerity in the United Kingdom has seen the closure of much local youth provision, of playing fields, and of leisure centres. At the same time, the 'one size fits all' specifications of schools' citizenship curricula, even in the best of circumstances, do not recognise the additional challenges faced by particular groups of pupils in accessing routes to power. It was exceptional if schools with a keen awareness of the needs of their pupils provided consistent opportunities for girls to develop the competencies to participate in civic life. It was interesting that the two schools appearing to do this in ways specifically tailored for their socially situated cohorts were the independent school which ensured girls were prepared to assume positions of authority in adult life and a state school serving the most marginalised catchments, which recognised the challenges of the multiple exclusions confronting girls and sought to equip them to meet those challenges.

The campaigns we examined that promote leadership role models in the public eye to girls are an attempt to intervene in the pedagogies of popular culture; any such attempt by adults to intervene in teen worlds is often both clumsy and ineffective.Sheryl Sandberg has the resources and the influence to recruit girl favourites such as Michelle Obama and Beyoncé to her 'Ban Bossy' and 'The Female Lead' campaigns, thus lending them a degree of credibility. In terms of their discursive address, these campaigns do resonate to an extent with girls, because they mobilise ubiquitous discourses of self-worth, possibility, and aspiration that are a mainstay of the girl-orientated popular feminisms circulating in online worlds, as evidenced in the memes girls shared with us. It is this discursive familiarity that is problematic. In their reproduction of neoliberal tenets of self-responsibility for overcoming gendered inequalities, their elision of other entrenched forms of structural disadvantage, and their reproduction of individualist models, leadership role model initiatives reinforce key tenets of neoliberalism and masculinised modes of power. Indeed, their popularity with adults may lie in their silence on issues of equality in an increasingly and frighteningly unequal world – as well as their economies of reproduction: in a prevailing economic orthodoxy that seeks to remove funding for public services, a logic that asserts that putting posters of Michelle Obama or Mary Earp on classroom walls will be just as effective in developing futures as providing girls with spaces and activities for community and civic engagement is bound to be welcomed. However, this goes to the heart of role model solutions themselves; they are more about the models than the roles, and cannot substitute for the learning and experience that girls recognise as central.

However, to focus solely on the problematic nature of the discourse for us is to reproduce the same fallacy of which we accuse the campaigns themselves: assuming that girls will read the meaning of texts in ways intended by the producers. We acknowledge the hegemonic weight of the gendered roles inscribed into these texts and the interpellative allure of their promise that power is being held out for girls if only they are bold enough to take it. However, this study has enabled us to recognise ways in which girls themselves find their promise of leadership roles problematic because leadership, for women, entails risks that girls do not wish to confront. The 'real conversations' about bias of 'Lean In Girls' and the aspirational pedagogies of 'The Female Lead' exhort girls to make themselves more heard, more visible, while never addressing the very real risks of visibility for women in the public eye. The girls in our study have shown us that their construction of power through the prism of risk is accurate and evidenced; they draw upon a deep well of examples of women who have been harmed as a consequence of the visibility that their public roles demanded, and of reasons why it matters that those who do have power neither represent nor listen to them and therefore do not understand them .The importance of listening as an ethical obligation of leaders emerged strongly in their naming of leadership traits;

their experiences of not being listened to themselves make this a priority in their own envisionings of both the leaders they wanted and the leaders they might like to become This is not merely the commonly cited problem of self-fulfilling prophecies, that if girls do not believe power is available, then the belief makes it so. Girls are not self-limiting in this way, but acquire a sense of limitation and personal responsibility for it through the wider patriarchal conditions which restrict both their possibilities of making change and their opportunities to challenge such restrictions. As we saw in chapter 1, the weight of confidence discourses turns girls' attention inward to resolve the performative inhibitions created by the wider conditions that they inhabit.

It is not only visibility which troubles girls when they attend to the idea of women leaders; the ideas of earned success emerged strongly in our data, especially in intense discussions of Meghan Markle as both the target of abuse and as representing the promise of meritocracy. Such possibilities are central to girls' investments in the possibilities for themselves, offering a high-profile instance of a 'popular parable' (Littler 2018) of social mobility (Dyer 1979). This discourse centred particularly strongly around the Black women leaders and celebrities they nominated, who were recognised as having achieved a particularly challenging form of overcoming. Tension between the promises of meritocratic discourse and their experiential perceptions of the limitations to their own probable success because of who they were, who they knew, and where they lived, was not fully resolved. Even as they experience limitation and exclusion along intensifying intersecting axes of disadvantage, they remained invested in stories and images suggesting that people like them could attain extraordinary success. The narratives they reproduced tended to exaggerate the 'ordinariness' (Dyer 1979) of the individuals involved and failed to recognise any existing advantage. This investment illustrates the tenacity of the meritocratic narrative in obscuring division and disadvantage. Tensions emerged particularly in participants' discussion of those that they saw as enjoying unearned privilege, particularly around monarchy. This is illustrative of a wider unease over increasing inequalities in the United Kingdom and a growing dissatisfaction with the British royal family as emblems of unearned privilege and excess in an era of prolonged austerity.

Individual aspiration is central to the meritocracy myth and thus to neoliberalism itself. It has transformed feminism from a social justice endeavour into one of self-actualisation, and (as, for example, in role model initiatives) offers girls in particular the promise of a mechanism that will enable them to overcome gender-related obstacles to success if only they invest hard. The affective dimensions of such investment are particularly problematic for girls who experience the attachments to future selfhood they promote as alienating. The requirement for girls and women in particular to demonstrate emotional attachment and 'passion' is one that can be exclusionary for girls who do not experience it. In itself, it becomes an apologia for those wishing to enter male-dominated fields, justifying such temerity through the strength of their feelings. At the same time, emotional commitment becomes a requirement for women leaders in service economies and under inclusive capitalism, where their Cartesian connection with feeling and with nature is transformed into labour.

Although individual aspiration has worked to edge discourses of collaboration and collectivism out of the public sphere (Amsler 2008), we saw evidence of girls preferring such models in their imaginative forays into leadership roles. Although these choices were in part demonstration of their desire for fairness and better representation, girls also preferred collaborative leadership because it left them less exposed to the risks for women in public roles than they would be as individuals. The very act of envisioning themselves in individual power roles exposed to participants their limitations. Some girls do indeed want power. They do not want the risk they understand as a condition of power and its attendant visibility.

What is at stake in the way girls construct ideas about power is their willingness and their capacity to occupy in future the decision-making roles that shape our society, our culture, and our economy. Women, especially women of colour, as we identify at the outset, are missing from such roles. We do not propose that girls take on this mantle to become the responsible saviours of this mess, but that the adults holding power in girls' lives map out and clear their paths to activism and engagement, whether in community, corporate, civic, or national realms, so that they might participate in decision-making on equal terms with the elites for whom the paths to power are often smooth and whose interests therefore dominate.

As well as examining how girls understand the power available to, and the specific challenges facing, women in the public eye, we have theorised girls' understanding of, and response to, masculine models of leadership and specific male leaders. We began in chapter 1 by demonstrating the tensions for girls as they are exhorted to feign confidence when they seek the tools and opportunities to build a track record of competence. We end in chapter 5 by demonstrating that, in girls' conceptions, male power is as performatively overconfident as it is dangerously under-competent. Not only is power felt to be out of reach for girls, but they also see it as poorly, irresponsibly wielded by the men for whom it is predominantly reserved. Chapter 4 articulated girls' collective hope, while chapter 5 pronounced their mistrust. 'Leadership theatre' enshrines power in masculinised signs and codes of specific locations, attire, aesthetics, and imagery; girls reject both the fabrication inherent in our gendered codes of power and legitimacy and the limiting discourses of domestication offered up to them as women's roles. Cultural misogyny constrains girls' opportunities and their voices and leaves them seeking strategies to circumvent the limits placed upon them. Ven*troll*oquism is one such strategy we have identified: the strategic disruption of the voice from its source to articulate unutterable anger and critique, using the voices of others to inhabit positions beyond (the strictures upon) one's own gender.

The logic of wanting more women in leadership roles is not just to count their numbers and reassure ourselves that equality is resolved, but is part of the broader aim of social justice to ensure the interests of all groups are represented in the shaping of social, cultural, and economic realms. This leaves us with the question of what conditions might encourage girls to become the leaders of the future and how such work this might help might bring them about. Calls for increased funding for girl-orientated youth services are easy to make but carry little weight in a context of ongoing economic gloom. Arguing for changes at the national curriculum level that might demystify routes to power and its operations may not fare better in the midst of ideological struggles over what should be taught and how, as neoconservative interests bring in new measures which co-opt the language of social justice and equity to promote neoliberal values of individual aspiration and social mobility (Bailey and Ball 2014; Neumann et al. 2020). In the meantime, legacy and social media prove resistant to reform when it appears in the shape of restraint, even if only self-imposed and self-regulated, and easily get caught up in arguments of harm and offence (Chick 2020) and the rights of expression (Merrin 2021). What, then, can this work do for girls now to make their entry into such roles more likely?

It is vital that policymakers and policy influencers have an understanding of barriers for girls in terms of developing as leaders. It is especially important for us to seek to intervene in these settings, as we know that hostility towards women in positions of power finds its own expression in the widespread harassment and assault of women MPs (The Fawcett Society 2023), in exclusive cultures of masculinity (Julios 2020; Blewett 2023), and more broadly in the ways that gender 'makes' parliament (Erikson and Verge 2022, 4). A legislative body that is characterised by the same kinds of gendered hostility that deters girls when they see it enacted on women in the public eye may not be receptive to necessary change. It is all the more important for us, therefore, that this work makes the implications of such cultures for girls clear.

While the live interactions girls have within their communities shape their understanding of power and its role, lack of opportunity leaves them frustrated in their desire for experience in decision-making roles. This book comprehensively evidences that media representations of women and power shape girls' perceptions of the pitfalls and possibilities for women in power and, as a consequence, for themselves. In cultures of media misogyny where the maltreatment, scrutiny, and risk of physical and sexual violence to women are witnessed by girls, these media representations operate more often as a caution from power and visibility than an inspiration towards it. As such, our current media landscape offers a very poor proxy, inadequately supplementing girls' lack of real-world experience. Our data is a resource for those working in industries contributing to representations and treatment of women in the public eye, who, we hope, will attend to the significant impact of their roles on the likelihood of girls feeling like future participation in public life is a safe possibility for them. As we have demonstrated, the cast from which girls draw their ideas of power and leadership goes far beyond traditionally conceived and culturally endorsed leaders such as politicians, historical figures, heads of business, royals, and sports stars; it includes fictional characters, singers, actors, TV personalities, influencers, and manifold other forms of celebrity. Media producers, editors, commissioners, and commentators whose work intersects any of these fields stand to benefit from our findings as they consider standards for industry practice in the representation and treatment of women in the public eye.

As we have demonstrated, girls lament the lack of opportunities to develop the skills and experience necessary to make paths towards holding positions of power, and the opacity of those paths in a culture that does not consider them legitimate candidates for the pursuit of power. This is especially the case for girls in state schools, those with poor access to extra-curricular opportunities, and girls who are considered marginalised by intersections of race, sexuality, regionality, disability, and class. Our findings have already been put into practice to address this lack of opportunity and offer intelligible and realisable pathways to power. From our data, we have developed a five-part course in collaboration with award-winning women's rights campaigner, Laura Coryton MBE, which has been delivered in forty schools and youth groups in the United Kingdom so far. Tools for Change offers the skills and knowledge required for campaigning, which is used by students to launch their own campaigns to lead change around any issue that matters to them. It is sobering that we had to shape the guidelines on strategies for achieving change to reflect the UK's draconian new rules limiting the right to protest and demonstrate. The 'Protest Powers: Police, Crime, Sentencing and Courts Act' (2022) can forbid protest on the subjective and ambiguous grounds of 'nuisance', and it specifically mentions protests outside schools. This heightens our awareness that any attempt to encourage girls to take up positions of power exposes them to risk.

Girls are routinely discussed as vulnerable and girl culture dismissed as trivial. We found girls to be highly sophisticated in their appraisal of social hierarchies and their navigation of complex, hostile cultural terrain. Theirs is an informed scepticism borne of experience rather than any relation of girlhood to intrinsic vulnerability. No amount of campaigns, socially approved role models, or girl-focused initiatives will make a difference as long as girls are witness to the abuse, scrutiny, and threat of physical harm that is a condition of public visibility for women. Will the girls of today grow up to close the gender leadership gap? Not unless the conditions in which they are invited to do so significantly change.

# Appendix

## *Notes on Methodology*

In this section we provide details of the study on which this book draws in terms of research design and sites, and wider context in terms of some ongoing tensions in research into girlhood that informed the project's methodology: these were tensions between the celebration of girls' agency and resilience, and anxieties over their vulnerability in their habitation of wider, hostile cultures, and between researchers' meaning-making and the voices of girls as research subjects.

### METHOD

We collected data via twelve semi-structured group interview workshops and online groups, conducted with 94 participants aged 13–15 in diverse geographical and socio-economic settings. Our twelve sites included nine comprehensive state secondary schools, an independent girls' school, a SEND school, and a Local Authority youth office. Sites were located in England, Wales, and Scotland. Despite our best efforts, we were unable to secure further research sites in Northern Ireland after the COVID-19 pandemic and ensuing lockdowns upset our initial arrangements there. Half of our focus groups took place before the first pandemic lockdown of 2020; it was not possible to resume until 2022 when schools were fully open and receptive to researchers once more. During the lockdown period when there was a hiatus in data collection, we were particularly attentive to representation of gender and leadership in mainstream and social media contexts; this attentiveness made it possible to identify resonances between young women's activity on TikTok during lockdown and the themes emerging in our data so far: these form the basis of chapter 5.

Access to the research sites was negotiated via local education authorities, academy chain executives, and head teachers. Participants were recruited with the help of local authority officers and schools' pastoral heads and, in schools, selected as broadly representative of pupil cohorts in terms of ethnicity and achievement profile. We specified 'achievement' rather than social class as schools can be reluctant to make judgements on this basis, even where they have data to support such categorisation. Nonetheless, evidence indicates the link between socio-economic status and school achievement (Sammons 1995; Blanchett 2008; Gillborn and Mirza 2000), meaning a 'mixed ability' sample is likely to represent a range of backgrounds. As a result of this recruitment process, the girls we spoke to offered a range of classed, raced, and regional perspectives, whether within groups or between schools. Within the scope of the study, we specifically wanted to talk to girls from groups under-represented in leadership roles, rather than those who already identified as activists or future leaders. We sought insights into how those girls whose lack of aspiration to leadership is the focus of popular concern were inhabiting and responding to discourses and representations that enjoin them to confidence, voice, and power.

The design was initially piloted in two schools before being adapted and rolled out to further sites. Each focus group lasted 60–90 minutes, depending on time available within the research sites. The interviews were semi-structured, entailing both prompt questions and free discussion of issues and images associated with women and leadership. Girls were enabled to access their preferred social media during the focus groups so that they could identify and discuss popular figures appearing on their feeds. We also set up a dedicated social media group for each school where girls could share and discuss images and memes that would form the prompts for discussion, and show us the kinds of texts that girls were engaging with. We chose Facebook for these groups due to the likelihood that students would already have accounts but were likely only to use them for specific purposes (Ofcom 2021; 2022). This pattern of use supported our ethical principle of renewed consent (Fuller, Shareck, and Stanley 2017) as participants were more likely to log into the groups – each of which was titled as a Research Group – with the awareness that they are participating in research. Facebook also offered the facility for setting up closed, undiscoverable groups, which were monitored daily as a condition of our ethical approval. Where girls were unable to access social media due to school firewalls, and for those who did not have existing profiles or preferred not to participate in this way, the girls were enabled to search for and share images during group discussion and we photographed their screens as a record of their chosen images. Online groups were open for up to four weeks after the initial interviews, which we found to be a natural cut-off point in the pilot schools. The focus groups were audio and video recorded and the data transcribed; the images, comments, and memes for the social media groups were downloaded; all data were then thematically coded using NViVO.

## THINKING THROUGH DESIGN

Our design aimed to reproduce, as far as possible, youth practices in engaging with prominent women and popular discourses through their everyday talk about their media consumption and through their online activities. The focus groups entailed both prompt questions and free discussion. At the start of each, we logged them all into the site-specific Facebook group we had set up for them and invited them to contribute images and comments around women leaders. Then we offered questions around the leaders they chose, associated with gender, power, and their own experiences, opportunities, and ambitions. We did not mention any specific public figures ourselves; the women discussed in this study were all raised in conversation and online by the girls themselves. The social media groups meant that girls could synchronously add images and communicate while other conversations were going on, helping to mitigate what can feel like artificial and painstaking turn-taking in group interviews. Keeping the groups open also meant that girls could contribute and discuss images and memes in their own time without the presence of the researcher. This element aimed to tap into adolescents' modes of online communication via posting and comment on images (Hamilton, Nesi, and Choukas-Bradley 2021).

We were particularly interested in the ways in which role models – both adult-endorsed and of their own choosing – might operate in girls' imaginings of leadership with regard to their own experiences and prospects. The focus on representations of women in the public eye as role models entailed attention to the epistemologies of audience research. As we discuss in chapter 2, the assumption that girls' attitudes and choices can be shaped by exposure to specific media texts reproduces central tenets of 'effects' research, which tends to cast audiences as passive receptors of media messages, and has traditionally been concerned with audiences low on the social hierarchy presumed to be less capable of resisting media meanings – particularly youth (Davison 1983; Gauntlett 2002). At the same time, role-model solutions assume that adult-endorsed representations of women in the public eye will be 'used' to fulfil specific needs for girls in terms of identity formation through fostering aspirations towards a future selfhood (McQuail 2010). Such assumptions ignore the ways that girls choose their own texts for their own particular uses and gratifications, and may read their own meanings into them, unlike 'active audience' theories – most famously Stuart Hall's (1980) 'Encoding/

Decoding' model – that frame the audience as the creator of meaning. Studies in this tradition have traditionally been interested in 'resistant' readings as demonstrations of agency (McRobbie 2009), but can ignore the hegemonic weight of mass media meanings in their optimistic celebration of the agency of the audience. Our project was designed to both enable interrogation of the simplistic assumptions of popular role model claims in terms of their pedagogic function, and to examine the use and significance for girls of women in the public eye of their own choosing. While focusing on the meanings girls make around leadership and representations of women in the public eye, we trace ways in which the girls such meanings are within available narratives of gender and power. In our data gathering and coding we were alert to ways in which girls articulated their attachments to their 'role models', and made sense of texts and figures via both hegemonic discourses and more local cultural codes in ways that recognise both the force of dominant cultural narratives and the (in)adequacy and selectiveness of their address.

## 'VOICE' AND THE RESEARCHER/RESEARCHED RELATIONSHIP

In designing the method, we were aware of ways in which 'participatory' youth methods, like active audience theories, can be over-optimistic in their assumptions of 'voice' and agency. Both can celebrate resistance while ignoring the hegemonic weight of dominant cultural structures and forces (McRobbie 2009); both can ignore the ways in which 'voice' itself 'both shapes and reflects the social discourses within which young people find themselves' (McGarry 2016). The issue of 'voice' in devising the method and in analysing and writing about our data was constantly present to us, particularly as 'voice' emerged as a recurrent theme in participants' discussions of 'voice' and power. While Linda Duits and Liesbet van Zoonen (2009) call for more studies giving girls themselves 'voice' in critiques of neoliberal girls' cultures, Orla Mcarry (2016) finds that the influential role of the researcher is rarely critically examined and often minimised in methods claiming empowerment. The claims of research to 'give voice' to youth can be reductive and ignore the many ways in which young people speak for themselves (Woodgate et al. 2020), while for youth, '"having your say" does not seem to mean "being listened to"' (Rheingold 2008, 98–99). Like Pam Alldred (1998, 5), we wish to 'avoid creating the illusion of "democratized" research through the fantasy of empowerment' in our method, while addressing a central question of how girls experience the lack of access to power. In our collection and reading of data, we sought to recognise the power dynamics at play both in the research relationship, and in girls' claims to 'voice' in wider discursive arenas. We attempted to navigate between a determinist view of the girl-as-discursive-subject and the optimism of girl-as-empowered-resistor through attention both to ways in which the discourses that coalesce around both leadership and girlhood are present in participant's discussion, and to the extent and manner in which such discourses are adequate to frame their embodied experiences.

Schools are not just convenience site for researchers to gain access to groups of young people, they are places where everyday performances of gender take place and in which wider, popular discourses are mobilised in commonplace interactions (Kehily and Nayak 2008, 326); They are also spaces with particular power effects, in which producing the 'right' kinds of answers to questions posed by adults is the prevailing culture (Epstein 1993). It is particularly important to be alert to this when entering as a researcher; while it is true that there is no established relationship of domination as there may be between teacher and pupils, there is also no existing relationship of trust and disclosure. We were aware of our status as conveyed by our adult-hood and whiteness, and of the claims to privilege that attach to the academic researcher identity. These factors inevitably shaped the stories that were told to us and the ways in which they were told. This wasn't necessarily negative – one participant told us that talking to researchers made her feel as if what she said mattered because of the status of the attention with which her words were treated.

We attempted to mitigate this power effect through the design: Both the workshop and online groups encouraged participant-led discussion, and were designed with the aim of reproducing ways that girls, in their peer group and social media interactions, produce and negotiate meanings as interpretive communities (Fish 1980; Barbour 2007; Allington 2007). Semi-structured group interviews themselves can replicate the dynamic social processes in which meaning is made and discourses circulated between individuals in social settings (Barbour 2007), while the online groups also offered the potential for unanticipated insights which can result from the researcher allowing participants to continue discussion independently and asynchro-nously (Gaiser 2008, 297). We also intended these groups to offer spaces in which girls might explore and express thoughts relating to gender and girl-hood, to power and inequality, and to their own imagined futures (Gonick 2003, 15).

In these ways and others, we aimed to align the method with the project's feminist aims (Hesse-Biber 2007; Phillips et al. 2013; Caretta and Vacchelli 2015). This entailed the recognition of tensions between the tendency of research to objectify participants as mere providers of data and the need to recognise subjectivity as central to the 'mapping of social experience' (Oak-ley 2018, xi). Within feminist research traditions, semi-structured interview-ing itself has been characterised as a 'principal means by which feminists have sought to achieve the active involvement of their respondents in the construction of data about their lives' (Graham 1984, 104). Our semi-structured interview design allowed for variation in response among diverse participants and provided opportunities for them to tell their own stories and foreground their priorities – priorities which did not always align with ours (Reinharz and Chase 2002). Furthermore, recognising that these stories themselves are formed 'in the process of the research conversation, as self-reflections instigated by our questions' (Frank 2005, 968), we devised our method to follow dialogically informed principles which aim to allow participants to engage reflexively in their own meaning-making through offering windows for further discussion and for qualification of previous statements. Thus, we included an element of 'circling back' in our interview questions, while the addition of online groups extending beyond the group interviews allowed for such further reflection. While most participants contributed posts within a short window of time (often the same day) on these groups, some did take the opportunity to offer further contributions. These online contributions were overwhelmingly images, some mediated by themselves or a third party, in the form of memes. Such postings allowed participants to contribute not just as traditional audiences commenting on texts, but as more participatory 'produsers' (Bruns 2006) in whose activities the traditional boundaries between text and audience/reader are destabilised. In the analysis of the 'texts' transcribed from interviews and those posted online, we position ourselves as a 'researcher audience' making meaning in a specific context as members of an interpretive community.

## OUR RESEARCH SITES

Site 1 is a comprehensive co-educational state school for students aged 11–16 located in a post-industrial conurbation in North-West England. The proportion of students from minority ethnic heritages, of students who speak English as an additional language, and of students known to be eligible for free school meals is significantly higher than that found nationally.

Site 2 is a comprehensive co-educational state secondary school s on the South coast of England catering for pupils aged 11–19. Most students are of white British heritage. The proportion of students with additional learning needs is lower than found nationally, as is the proportion of students known to be eligible for free school meals.

Site 3 is a comprehensive co-educational state secondary school in rural South-East England. Its catchment includes less advantaged estates and villages in an authority where many children attend independent schools or other state schools sitting higher in examination league tables. The levels of attainment of pupils coming into the school are below the national average. Almost all pupils are from white ethnic families and the percentage of pupils speaking English as an additional language is low. The proportion of pupils on the special educational needs register is above the national average.

Site 4 is a comprehensive co-educational state secondary school in North West London. The majority of pupils speak English as an additional language and are from minority ethnic backgrounds. The proportion of students known to be eligible for free school meals is much higher than that found nationally. A higher-than-average number of students needs additional support with learning.

Site 5 is a comprehensive co-educational state secondary school in rural Western England. The levels of attainment of pupils coming into the school are below the national average. Most pupils are from white ethnic families and the percentage of pupils speaking English as an additional language is low. The proportion of pupils on the special educational needs register and of those entitled to free school meals is above the national average.

Site 6 is a secondary comprehensive Church of England faith school for girls in South West London. Two-thirds of students are from minority ethnic groups, of which the largest are groups with Black African or Black Caribbean heritage. One-third of students speak a first language other than English but few are at an early stage of learning English. Students come from a range of socio-economic backgrounds, with the proportion eligible for free school meals in line with national averages. A lower-than-average number of students has learning difficulties and/or disabilities,

Site 7 is an English-medium suburban comprehensive school in Wales. Around one-third of pupils come from a minority ethnic background although the majority of pupils speak English as their first language. A very small minority speak Welsh as their first language. The percentage of pupils eligible for free school meals is much lower than the national average, and of those with special education in line with the national average.

Site 8 is a children's centre in North-East London, where we spoke to girls in local authority care. The girls were all in mainstream state schools for the majority of their education but received additional support through childrens' services.

Site 9 is a state secondary comprehensive Muslim faith school in a post-industrial Midlands setting. The overwhelming majority of students are from minority ethnic backgrounds, particularly South-East Asia. The proportion of pupils who are known to be eligible for free school meals is well above the national average. A large proportion of pupils speak English as an additional language. A lower-than-average number of students has additional learning needs.

Site 10 is a state secondary school in an urban Scottish setting. Its pupils are overwhelmingly drawn from the city's poorest postcodes. The overwhelming majority of pupils are of white ethnic backgrounds. A large majority of pupils are eligible for free school meals. More than half have additional learning needs.

Site 11 is a Local Authority SEND setting catering for pupils with additional learning needs.

Site 12 is an independent day school for girls aged 7–18. The majority of pupils come from affluent professional backgrounds. The attainment levels on entry are higher than the national average. A lower-than-average number of students has additional learning A lower proportion than the national average of pupils speak English as an additional language.

# Bibliography

50:50 Parliament. https://5050parliament.co.uk.

Aapola, S., Gonick, M. and Harris, A. 2005. *Young Femininity: Girlhood, Power and Social Change*. Basingstoke: Deakin University.

Adams, E.M. 1999. 'An economy fit for human beings: Capitalism at the end of the century'. *Vital Speeches of the Day, 65*(14): 426.

Adamson, M. 2017. 'Postfeminism, neoliberalism and a 'successfully' balanced femininity in celebrity CEO autobiographies'. *Gender, Work & Organization, 24*: 314–27.

Adamson, M. and Kelan, E. 2018 ''Female heroes': Celebrity executives as postfeminist role models'. *British Journal of Management, 30*(4): 981–96. https://onlinelibrary.wiley.com/doi/abs/10.1111/1467-8551.12320.

Ahmed, S. 2010. 'This other and other others'. *Economy and Society, 31*(4): 558–72.

Alcadipani, R. 2020. 'Pandemic and macho organizations: Wake-up call or business as usual?' *Gender, Work & Organization, 27*(5): 734–46.

Aldrich, A.S. and Lotito, N.J. 2020. 'Pandemic performance: Women leaders in the Covid-19 crisis'. *Politics & Gender, 16*(4): 960–67.

Alldred, P. 1998. 'Ethnography and discourse analysis: Dilemmas in representing the voices of children'. In *Feminist Dilemmas in Qualitative Research*, edited by J. Ribbens and R. Edwards, 147–70. Thousand Oaks: Sage.

Allen, Charles. 1760. 'The polite lady: Or, a course of female education in a series of letters, from a mother to her daughter'. In *Conduct Literature for Women: Part III: 1720–1770*. 6 vols, edited by Pam Morris, 5–197. London: Pickering & Chatto, 2004.

Allen, Kim. 2014. 'Blair's children'. *The Sociological Review, 62*: 760–79.

Allen, Kim. 2016. 'Top girls navigating austere times: Interrogating youth transitions since the "crisis"'. *Journal of Youth Studies, 19*(6): 805–20.

Allen, Kim and Hollingworth, Sumi. 2013. '"Sticky subjects" or "cosmopolitan creative"? Social class, place and young people's aspirations for work in the knowledge economy'. *Urban Studies, 50*(3), 499–517.

Allen, Kim and Mendick, Heather. 2012. 'Young people's uses of celebrity: Class, gender and 'improper' celebrity'. *Discourse: Studies in the Cultural Politics of Education, 34*(1): 77–93.

Allen, P. 2018. 'Sexy footage of Meghan Markle stripping off shows Kate Middleton was not entitled to £92, 000 compensation'. *Daily Mail.* https://www.dailymail.co .uk/news/article-5833837/Sexy-footage-Meghan-proves-Kate-did-not-deserve-92k -payout-topless-snaps-French-lawyers-say.html.

Allington, D. 2007. 'How come most people don't see it?: Slashing The Lord of the Rings'. *Social Semiotics, 17*(1): 43–62.

Althusser, Louis. 1971. 'Ideology and State apparatuses'. In *Lenin and Philosophy and Other Essays,* translated by Ben Brewster, 155–65. London: New Left Books.

Amnesty International. 2018. 'Women abused on Twitter every 30 seconds: New research reveals the staggering level of abuse against women journalists and politicians from the UK and US on Twitter last year'. 18 December. https://www.amnesty .org.uk/press-releases/women-abused-twitter-every-30-seconds-new-study.

Amsler, Sarah S. 2008. 'Pedagogy against "dis-utopia": From conscientization to the education of desire.' In *No Social Science without Critical Theory (Current Perspectives in Social Theory, Vol. 25),* edited by H. Dahms, 291–32. Bingley: Emerald Group Publishing Limited.

Andrew Walker (@bigboithebard). 2020. 'World would be a better place with woman in charge absolutely zero doubt about that in my mind. Ego is the bane of humanity and guys excell at being egotistical'. *Twitter.* April 9. https://twitter.com/bigboithe-bard/status/1248193153619853317.

Ansell, N., Froerer, P. and Huijsmans, R. 2022. 'Young people's aspirations in an uncertain world: Taking control of the future?' *Sociological Research Online,* 27(4): 795–802.

Antonopoulos, N., Veglis, A., Gardikiotis, A., Kotsakis, R. and Kalliris. G. 2015. 'Web third-person effect in structural aspects of the information on media websites'. *Computers in Human Behavior, 44*(3): 48–58.

Applebaum, Anne. 2008. 'Irrational ambition is Hillary Clinton's flaw'. *Daily Telegraph.* Available at https://www.telegraph.co.uk/comment/3558075/Irrational -ambition-is-Hillary-Clintons-flaw.html.

Archard, Nicole. 2012. 'Developing future women leaders: The importance of mentoring and role modeling in the girls' school context'. *Mentoring & Tutoring: Partnership in Learning, 20*(4): 451–72.

Ashman, R., Radcliffe, L., Patterson, A. and Gatrell, C. 2022. 'Re-ordering motherhood and employment: Mobilizing 'Mums Everywhere' during Covid-19'. *British Journal of Management, 33*(3): 1125–43.

Atkinson, Emily. 2022. 'Eton College apologises after claims visiting schoolgirls were subjected to misogynistic and racial slurs'. *The Independent.* 19 November. https://www.independent.co.uk/news/uk/home-news/eton-college-misogynistic -racial-slurs-b2228593.html

Awan, F. 2008. *Young People, Identity and the Media: A Study of Conceptions of Self Identity among Youth in Southern England,* (Unpublished Doctoral Thesis, Bournemouth University). http://eprints.bournemouth.ac.uk/10466.

Bailey, P.L.J. and Ball, S. 2015. 'The coalition government, the general election and the policy ratchet in education: A reflection on the 'ghosts' of policy past, present and yet to come'. In *The Coalition Government and Social Policy: Restructuring the Welfare State'*, edited by H. Bochell and M. Powell, 127–52. Bristol: Policy Press.

Baker, P. 2004. *Fantabulosa: A Dictionary of Polari and Gay Slang*. London: Bloomsbury Publishing.

Baker, Ashley A. and Kimberly Kelly. 2016. 'Live like a king, y'all: Gender negotiation and the performance of masculinity among Southern drag kings'. *Sexualities, 19*: 1–2.

Bakhtin, Mikhail. 1965. *Rabelais and His World*. Bloomington: Indiana University Press.

Bakhtin, M.M. 1986. *Speech Genres and Other Late Essays*. Vol. 17. Edited by C. Emerson and M. Holquist. Texas: University of Texas Press.

Ban Bossy. no date. *Leadership Tips for Teachers*. http://banbossy.com/teacher-tips/ Accessed 2nd January 2021.

Ban Bossy. no date. *Lean in Girls | Girls Leadership Program*. http://banbossy.com/ Accessed 2nd January 2022.

Ban Bossy (@Ban_Bossy). no date. *Twitter account*. https://twitter.com/Ban _Bossy.

Bandura, A. 1965. 'Influence of models' reinforcement contingencies on the acquisition of imitative responses'. *Journal of personality and social psychology, 1*(6): 589.

Banet-Weiser, Sarah. 2013. *Authentic TM: The Politics of Ambivalence in a Brand Culture*. New York: New York University Press.

Banet-Weiser, Sarah. 2014. 'Am I pretty or ugly? Girls and the market for self-esteem'. *Girlhood Studies, 7*(1): 83–101.

Banet-Weiser, Sarah. 2015. ''Confidence you can carry!': Girls in crisis and the market for girls' empowerment organizations'. *Continuum 29*(2): 182–93.

Banet-Weiser, Sarah and Portwood-Stacer, Laura. 2017. 'The traffic in feminism: An introduction to the commentary and criticism on popular feminism'. *Feminist Media Studies, 17*(5): 884–88.

Banet-Weiser, Sarah. 2018. *Empowered: Popular Feminism and Popular Misogyny*. Durham: Duke University Press.

Barbour, R. 2007. *Doing Focus Groups*. London: Sage.

Barker, Kim. and Olga Jurasz. 2019. 'Online misogyny'. *Journal of International Affairs, 72*(2): 95–114.

Barnes, M., Holmes, S. and Ralph, S. 2015. 'Audiences for stardom and celebrity'. *Celebrity Studies, 6*(1): 1–5.

Bates, S. 2010. 'Sarah Ferguson offered access to Prince Andrew for cash, says tabloid'. *The Guardian*. May 23rd 2010. https://www.theguardian.com/uk/2010/may /23/sarah-ferguson-andrew-cash-tabloid.

Batsleer, Janet and McMahon, Gráinne. 2017. 'Girls, 'leaning in' and faux-empowerment'. Presented at: Who Runs the World? Girls, Leadership and Celebrity, 16th June 2017, Senate House, London. http://eprints.hud.ac.uk/id/eprint/32273/

Battersby, Christine. 1988. 'Gender and Genius: Towards a Feminist Aesthetics'. London: Women's Press.

Baumgardner, Jennifer, and Richards, Amy. 2004. 'Feminism and femininity: Or how we learned to stop worrying and love the thong'. In *All About the Girl,* edited by Anita Harris, 85–94. London: Routledge.

Baxter, Judith. 2006. *Speaking Out: The Female Voice in Public Contexts.* Basingstoke: Palgrave Macmillan.

Baxter, Judith. 2012. 'Jokers in the pack: Why boys are more adept than girls at speaking in public settings'. *Language and Education, 16*(2): 81–96.

BBC.co.uk. 2016. 'Role model campaign to encourage female leaders'. *BBC News Online,* 29 August. Available at: https://www.bbc.co.uk/news/uk-scotland-37209280

BBC.co.uk. 2017. 'BBC pay: Male stars earn more than female talent'. *BBC News.* 19 July 2017.https://www.bbc.co.uk/news/entertainment-arts-40661179

BBC.co.uk. 2020. 'Coronavirus: How New Zealand relied on science and empathy'. www.bbc.co.uk/news/world-asia-52344299 Accessed 12th January 2024.

BBC.co.uk. 2021. Pink is UK's most-played female artist of 21st Century, says PPL. https://www.bbc.co.uk/news/entertainment-arts-58869041

Beal, J.C. 2008. '"Shamed by your English?": The market value of a "good" pronunciation'. In *Perspectives on Prescriptivism,* edited by Joan C. Beal, Carmela Nocera, Massimo Sturiale, 21–40. Bern: Peter Lang.

Beard, Mary. 2017a. 'Women in power'. *London Review of Books, 39*(6): 9–14.

Beard, Mary. 2017b. *Women and Power: A Manifesto.* London: Profile Books.

Belam, M. 2019. '"You great big girl's blouse' – Johnson appears to insult Corbyn during PMQs'. *The Guardian,* September 4. www.theguardian.com/politics/2019/sep/04/you-great-big-girls-blouse-boris-johnson-appears-to-insult-corbyn-during-pmqs Accessed 12th Januray 2024.

Bell, D. 2020. 'Why female leaders are faring better than 'wartime presidents' against COVID-19'. *Fortune Magazine.* August 20. https://fortune.com/2020/08/20/women-female-leaders-vs-wartime-president-trump-jacinda-ardern-angela-merkel-covid-19-coronavirus/ Accessed 12th Januray 2024.

Ben Smith (@football_ben). 2022. 'Coffee carrots bean 100 in Welsh'. *TikTok,* 27 April.tiktok.com/@football_ben/video/7091547477320518918.

Bennett, John. 1795. *Letters to a Young Lady: On a Variety of Useful and Interesting Subjects, Calculated to Improve the Heart, to Form the Manners, and Enlighten the Understanding. In two Volumes: By the Rev. John Bennett, Author of Strictures on Female Education. 1784.* (2nd Edition). London: T. Cadell Jr. and W. Davies.

Bent, E. 2013. 'A different girl effect: Producing political girlhoods in the 'Invest in Girls' climate'. In *Youth Engagement: The Civic-Political Lives of Children and Youth,* edited by Sandi Kawecka Nenga and Jessica K. Taft, 3–20. Leeds: Emerald Group Publishing Limited.

Berlant, Lauren. 2007. 'Cruel optimism: On Marx, loss and the senses'. *New Formations, 63*: 33–51.

Berlant, Lauren. 2011. *Cruel Optimism.* London: Duke University Press.

Berrington, Ann, Roberts, Steven and Tammes, Peter. 2016. 'Educational aspirations among UK young teenagers: Exploring the role of gender, class and ethnicity'. *British Educational Research Journal, 42:* 729–55.

Berry, A.J. 2000. 'Leadership in a new millennium: The challenge of the 'risk society''. *Leadership & Organization Development Journal, 21*(1): 5–12.

Bettie, J. 2014. *Women without Class: Girls, Race, and Identity.* Berkeley: University of California Press.

Biddle, S., Riberiro, P.V. and Dias, T. 2020,. 'Invisible censorship: TikTok told moderators to suppress posts by "ugly" people and the poor to attract new users'. *The Intercept.* https://theintercept.com/2020/03/16/TikTok-app-moderators-users-discrimination/ Accessed 12 January 2024.

Bierema, Laura L. 2017. 'Foreword'. In *Theorising Women and Leadership,* edited by Julia Storberg-Walker and Paige Haber-Curran, vii–xii. Charlotte: IAP Inc.

Bigio, J. and Vogelstein, R. 2020. 'Women under attack'. *Foreign Affairs, 99*(1): 131–38.

Billig, M. (1992) 2002. *Talking of the Royal Family.* London: Routledge.

Billing, Y.D. and Alvesson, M. 2000. 'Questioning feminine leadership'. *Gender, Work and Organization, 7*: 144–57.

Biressi, A.R. 2018. 'From the girl to the world: Good girls as political endorsers and agents of change'. *Communication Culture & Critique, 11*(3): 399–417.

Bishop, E.C. and Willis, K., 2014. 'Without hope everything would be doom and gloom': young people talk about the importance of hope in their lives. *Journal of Youth Studies, 17*(6): 778–93.

Blader, S.L. and Chen, Y.R. 2012. 'Differentiating the effects of status and power: A justice perspective'. *Journal of Personality and Social Psychology, 102*(5): 994–1014.

Blanchett, W.J. 2008. ' Educational inequities: The intersection of disability, race and class'. In *Urban Narratives: Portraits in Progress, Life at the Intersection of Learning Disability, Race and Social Class,* edited by D. J. Connor, xi–xvii. New York: Peter Lang.

Blewett, Sam. 2023. 'Covid inquiry will be the thorough investigation the UK deserves, chair vows'. *The Independent.* 13 June. https://www.independent.co.uk/news/uk/covid-court-of-appeal-scottish-b2356509.html

Block, Ray Jr. 2017. 'Race, gender, and media coverage of Michelle Obama'. *Politics, Groups, and Identities, 5*(1): 161–65.

Blumer, H. and Hauser, P.M. 1933. *Movies, Delinquency, and Crime.* (Vol. 8). New York: Macmillan.

Bodie, G.D. 2012. 'Listening as positive communication'. *The Positive Side of Interpersonal Communication,* edited by Thomas Socha and Margaret J. Pitts, 109–25. New York: Peter Lang.

Bourdieu, P. 1984. *Distinction.* London: Routledge.

boyd, d. 2011. 'Affordances, dynamics, and implications'. In *A Networked Self: Identity, Community, and Culture Network Sites,* edited by Zizi Papacharissi, 39–58. London: Routledge .

Boyle, Karen. 2011. 'Producing abuse: Selling the harms of pornography'. *Women's Studies International Forum, 34*: 593–602.

Bradby, T. 2020. 'Harry and Meghan's escape from the poisonous palace'. *The Times*. https://www.thetimes.co.uk/article/harry-and-meghans-escape-from-the-poisonous-palace-rg75t9rxc.

Bradford, Simon and Cullen, Fin. 2014. 'Youth policy in austerity Europe'. *International Journal of Adolescence and Youth, 19*(sup1): 1–4.

Bramall, Rebecca. 2016. 'Introduction: Thefuture of austerity'. *New Formations, 87*: 1–10. http://ualresearchonline.arts.ac.uk/9677/1/Bramall%20Introduction.pdf.

Brave In Bloom. 2024. 'How women are inspiring the next generation: Great role models'. https://braveinbloom.com/blogs/brave-in-bloom-journal/how-women-are-inspiring-the-next-generation-great-role-models.

Brickman, Barbara J. 2016. 'This charming butch: The male pop idol, girl fans, and lesbian (in)visibility'. *Journal of Popular Music Studies, 28*: 443–59. https://doi.10.1111.jpms.12193.

Brickman, Barbara J. 2019. 'Guest editorial: Queering girlhood'. *Girlhood Studies, 12*(1): vi–xv.

Bright, Geoffrey N. 2011. ''Off the model': Resistant spaces, school disaffection and 'aspiration' in a former coal-mining community'. *Children's Geographies, 9*(1): 63–78.

Briton, N.J. and Hall, J.A. 1995. 'Beliefs about female and male nonverbal communication'. *Sex Roles, 32*: 79–90.

Brooks, Libby. 2024. 'Nicola Sturgeon Called Boris Johnson a Clown, UK Covid Inquiry Hears'. *The Guardian*, 25 January. www.theguardian.com/uk-news/2024/jan/25/nicola-sturgeon-called-boris-johnson-a-clown-uk-covid-inquiry-hears.

Brooks, T. 2019. 'The Life in the UK citizenship test and the urgent need for its reform'. In *Citizenship in Times of Turmoil?*, edited by Devyani Prabhat, 22–60. Cheltenham: Edward Elgar Publishing.

Broome, J. 1990. 'Fairness'. In *Proceedings of the Aristotelian Society* (Vol. 91), 87–101. Aristotelian Society, Wiley.

Brown, Wendy. 2003. 'Neo-liberalism and the end of liberal democracy'. *Theory & Event, 7*(1):15–18. 10.1353/tae.2003.0020

Brown, Wendy. 2015. *Undoing the Demos: Neoliberalism's Stealth Revolution*. Cambridge: MIT Press

Bruckmüller, S. and Branscombe, N.R. 2010. 'The glass cliff: When and why women are selected as leaders in crisis contexts'. *British Journal of Social Psychology, 49*(3): 433–51.

Bruns, A. 2006. 'Towards produsage: Futures for user-led content production.' In *Proceedings Cultural Attitudes towards Communication and Technology*, edited by F. Sudweeks, H. Hrachovec and C. Ess, 275–84. https://eprints.qut.edu.au/4863/.

Bruns, Axel. 2008. *Blogs, Wikipedia, Second Life, and Beyond: From Production to Produsage*. New York: Peter Lang.

Butler, Judith. 1990. *Gender Trouble: Feminism and the Subversion of Identity*. New York: Routledge.

Cabinet Office. 2022. *Gender Pay Gap Report*. Available. at: https://www.gov.uk/government/publications/cabinet-office-gender-pay-gap-report-2022/2022-cabinet-office-gender-pay-gap-report-html

Calás, M.B. and Smircich, L. 1991. 'Voicing seduction to silence leadership'. *Organization Studies, 12*(4): 567–601.

Calkin, S. 2015. 'Post-feminist spectatorship and the girl effect: "go ahead, really imagine her"'. *Third World Quarterly, 36*(4): 654–69.

Cameron, D., 2006. 'Theorising the female voice in public contexts'. In *Speaking Out: The Female Voice in Public Contexts*, edited by Judith Baxter,3–20. London: Palgrave Macmillan.

Campbell, R. and Childs, S. 2010. '"Wags", "Wives" and "Mothers" . . . But what about women politicians?' *Parliamentary Affairs, 63*(4): 760–77.

Campus, D. 2013. *Women Political Leaders and the Media.* Basingstoke: Palgrave Macmillan.

Capraro, Valerio and Hélène Barcelo. 2020. 'The effect of messaging and gender on intentions to wear a face covering to slow down COVID-19 transmission'. *Journal of Behavioral Economics for Policy, 4*(2) 45–55. *arXiv preprint arXiv:2005.05467.* https://osf.io/preprints/psyarxiv/tg7vz.

Card, K.G. and Hepburn, K.J. 2023. 'Is neoliberalism killing us? A cross sectional study of the impact of neoliberal beliefs on health and social wellbeing in the midst of the COVID-19 pandemic'. *International Journal of Social Determinants of Health and Health Services, 53*(3): 363–73.

Caretta, Martina Angela and Vacchelli, Elena. 2015. 'Re-thinking the boundaries of the focus group: A reflexive analysis on the use and legitimacy of group methodologies in qualitative research'. *Sociological Research Online, 20*(4): 58–70.

Carling, Jørgen and Collins, Francis. 2018. 'Aspiration, desire and drivers of migration'. *Journal of Ethnic and Migration Studies, 44*(6): 909–26.

Cassell, J., Huffaker, D., Tversky, D. and Ferriman, K. 2006. 'The language of online leadership: Gender and youth engagement on the Internet'. *Developmental Psychology, 42*(3): 436.

Castoriadis, C. 1987. *The Imaginary Institution of Society.* Cambridge: Polity Press.

Cavalieri, S. 2019. 'On amplification: Extralegal acts of feminist resistance in the# MeToo Era'. *Wisconsin Law Review, 2019*(6): 1489–549.

Cawston, A. 2016. 'Are feminism and competition compatible?' *Hypatia: A Journal of Feminist Philosophy, 31*(1): 204–20.

Chan, E. 2018. 'Prince Harry is 'worried there's too much hysteria around Meghan'. *Daily Mail.* https://www.dailymail.co.uk/femail/article-6023423/Prince-Harry-worried-theres-hysteria-Meghan-Markle.html.

Chant, S. 2006. 'Re-thinking the "feminization of poverty" in relation to aggregate gender indices'. *Journal of Human Development, 7*(2): 201–20.

Chatman, D. 2015 'Pregnancy, then it's 'back to business'. *Feminist Media Studies, 15*(6): 926–41.

Chauncey, G. 2008. *Gay New York: Gender, Urban Culture, and the Making of the Gay Male World, 1890–1940.* London: Hachette UK.

Chen, J.M. and Moons, W.G. 2015. 'They won't listen to me: Anticipated power and women's disinterest in male-dominated domains.' *Group Processes & Intergroup Relations, 18*(1): 116–28. https://doi.org/10.1177/1368430214550340.

Chick, K. 2020. 'Harmful comments on social media'. *York Law Review, 1*: 83–110. White Rose Research Online https://doi.org/10.15124/yao-m4xsmhb5.

Childs, S. and Krook, M.L. 2008. 'Critical mass theory and women's political representation'. *Political Studies, 56*(3): 725–36.

Chin, Jean Lau. 2004. 'Division 35 Presidential address: Feminist leadership: Feminist visions and diverse voices'. *Psychology of Women Quarterly, 28*(1): 1–8.

Chin, J.L. 2007. 'Overview: Women and leadership: Transforming visions and diverse voices'. In *Women and Leadership: Transforming Visions and Diverse Voices,* edited by Jean Lau Chin, Bernice Lott, Joy K. Rice, and Janis Sanchez-Hucles, 1–17. Malden, MA: Blackwell.

Christiansen, Lene Bull and Richey, Lisa Ann. 2015 'Celebrity-black: The meanings of race and performances of aid celebrity outside the mainstream Hollywood/UK circuit'. *Celebrity Studies, 6*(4): 505–18.

Chu, H., Yang, J.Z. and Liu, S. 2021. 'Not my pandemic: Solution aversion and the polarized public perception of COVID-19'. *Science Communication, 43*(4): 508–28.

Clack, Beverley and Paule, Michele. (eds). 2019. *Interrogating the Neoliberal Lifecycle: The Limits of Success.* Basingstoke: Palgrave Macmillan.

Clancy, L. 2015. Baby's first photo call: how the royals learned to act normal'. *The Conversation, 2.* https://theconversation.com/babys-first-photo-call-how-the-royals-learned-to-act-normal-40809

Clinton, Hillary (@HillaryClinton). 2016. *Twitter Post.* June 8, 2:08 AM. https://twitter.com/hillaryclinton/status/740349871073398785?lang=en.

Coates, Sam. 2019. 'Boris Johnson called David Cameron 'girly swot', leaked documents reveals'. *Sky News.* 7 September. https://news.sky.com/story/boris-johnson-branded-david-cameron-girly-swot-leaked-document-reveals-11803807 Accessed 12th January 2024.

Cochran, S. 2021. 'Give me body! Race, gender, and corpulence identity in the artistry and activism of queen Latifah'. *Journal of Hip Hop Studies, 8*(1): 14–34.

Coleman, R. 2008. 'The becoming of bodies'. *Feminist Media Studies, 8*(2): 163–79.

Collins, M. 2004. 'Sport, physical activity and social exclusion'. *Journal of Sports Sciences, 22*(8): 727–40.

Connor, Steven. 2000. *Dumbstruck-A Cultural history of ventriloquism.* Oxford: OUP Oxford.

Cooper, Sarah (@sarahcpr). 2020. 'How to medical'. *Twitter.* April 24. https://twitter.com/sarahcpr/status/1253474772702429189?lang=en.

Couldry, N. 2004. 'Theorising media as practice'. *Social Semiotics, 14*(2): 115–32.

Covay, Elizabeth and Carbonaro, William. 2010. 'After the bell: Participation in extracurricular activities, classroom behavior, and academic achievement'. *Sociology of Education, 83*(1): 20–45.

Cover, Rob, Prosser, R. and Duc, D. 2022. 'The corporeality of sound: Drag performance, lip-synching and the popular critique of gendered theatrics in Australian film and television.' *Media International Australia, 182*: 81–94.

Crace. 2020. 'Boris Johnson resorts to bluster under Starmer's cross-examination'. *The Guardian.* https://www.theguardian.com/politics/2020/may/13/boris-johnson-resorts-to-bluster-under-keir-starmer-cross-examination.

Crenshaw, K. 1991. 'Mapping the margins: Intersectionality, identity politics, and violence against women of color'. *Stanford Law Review, 43*: 1241–299.

Crocker, J., Major, B. and Steele, C. 1998. 'Social stigma'. In *The Handbook of Social Psychology* (4th ed.), Vol.1–2, edited by T. Gilbert, T. Fiske and G. Lindzey, 504–53. New York: McGraw-Hill.

Curriculum for Wales. 2016. *Languages, Literacy and Communication*. https://hwb .gov.wales/curriculum-for-wales/languages-literacy-and-communication/

Currid-Halkett, Elizabeth. 2013. 'The geography of celebrity and glamour: Reflections on economy, culture, and desire in the city.' *City, Culture and Society, 4*(1): 2–11.

Currie, D.H. 2015. 'From girlhood, girls to girls' studies the power of the text.' In *Girls, Texts, Cultures,* edited by C. Bradford and M. Reimer, 1–29. Waterloo: Wilfrid Laurier University Press.

Currie, D.H., Kelly, D.M. and Pomerantz, S. 2007. '"The power to squash people": Understanding girls' relational aggression'. *British Journal of Sociology of Education, 28*(1): 23–37.

Cushion, S., Morani, M., Kyriakidou, M. and Soo, N. 2022. '(Mis) understanding the coronavirus and how it was handled in the UK: An analysis of public knowledge and the information environment'. *Journalism Studies, 23*(5–6): 703–21.

Dahmer, C. 2016. 'Still, however, it is certain that young ladies should be more apt to hear than to speak: Silence in eighteenth century conduct books for young women'. *XVII–XVIII. Revue de la Société d'études anglo-américaines des XVIIe et XVIIIe siècles, 73*: 123–45.

Daniels, J. 2015. 'The trouble with white feminism: Whiteness, digital feminism and the intersectional internet'. *Digital Feminism and the Intersectional Internet.* February 16. Accessed 2 January 2021.

Davis, Jenny L. 2020. *How Artifacts Afford: The Power and Politics of Everyday Things*. Cambridge: MIT Press.

Davison, W. 1983. 'The third-person effect in communication'. *Public Opinion Quarterly, 47*(1): 1–15.

De Henau, J. and Reed, H. 2013. 'A cumulative gender impact assessment of ten years of austerity policies'. *Women's Budget Group.* https://wbg.org.uk/wp-content/uploads/2016/03/De_HenauReed_WBG_GIAtaxben_briefing_2016_03_06 .pdf Accessed 2 January 2022.

de Jong, M., 2021. 'Inclusive capitalism: The emergence of a new purpose paradigm in economics and business administration and its implications for public policy'. *Global Public Policy and Governance, 1*(2): 159–74.

Debray, C., Schnurr, S., Loew, J. and Reissner-Roubicek, S. 2024. 'An 'attractive alternative way of wielding power'? Revealing hidden gender ideologies in the portrayal of women Heads of State during the COVID-19 pandemic'. *Critical Discourse Studies, 21*(1): 52–75.

DeCotis, Maria (@mariadecotis). 2023. 'Breaking News: Andrew Cuomo and his daughter Michaela's "adult life".' *TikTok,* October 7. https://www.tiktok.com/@ mariadecotis/video/7287303981884362027.

Demos. 2016. 'New Demos study reveals scale of social media misogyny'. 26 May. https://demos.co.uk/press-release/staggering-scale-of-social-media-misogyny-mapped-in-new-demos-study. Accessed 2 January 2021.

Devereux, C. 2014. 'Hysteria, feminism, and gender revisited: The case of the second wave'. *ESC: English Studies in Canada, 40*(1): 19–45.

DiBranco, A. 2022. 'Mobilizing misogyny'. In *Male Supremacism in the United States*, edited by Emily K. Carian, Alex DiBranco, Chelsea Ebin, 3–20. London: Routledge.

Drenten, Jenna and Evie Psarras. D. 2023. 'Digital ventriloquism and celebrity access: Cameo and the emergence of paid puppeteering on digital platforms'. *New Media & Society, 25*(12): 3350–69.

Dolan, K., 2018. *Voting for Women: How the Public Evaluates Women Candidates.* New York: Routledge.

Drummond, R. 2017. '(Mis) interpreting urban youth language: White kids sounding black?'. *Journal of Youth Studies, 20*(5): 640–60.

Drysdale, Kerryn. 2019. *Intimate Investments in Drag King Cultures.* New York: Springer International Publishing.

Du Plooy, B. 2021. 'The return of Rosie the Riveter: Contemporary popular reappropriations of the iconic World War II image'. *Image & Text, 35:* 1–33. Available at https://www.scielo.org.za/scielo.php?pid=S1021-14972021000100009&script=sci_arttext.

Dudman, Jane. 2020. Female leaders make a real difference. Covid may be the proof. 16 December. https://www.theguardian.com/society/2020/dec/16/female-leaders-make-a-real-difference-covid-may-be-the-proof

Duffett, M. 2013. *Understanding Fandom: An Introduction to the Study of Media Fan Culture.* New York: Bloomsbury Publishing USA.

Duits, L. and van Romondt Vis, P. 2009. 'Girls make sense: Girls, celebrities and identities'. *European Journal of Cultural Studies, 12*(1): 41–58.

Dunn, Edwina. 2017. *The Female Lead: Women Who Shape Our World.* New York City: Random House.

Duster, Chadelis. 2019. 'Gov. Andrew Cuomo uses 'n-word' to make point about derogatory terms against Italians'. *CNN.* October 15https://www.cnn.com/2019/10/15/politics/andrew-cuomo-racial-slur/index.html Accessed 1 December 2022.

Dyer, Richard. 1979. *Stars.* London: British Film Institute.

Eagleton, M. 2017. 'Angry young women: Education, class, and politics'. *The History of British Women's Writing, 1945–1975*, edited by Clare Hanson and Susan Watkins, 91–107. Basingstoke: Palgrave MacMillan.

Eagly, Alice H., and Linda L. Carli. 2003. 'The female leadership advantage: An evaluation of the evidence'. *The Leadership Quarterly 14*(6): 807–83

Edmondson, Amy C. and Tomas Chamorro-Premuzic. 2021. 'Leadership in times of upheaval: The rise of the empathic leader'. In *Social Scientists Confronting Global Crises,* edited by Jean M. Bartunek, 97–105. Abingdon: Routledge.

Education Scotland. 2016. Curriculim for Excellence: Literacy Experiences and Outcomes. https://education.gov.scot/curriculum-for-excellence/curriculum-for-excellence-documents/experiences-and-outcomes/#all

Eek-Karlsson, L. 2021. 'The importance of belonging: A study about positioning processes in youths' online communication'. *SAGE Open*, *11*(1): 2158244020988860.

Eilperin, J. 2016. How a White House women's office strategy went viral. *Washington Post*. https://www.washingtonpost.com/news/powerpost/wp/2016/10/25/how-a -white-house-womens-office-strategy-went-viral/ Accessed 12 January 2024.

Eksi, Betul and Wood, Eilzabeth A. 2019. 'Right-wing populism as gendered performance: Janus-faced masculinity in the leadership of Vladimir Putin and Recep T. Erdogan'. *Theory and Society, 48*(5): 733.

Elgot, Jessica. 2018. 'Boris Johnson accused of 'dog-whistle' Islamophobia over burqa comments'. *The Guardian.* August 07. https://www.theguardian.com/poli-tics/2018/aug/06/boris-johnsons-burqa-remarks-fan-flames-of-islamophobia-says -mp Accessed 12 January 2024.

Elliott, C. and Stead, V. 2018. 'Constructing women's leadership representation in the UK press during a time of financial crisis: Gender capitals and dialectical tensions'. *Organization Studies*, *39*(1): 19–45.

Ellis, K. 2018. 'Contested vulnerability: A case study of girls in secure care'. *Children and Youth Services Review*, *88*, 156–63.

Ely, R.J., Ibarra, H. and Kolb, D.M. 2011. 'Taking gender into account: Theory and design for women's leadership development programs'. *Academy of Management Learning & Education*, *10*(3): 474–93.

Enderstein, A.M. 2018. 'Not just a girl: Reworking femininity through women's leadership in Europe'. *European Journal of Women's Studies, 25*(3): 325–40.

English, R. 2018. 'Meghan's Manifesto: 'Proud feminist' the Duchess of Sussex will take the royals in a striking new direction'. *Daily Mail*: 1–3. 21 May.

Epstein, D. 1993. 'Sexual subjects: Some methodological problems in researching sexuality in schools'. Paper for AARE Conference November 1993. www.aare .edu.au.

Epstein, D. 2014. 'Race-ing class ladies: Lineages of privilege in an elite South African school'. *Globalisation, Societies and Education*, *12*(2): 244–61.

Erikson, J. and Verge, T. 2022. 'Gender, power and privilege in the parliamentary workplace'. *Parliamentary Affairs*, *75*(1): 1–19.

Estrada, Juan Diego, García-Ael, Cristina and Martorell, José LuiS. 2015. 'Gender differences in adolescents' choice of heroes and admired adults in five countries'. *Gender and Education, 27*(1): 69–87.

European Commission. 2018. 'Gender balance in decision-making positions: Initiatives for ending the EU gender gap in decision-making positions'. https://ec.europa .eu/info/policies/justice-and-fundamental-rights/gender-equality/gender-balance -decision-making-positions_en Accessed 13 January 2024.

European Commission. 2024. 'Report on gender equality in the EU: Equality between women and men in decision-making'. https://commission.europa .eu/document/download/965ed6c9-3983-4299-8581-046bf0735702_en?filename =2024%20Report%20on%20Gender%20Equality%20in%20the%20EU_coming %20soon.pdf.

European Women's Lobby. 2018. 'Manifesto for a feminist Europe'. https://women-lobby.org/Our-Manifesto-for-a-Feminist-Europe.

Eva, N., De Cieri, H., Murphy, S.E. and Lowe, K.B. 2021. 'Leader development for adolescent girls: State of the field and a framework for moving forward'. *The Leadership Quarterly*, *32*(1): 101457.

Evans, L. 2020. '£Keir Starmer's big weakness was exposed at PMQs'. *The Spectator*. 20 May. https://www.spectator.co.uk/article/keir-starmer-s-big-weakness-was-exposed-at-pmqs.

Eveland, Jr. William P. and McLeod, Douglas M. 1999. 'The effect of social desirability on perceived media impact: Implications for third-person perceptions'. *International Journal of Public Opinion Research, 11*(4): 315–33.

Fabricius, A.H. 2000. 'T-glottalling between stigma and prestige: A sociolinguistic study of Modern RP', (PhD dissertation, Copenhagen Business School). Advance online publication. chrome-extension://efaidnbmnnnibpcajpcglclefindmkaj/https://forskning.ruc.dk/files/63117207/Fabricius_2000_Ph.D._thesis.pdf.

Faludi, Susan. 2013. 'Facebook feminism, like it or not'. *The Baffler*. https://thebaffler.com/salvos/facebook-feminism-like-it-or-not Accessed 13 January 2024.

Farrier, Stephen. 2016. 'That lip-synching feeling: Drag performance as digging the past'. In *Queer Dramaturgies: International Perspectives on Where Performance Leads Queer*, edited by Campbell Alyson and Stephen Farrier, 192–209. London: Palgrave Macmillan UK.

Faulkner, L.J. 1997. 'Shades of discipline: Princess Diana, the US media, and whiteness'. *Lowa Journal of Cultural Studies, 1997*(16): 16–31.

fawcettsociety.org. 2024. WHAT DO THE ELECTION RESULTS MEAN FOR WOMEN'S REPRESENTATION? 10 July. https://www.fawcettsociety.org.uk/what-do-the-election-results-mean-for-womens-representation

Feldkamp, Jana. 2021. 'The rise of TikTok: The evolution of a social media platform during COVID-19'. *Digital Responses to Covid-19: Digital Innovation, Transformation, and Entrepreneurship During Pandemic Outbreaks*, edited by C. Hovestadt, C. Recker, J. Richter, and K. Werder, 73–85. Cham: Springer Nature.

Ferchaud, A., Grzeslo, J., Orme, S. and LaGroue, J. 2018. 'Parasocial attributes and YouTube personalities'. *Computers in Human Behavior, 80*: 88–96.

Finlayson, L.. 2018. 'The thirdshift: The politics of representation and the psychological turn'. *Signs: Journal of Women in Culture and Society, 43*(4): 775–95.

Finneran, R., Mayes, E. and Black, R. 2023. 'Pride and privilege: The affective dissonance of student voice. *Pedagogy, Culture & Society, 31*(1): 1–16.

Fisanick, Christina. 2007. '"They are weighted with authority": Fat female professors in academic and popular cultures'. *Feminist Teacher, 17*(3): 237–55.

Fischer, T. 2013. 'The roles of listening and non-listening in the formation of organizational hierarchies'. *Cybernetics & Human Knowing, 20*(1–2): 83–92.

Fish, Stanley. 1980. *Is There a Text in This Class? The Authority of Interpretive Communities*. Cambridge: Harvard University Press.

Flesher Fominaya, Cristina. 2010. 'Collective identity in social movements: Central concepts and debates'. *Sociology Compass, 4*(6): 393–404.

Fletcher, J.K. 2004. 'The paradox of postheroic leadership: An essay on gender, power, and transformational change'. *The Leadership Quarterly, 15*(5): 647–61.

Flechtner, S. 2014. 'Aspiration traps: When poverty stifles hope'. *Inequality in Focus*, 2(4): 1–4.

Flynn, A.V. 2022. 'Solidarity and collectivism in the context of COVID-19'. *Nursing Ethics*, 29(5): 1198–208.

Folbre, N. 1991. 'The unproductive housewife: Her evolution in nineteenth-century economic thought'. *Signs: Journal of Women in Culture and Society*, 16(3): 463–84.

Ford, Jackie. 2016. *Gendered Relationships and the Problem of Diversity in Leadership-as-practice*. London, UK: Routledge.

Ford, J. and Morgan, J. 2023. 'Critiquing leadership and gender research through a feminist lens'. *The SAGE Handbook of Leadership*, edited by A. Bryman, 247–61. Los Angeles: Sage.

Foster, Meggie (@meggiefoster). 2020. 'Bedtime with Boris: 'Stay Alert' ft. Theresa'. *TikTok*, May 11. https://www.tiktok.com/@meggiefoster/video /6825501817766563078.

Foucault, Michel. 1969. *The Archaeology of Knowledge*. Translated by A. *Sheridan*. London and New York: Routledge.

Foucault, M. 1988. 'Technologies of the self'. In *Technologies of the Self: A Seminar with Michel Foucault* (Vol. 18), edited by Luther H., Martin, Huck Gutman and Patrick H. Hutton, 170–366. London: Tavistock.

Foucault, Michel. 2008. *The Birth of Biopolitics: Lectures at the Collège de France 1978–1979*. Translated by Graham Burchell. New York: Palgrave Macmillan

Fradley, M. 2022. '"So you want to be a# GIRLBOSS?" Millennial femininity and entrepreneurial selfhood in girlboss and the girlfriend experience'. *Journal of Popular Television*, 10(3): 247–67.

Fraile, M. and Sánchez-Vítores, I. 2020. 'Tracing the gender gap in political interest over the life span: A panel analysis'. *Political Psychology*, 41(1): 89–106.

Francis, Becky and Hey, Valerie. 2009. 'Talking back to power: Snowballs in hell and the imperative of insisting on structural explanations'. *Gender and Education*, 21(2): 225–32.

Francis, Becky and Skelton, Christine. 2005. *Reassessing Gender and Achievement: Questioning Contemporary Key Debates*. London: Routledge.

Francis, Becky, Skelton, Christitne and Read, Barbara. 2010. 'The simultaneous production of educational achievement and popularity: How do some pupils accomplish it?'. *British Educational Research Journal*, 36(2): 317–340.

Frank Hester (@HesterObe). 2024. 'Statement regarding recent media reports'. *Twitter*. March 11. https://twitter.com/HesterObe/status/1767248542651781271.

Frank, J. 1990. 'You call that a rhetorical question?: Forms and functions of rhetorical questions in conversation'. *Journal of Pragmatics*, 14(5): 723–738.

Frank, A.W. 2005. 'What is dialogical research, and why should we do it?'. *Qualitative Health Research*, 15(7): 964–74.

Fraser, Nancy. 2009. 'Feminism, Capitalism and the Cunning of History'. *New Left Review 56:* 97–110.

Fraser, Helen. 2014. 'Young women need female role models to inspire success'. *The Guardian*. 22 October. https://www.theguardian.com/women-in-leadership/ women-leadership-blog/2014/oct/22/women-role-model-penguin.

Freeman, H. 2018. 'Are republicans allowed to be interested in Meghan Markle's pregnancy'. *The Guardian.* October 17. https://www.theguardian.com/fashion/2018/oct/17/are-republicans-allowed-to-be-interested-in-meghan-markles-pregnancy).

Frisby, C.M. 2017. 'Misrepresentations of lone shooters: The disparate treatment of Muslim, African American, Hispanic, Asian, and white perpetrators in the US news media'. *Advances in Journalism and Communication, 5*(2): 162.

Fuller, D., Shareck, M. and Stanley, K. 2017. 'Ethical implications of location and accelerometer measurement in health research studies with mobile sensing devices'. *Social Science & Medicine, 191:* 84–8.

Furness, H. 2019. 'Famous friends rally to support Duke and Duchess of Sussex'. *The Telegraph.* August 20. https://www.telegraph.co.uk/royal-family/2019/08/20/famous-friends-rally-support-duke-duchess-sussex-trying-do-make/.

Gaiser, T.J. 2008. 'Online focus groups'. In *The Sage Handbook of Online Research Methods*, edited by N. Fielding, R.M. Lee and G. Blank, 290–306. London: Sage.

García-Beaudoux, V., Berrocal, S., D'Adamo, O. and Bruni, L. 2023. 'Female political leadership styles as shown on Instagram during COVID-19'. *Comunicar, 31*(75): 125–34.

Garcia-Blanco, Iñaki and Karin Wahl-Jorgensen. 2012. 'The discursive construction of women politicians in the european press'. *Feminist Media Studies, 12*(3): 422–41.

Garikipati, Supriya and Uma Kambhampati. 2021. 'Leading the fight against the pandemic: Does gender really matter?' *Feminist Economics, 27*:1–2.

Gauntlett, D. 2002. *Media, Gender and Identity: An introduction.* London: Routledge.

Gavey, N. 2012. 'Beyond "empowerment"? Sexuality in a sexist world'. *Sex roles, 66*: 718–24.

Gershon, Sarah Allen. 2012. 'When race, gender, and the media intersect: Campaign news coverage of minority congresswomen'. *Journal of Women, Politics & Policy, 33*(2): 105–25.

Gibson, D.E. 2003. 'Developing the professional self-concept: Role model construals in early, middle, and late career stages'. *Organization Science, 14*: 591–610.

Gill, Rosalind C. 2007. 'Critical respect: The difficulties and dilemmas of agency and 'choice' for feminism'. A reply to Duits and van Zoonen'. *European Journal of Women's Studies, 14*(1): 69–80.

Gill, Rosalind C. 2008. 'Empowerment/sexism: Figuring female sexual agency in contemporary advertising'. *Feminism and Psychology, 18*(1): 35–60.

Gill, Rosalind C. 2016. 'Post-postfeminism?: New feminist visibilities in postfeminist times'. *Feminist Media Studies, 16*(4): 610–30.

Gill, Rosalind and Orgad, Shani. 2017. 'Confidence culture and the remaking of feminism'. *New Formations, 91*: 16–34. ISSN 0950-2378.

Gillborn, D. and Mirza, H.S. 2000. 'Educational inequality: Mapping race, class and gender—A synthesis of research evidence'. Report #HMI 232. London: Office for Standards in Education.

Gilligan, C. 1993. *In a Different Voice: Psychological Theory and Women's Development.* Cambridge: Harvard University Press.

GirlGuiding. 2018. 'Girls' attitudes survey'. https://www.girlguiding.org.uk/girls -making-change/girls-attitudes-survey/ Accessed 2nd January 2022.

Giroux, Henry A. 2004. 'Cultural studies, public pedagogy, and the responsibility of intellectuals'. *Communication and Critical/Cultural Studies*, *1*(1): 59–79.

Goldblatt, David. (2006) 2014. *Art and Ventriloquism*. New York: Routledge.

Gonick, Marnina. 2003. *Between Femininities: Ambivalence, Identity, and the Education of Girls*. New York: SUNY.

Gonick, Marnina. 2006. 'Between girl power and reviving Ophelia: Constituting the neo-liberal girl subject'. *National Women's Studies Association Journal*, *18*(2): 1–23.

Goswami, Nina. 2020. 'Have female CEOs coped better with Covid than men?' November 2020. *BBC News*. https://www.bbc.co.uk/news/business-54974132

Government Equalities Office. 2017. 'Gender pay gap reporting'. Available at https:// www.gov.uk/guidance/gender-pay-gap-reporting-overview Accessed 2 January 2022.

Gov.uk. 2024. 'Deaths with COVID-19 on the death certificate'. Accessed 12 January 2024. https://coronavirus.data.gov.uk/details/deaths

Graeber, David. 2011. *Revolutions in Reverse: Essays on Politics, Violence, Art and Imagination*. London: Minor Compositions.

Graham, Hilary. 1984. 'Surveying through stories'. In *Social Researching: Politics, Problems, Practice*, edited by Colin Bell and Helen Roberts, 104–24. London: Routledge.

Grant, Thomas. 2017. 'The complexity of aspiration: The role of hope and habitus in shaping working-class young people's aspirations to higher education'. *Children's Geographies*, *15*(3): 289–303.

Gray, Sue. 2022. 'Findings of second permanent secretary's investigation into alleged gatherings on government premises during covid restrictions'. https://assets.publishing.service.gov.uk/government/uploads/system/uploads/attachment_data/file /1078404/2022-05–25_FINAL_FINDINGS_OF_SECOND_PERMANENT_SECRETARY_INTO_ALLEGED_GATHERINGS.pdf.

Greenaway, Naomi. 2014. 'Women are better listeners, study says'. *The Daily Mail*. December 15. https://www.dailymail.co.uk/femail/article-2874213/Men-finally -admit-bad-listeners-pay-attention-talking-women-sport.html Accessed 2 January 2021.

Gregory, S.M. 2010. 'Disney's second line: New Orleans, racial masquerade, and the reproduction of whiteness in The Princess and the Frog'. *Journal of African American Studies*, *14*(4): 432–49.

Gronn, P. 2008. 'The future of distributed leadership'. *Journal of Educational Administration, 46*(2): 141–58.

Gunew, S. 2008. 'Serial accommodations: Diasporic women's writing'. *Canadian Literature, 196*: 6–15.

Hains, R. 2012. *Growing up with Girl Power: Girlhood on Screen and in Everyday Life*. Bern: Peter Lang.

Halberstam, Jack. 2019. *Female Masculinity*. Durham: Duke University Press.

Hall, Stuart. 1980. 'Encoding / Decoding'. In *Culture, Media, Language: Working Papers in Cultural Studies, 1972–79*, edited by S. Hall, D. Hobson, A. Lowe, and P. Willis, 128–38. London: Hutchinson.

Hall, S.M. 2019. *Everyday Life in Austerity: Family, Friends and Intimate Relations*. London: Palgrave Macmillan.

Hall, S.M. 2022. 'For feminist geographies of austerity'. *Progress in Human Geography, 46*(2): 299–318.

Hamilton, J.L., Nesi, J. and Choukas-Bradley, S. 2021. 'Reexamining social media and socioemotional well-being among adolescents through the lens of the COVID-19 pandemic: A theoretical review and directions for future research'. *Perspectives on Psychological Science, 17*(3): 662–79.

Hancock, D., Dyk, P.H. and Jones, K. 2012. 'Adolescent involvement in extracurricular activities: Influences on leadership skills'. *Journal of Leadership Education, 11*(1): 84–101.

Hansen, C.E. 2019. *Exploring the Impact of Positive Peer Views of Girls on School Engagement in Middle School Girls,* (PhD dissertation, Utah State University).

Harrington, C. and Dillahunt, T.R. 2021. 'Eliciting tech futures among Black young adults: A case study of remote speculative co-design'. *Proceedings of the 2021 CHI Conference on Human Factors in Computing Systems*, 1–15.

Harris, P.J. 2003. 'Gatekeeping and remaking: The politics of respectability in African American women's history and Black feminism'. *Journal of Women's History, 15*(1): 212–20.

Harris, Anita. 2004. 'The "can-do" girl versus the "at-risk" girl'. *Future Girl: Young Women in the Twenty-First Century,*help_outline 13–36. London: Routledge.

Harris, Anita. 2004. 'Jamming girl culture: Young women and consumer citizenship'. *All About the Girl: Culture, Power, and Identity,* edited by Anita Harris, 189–98. London: Psychology Press.

Harris, Anita. 2008. 'Young women, late modern politics, and the participatory possibilities of online cultures'. *Journal of Youth Studies, 11*(5): 481–49

Harris, Anita and Dobson, Amy Shields. 2015. 'Theorizing agency in post-girlpower times'. *Continuum, 29*(2): 145–56.

Hart, S.L. 2005. *Capitalism at the Crossroads: The Unlimited Business Opportunities in Solving the World's Most Difficult Problems*. London: Pearson Education.

Hasinoff, A. 2009. 'It's Sociobiology, Hon!: Genetic Gender Determinism in Cosmopolitan Magazine'. *Feminist Media Studies, 9*(3): 267–283.

Haste, H. 2010. 'Citizenship education: A critical look at a contested field'. In *Handbook of Research on Civic Engagement in Youth*, edited by Lonnie R. Sherrod, Judith Torney-Purta, and Constance A. Flanagan, 161–88. Hoboken: John Wiley & Sons.

Helmore, Edward. 2023. 'Andrew Cuomo accused of sexual assault as 'look-back' window closes'. *The Guardian*. November 24. https://www.theguardian.com/us-news/2023/nov/24/andrew-cuomo-sexual-assault-claim-new-york Accessed 5 January 2024.

Hess, A. 2015. 'Women aren't welcome here'. In *The Best American Magazine Writing,* edited by Sid Holt, 51–74. New York: Columbia University Press.

Hesse-Biber, Sharlene Nagy. 2007. 'The practice of feminist in-depth interviewing'. In *Feminist Research Practice: A Primer,* edited by Sharlena Nagy Hesse-Beiber and Patricia Lina Levy, Ch.5, 111–48. Thousand Oaks: Sage.

Hilliard, A.G. 1995. 'Mathematics excellence for cultural "minority" students: What is the problem?'. In *Prospects for School Mathematics,* edited by Iris M. Carl, 99–113. Reston, VA: National Council of Teachers of Mathematics.

Hirsch, A. 2020. 'Black Britons know why Meghan wants out'. *New York Times.* https://www.nytimes.com/2020/01/09/opinion/sunday/meghan-markle-prince -harry.html.

Hirsh, Jennie and Lorring W., Isabelle. 2023. 'Introduction'. In *Ventriloquism, Performance, and Contemporary Art*, edited by Jennie Hirsh and Isabelle Loring Wallace, 1–22. New York: Routledge.

Hitchens, P. 2020. 'Lord sumption speaks against Hysteria-Driven government coronavirus policy'. *Hitchens Blog. Mail on Sunday.* March 30. https://hitchensblog .mailonsunday.co.uk/2020/03/lord-sumption-speaks-against-hysteria-driven-government-policy-.html Accessed 12 January 2024.

Holmes, S. 2004. '"All you've got to worry about is the task, having a cup of tea, and what you're going to eat for dinner": Approaching celebrity in Big brother'. In *Understanding Reality Television*, edited by S. Holmes and D. Jermyn, 111–35. London: Routledge.

Holmes, Su. 2005. 'Off-guard, unkempt, unready'?: Deconstructing contemporary celebrity in heat magazine'. *Continuum: Journal of Media & Cultural Studies, 19*(1): 21–38.

Holmes, Su and Diane Negra. 2011. 'Introduction'. In *In the Limelight and Under the Microscope: Forms and Functions of Female Celebrity,* edited by Su Holmes and Diane Negra, 1–16. New York: Continuum.

Holtzman, D. 2017. 'Close-Up: Beyoncé: Media and cultural icon: Ass you lick it: Bey and jay eat cake'. *Black Camera: An International Film Journal, 9*(1): 179–88.

Home Office. 2023. *Life in the United Kingdom: A Guide for New Residents.* Great Britain: Home Office.

hooks, b. 2016. 'Moving beyond pain'. http://www.bellhooksinstitute.com/blog/2016 /5/9/moving-beyond-pain.

Hopkins, S. 2002. *Girl Heroes: The New Force in Popular Culture.* London: Pluto Press.

Horton, D. and Richard Wohl, R. 1956. 'Mass communication and para-social interaction: Observations on intimacy at a distance'. *Psychiatry, 19*(3): 215–29.

Hoyt, M.A. and Kennedy, C.L. 2008. 'Leadership and adolescent girls: A qualitative study of leadership development'. *American Journal of Community Psychology, 42*(3–4): 203–19. https://www.dailymail.co.uk/news/article-9100835/Prince-Harry -Meghan-Markles-episode-30m-podcast-ranked-whale-noises.html.

Hoyt, C.L. and Simon, S. 2011. 'Female leaders: Injurious or inspiring role models for women?' *Psychology of Women Quarterly, 35*(1): 143–57.

Huang, P.H. 2021. 'Put more women in charge and other leadership lessons from COVID-19'. *FIU Law Review, 15*: 353.

Hunt, Elle. 2020. 'People still need to laugh': How lipsyncing spoofs saved lockdown'. *The Guardian.* May 16. https://www.theguardian.com/technology /2020/may/16/people-still-need-to-laugh-how-lip-syncing-spoofs-saved-lockdown Accessed 12 January 2024.

Hussein, D. 2018. 'Meghan Markle to lose SECOND close aide'. *Daily Mail.* 9 December. https://www.dailymail.co.uk/news/article-6475701/Meghan-Markle-lose-SEC-OND-close-aide-private-secretary-announces-leave.html Accessed 12 January 2024.

I Am Spindlicus (@IanSpindley). 2020. 'Are more male leaders privately educated than women and so believe they are more entitled to be decision makers?' *Twitter.* April 9. https://twitter.com/IanSpindley/status/1248185653185187840&sa=D&source =docs&ust=1711039074097590&usg=AOvVaw1NJ_fY1ugJX5pleM3b7Vmj.

Illiashenko, P. 2019. '"Tough Guy" vs. "Cushion" hypothesis: How does individualism affect risk-taking?' *Journal of Behavioral and Experimental Finance, 24:* 100212.

Ipsos Mori. 2016. 'Monarchy popular as ever ahead of Queen's 90th Birthday celebrations'. 15 April. https://www.ipsos.com/ipsos-mori/en-uk/monarchy-popular -ever-ahead-queens-90th-birthday-celebrations Accessed 12 January 2024.

Iverson, Susan V., Allan, Elizabeth J. and Gordon, Suzanne P. 2017. 'Constructing the double bind: The discursive framing of gendered imaginings of leadership in the chronicle of higher education'. In *Theorising Women and Leadership,* edited by Julia Storberg-Walker and Paige Haber-Curran, 51–68. Charlotte: IAP Inc.

Jackson, S. 2014. *Black Celebrity, Racial Politics, and the Press: Framing Dissent.* New York: Routledge.

Jackson, S. 2021. 'A very basic view of feminism: Feminist girls and meanings of (celebrity) feminism'. *Feminist Media Studies, 21*(7): 1072–90.

Jackson, S. and Vares, T. 2016. 'Too many bad role models for us girls': Girls, female pop celebrities and 'sexualization''. *Sexualities, 18*(4): 480–98.

Jackson, S., Goddard, S. and Cossens, S. 2016. 'The importance of [not] being Miley: Girls making sense of Miley Cyrus'. *European Journal of Cultural Studies, 19*(6): 547–64.

Jacobs, S. 2020. 'Despite liberal bubble hysteria, the public will back Boris over lockdown crunch-time'. *The Telegraph.* April 23. https://www.telegraph.co.uk /politics/2020/04/23/despite-liberal-bubble-hysteria-public-will-back-boris-lock-down/ Accessed 13 January 2024.

Jaffe, Sarah. 2013. 'Trickle-down feminism'. *Dissent.* Winter. https://www.dissent-magazine.org/article/trickle-down-feminism.

Johns, S. 2020. 'Neil Ferguson talks modelling, lockdown and scientific advice with MPs'. *Imperial News.* London: Imperial College London. June 10. https://www .imperial.ac.uk/news/198155/neil-ferguson-talks-modelling-lockdown-scientific/ Accessed 12 January 2024.

Johnson, L. 1993. T*he Modern Girl: Girlhood and Growing Up.* Buckingham: Open University Press.

Johnson, C. 2022. 'Feeling protected: Protective masculinity and femininity from Donald Trump and Joe Biden to Jacinda Ardern'. *Emotions and Society, 4*(1): 7–26.

Jones, Owen. 2012. *Chavs*. London: Verso.

Josh Marshall (@joshtpm). 2020. 'Trump: Antibiotics used to save every problem and now one of the biggest problems the world has is the germ has gotten to brilliant that the anti-antibiotic can't keep up with it'. *Twitter*. 20 April. https://twitter .com/joshtpm/status/1248699275355328512?lang=en.

Jung, Jogn. 1986. 'How useful is the concept of "role model"? A critical analysis'. *Journal of Social Behaviour and Psychology, 1*(4): 525–36.

Kabengele, M.C., Keller, L. and Gollwitzer, P. 2023. 'Gendered leadership perception and the COVID-19 Pandemic: Are women perceived as better leaders in a health crisis?' PsyArXiv: Cornell University. https://doi.org/10.31234/osf.io/nstv7 Accessed 12 January 2024.

Kale, S. 2020. 'How coronavirus helped TikTok find its voice'. *The Guardian*. April 26. https://www.theguardian.com/technology/2020/apr/26/how-coronavirus -helped-tiktok-find-its-voice Accessed 12 January 2024.

Kaminski, Elizabeth and Verta Taylor. 2008. '"We're not just lip-synching up here': Music and collective identity in drag performances'. In *Identity Work in Social Movements*, edited by J. Reger, D.J. Myers and R.L. Einwohner, 47–76. Minnesota: University of Minnesota Press.

Karikis, Mikhail. 2015. 'Nonsense: Towards a vocal conceptual compass for art'. In *Voice Studies: Critical Approaches to Process, Performance and Experience*, edited by Konstantinos Thomaidis and Ben Macpherson, 79–89. Oxon: Routledge.

Kaul, N. 2021. 'The misogyny of authoritarians in contemporary democracies'. *International Studies Review, 23*(4): 1619–45.

Kavanagh, T. 2020. 'Hysteria has forced the UK into lockdown, crashed the economy and will kill more than coronavirus'. *The Sun*. March 29. https://www.thesun.co.uk /news/11282990/hysteria-has-forced-the-uk-into-lockdown-crashed-the-economy -and-will-kill-more-than-coronavirus/ Accessed 12 January 2024.

Kavka, Misha. 2014. 'Hating Madonna and loving Tom Ford: Gender, affect and the 'Extra-curricular' celebrity'. *Celebrity Studies, 5*(1–2): 59–74.

Kay, Jilly Boyce. 2020a. *Gender, Media and Voice: Communicative Injustice and Public Speech*. Cham: Palgrave Macmillan.

Kay, Jilly Boyce. 2020b. '"Stay the fuck at home!": Feminism, family and the private home in a time of coronavirus'. *Feminist Media Studies, 20*(6): 883–88.

Kearney, Mary Celeste. 2011. 'Girls' media studies 2.0'. In *Mediated Girlhoods: New Explorations of Girls' Media Culture*, edited by Mary Celeste Kearney, 1–14. New York: Peter Lang.

Kelan, E.K. and Wratil, P. 2018. 'Post-heroic leadership, tempered radicalism and senior leaders as change agents for gender equality'. *European Management Review, 15*(1): 5–18.

Keller, J. 2015. 'Girl power's last chance? Tavi Gevinson, feminism, and popular media culture'. *Continuum, 29*(2): 274–85.

Keller, J. and Ringrose, J. 2015. 'But then feminism goes out the window!': Exploring teenage girls' critical response to celebrity feminism'. *Celebrity Studies, 6*(1): 132–35.

Kennedy, Melanie. 2020. "If the rise of the TikTok dance and e-girl aesthetic has taught us anything, it's that teenage girls rule the internet right now': TikTok celebrity, girls and the Coronavirus crisis'. *European Journal of Cultural Studies, 23*(6): 1069–76.

Kerswill, P. 2013. 'Identity, ethnicity and place: the construction of youth language in London'. *Space in Language and Linguistics: Geographical, Interactional, and Cognitive Perspectives, 24*: 28–164.

Kim, S., 2004. 'Rereading David Morley's the 'nationwide'audience'. *Cultural Studies, 18*(1): 84–108.

Klapp, O.E. 2017. *Symbolic Leaders: Public Dramas and Public Men.* New York: Routledge.

Kleist, Nauja. 2016. 'Introduction: Studying hope and uncertainty in African migration'. In *Hope and Uncertainty in Contemporary African Migration*, edited by Nauja Kleist and Dorte Thorsen, 1–20. New York: Routledge.

Knowles, Kristen K. and Little, Anthony C. 2019. 'Leadership perception in candidate faces: Scotland's unionists prefer dominant leaders, and so do nationalists – but only if they are economic pessimists'. *Scottish Affairs, 28*(4): 434–58.

Koenig, A.M., Eagly, A.H., Mitchell, A.A. and Ristikari, T. 2011. 'Are leader stereotypes masculine? A meta-analysis of three research paradigms'. *Psychological Bulletin, 137*(4): 616–42.

Koffman, O. and Gill, R. 2013. '"The revolution will be led by a 12-year-old girl": Girl power and global biopolitics'. *Feminist Review, 105*(1): 83–102.

Kokoli, Alexandra M. and Winter, Aaron. 2015. 'What a girl's gotta do: The labour of the biopolitical celebrity in austerity Britain'. *Women & Performance: A Journal of Feminist Theory, 25*(2): 157–74.

Kristeva, J. 1982. 'Approaching abjection'. *Oxford Literary Review*, 5(1\2): 125–49.

Kyriakides, Theodoros. 2014. 'Stillness as a Form of Imaginative Labour'. *The Unfamiliar, 4*(1): 47–55.

Lady, C. (@CazzyRNF). 2020. 'Is there an 'empathy' angle to this too? Are women leaders perhaps more empathetic, prioritising 'protecting lives' above anything else??' *Twitter.* April 9. https://twitter.com/CazzyRNF/status /1248179099450867714&sa=D&source=docs&ust=1711038725949313&usg =AOvVaw2VIvbqq5RCI1YZSh-27Lpf.

Latu, I., Schmid Mast, M., Bombari, D., Lammers, J. and Hoyt, C. 2019. 'Empowering mimicry: Female leader role models empower women in leadership tasks through body posture mimicry'. *Sex Roles, 80*(1–2): 11–24.

Latu, I., Schmid Mast, M., Lammers, J. and Bombari, D. 2013. 'Successful female leaders empower women's behavior in leadership tasks'. *Journal of Experimental Social Psychology, 49*: 444–48.

Lawson, M. 2020. 'Vision: How Covid news topped the TV ratings'. *The Guardian.* December 23. https://www.theguardian.com/tv-and-radio/2020/dec/23/tv-news -2020-covid-ratings-dominic-cummings Accessed 13 January 2024.

Le Doeuff, M. 2005. *The Sex of Knowing.* London: Routledge.

Lean in Girls (@leaningirls). no date. Twitter account. https://twitter.com/leaningirls.

Lean In Girls. 2023a. https://www.leaningirls.org/ Accessed 11 November 2023.

Lean In Girls. 2023b. *Challenging Stereotypes & Inspiring Girls to Go for It.* https://www.leaningirls.org/program-curriculum#_ Accessed 11 November 2023.

Lee, Kyung Sen and Chen, Wenhong. 2017. 'A long shadow: Cultural capital, techno-capital and networking skills of college students'. *Computers in Human Behavior,* 70: 67–73.

Lee-Koo, K. and Pruitt, L. 2020. 'Building a theory of young women's leadership'. In *Young Women and Leadership*, edited By Katrina Lee-Koo and Lesley Pruitt,7–25. London: Routledge.

Leonard, Tom. 2019. 'How Meghan's favourite avocado snack - beloved of all millennials - is fuelling human rights abuses, drought and murder'. 22 January. *Mail Online.* https://www.dailymail.co.uk/news/article-6621047/How-Meghans-favourite-avocado-snack-fuelling-human-rights-abuses-drought-murder.html

Lewis, P. 2014. 'Postfeminism, femininities and organization studies: Exploring a new agenda'. *Organization Studies, 35*: 1845–66.

Lipsitz, G. 2013. '"Home is where the hatred is": Work, music, and the transnational economy'. In *Home, Exile, Homeland*, edited by Hamid Namicy, 193–212. London: Routledge.

Littler, Jo. 2004. 'Celebrity and 'meritocracy''. *Soundings: A Journal of Politics and Culture, 26*: 118–30.

Littler, Jo. 2018. *Against Meritocracy: Culture, Power and Myths of Mobility.* Abingdon: Routledge.

Litwiller, Fenton. 2020. 'Normative drag culture and the making of precarity'. *Leisure Studies, 39*(4): 600–12.

Liu, Y., Wu, Z., Wang, Y., Dong, Z., Sun, Z. and Gan, Y. 2023. 'Neoliberalism and governmental and individual responses to the COVID-19 pandemic: A cross-national analysis'. *Political Psychology, 45*(2): 363–82.

Livingstone S., Bober M. and Helsper E.J. 2005. 'Active participation or just more information? Young people's take up of opportunities to act and interact on the internet'. *Information, Communication & Society, 8:* 287–314.

Lorde, Audre. 1984. *The Master's Tools Will Never Dismantle the Master's House Sister Outsider: Essays and Speeches*, 110–13. Berkeley: Crossing.

Lordi, E. 2017. 'Close-up: Beyoncé: Media and cultural icon: Surviving the hustle: Beyoncé's performance of work'. *Black Camera: An International Film Journal, 9*(1): 131–45.

Louise Cook (@CookeLouise). 2020. 'Investment funds managed by women are more careful, more risk averse'. *Twitter.* April 9. https://twitter.com/CookeLouise/status/1248190809201152005.

Lu, J.H. and Steele, C.K. 2019. 'Joy is resistance': Cross-platform resilience and (re)invention of Black oral culture online'. *Information, Communication & Society, 22*(6): 823–37.

Lumsden, K. and Morgan, H.M. 2018. 'Cyber-trolling as symbolic violence: Deconstructing gendered abuse online'. In *The Routledge Handbook of Gender and Violence,* edited by Nancy Lombard, 1–132. London: Routledge.

Lybbert, Travis J. and Wydick, Bruce 2019. 'Hope as aspirations, agency, and pathways: Poverty dynamics and microfinance in Oaxaca, Mexico'. In *The Economics of Poverty Traps,* edited by Christopher B. Barrett, Michael R. Carter and Jean-Paul Chavas, 153–77. National Bureau of Economic Research. Available at https://www.nber.org/books/barr-3.

MacKenzie, C. and Garavan, T. 2023. 'Political leadership during the COVID-19 pandemic: Paradox, politics, power and compassion'. *Leadership in a Post-COVID Pandemic World*, edited by David McGuire and Marie-Line Germain,125. Berlin: De Gruyter.

Maira, S. and Soep, E. 2004. 'United States of adolescence? Reconsidering US youth culture studies'. *Young, 12*(3): 245–69.

Malik, K. 2019. 'Sure, defend Meghan from racists, but let's not bow to the monarchy'. *The Guardian.* August 24. https://www.theguardian.com/commentisfree/2019/aug/24/sure-defend-meghan-markle-from-racists-but-lets-not-bow-to-monarchy Accessed 12 January 2024.

Malik, N. 2020. 'Britain's racism pantomime: Now starring Meghan and Harry'. *The Guardian.* https://www.theguardian.com/commentisfree/2020/jan/13/britain-racism-media-harry-meghan Accessed 12 January 2024.

Malveaux, E. 2015. *The Color Line: A History.* Bloomingtoton: Xlibris Corporation.

Mance, H. 2016. 'Britain has had enough of experts, says Gove'. *Financial Times.* June 3. www.ft.com/content/3be49734-29cb-11e6–83e4-abc22d5d108c Accessed 12 January 2024.

Manne, Kate. 2018. *Down Girl: The Logic of Misogyny.* Oxford: OUP.

Mantilla, Karla. 2013. 'Gendertrolling: Misogyny adapts to new media'. *Feminist Studies, 39*(2): 563–70.

Marren, C. and Bazely, A. 2022. 'Sex and Power 2022'. *The Fawcett Society.* https://equalityleaders.com/wp-content/uploads/2022/02/Sex-and-Power2022-min.pdf

Markham, T. 2015. 'Celebrity advocacy and public engagement: The divergent uses of celebrity'. *International Journal of Cultural Studies, 18*(4): 467–80.

Martin, D.G., Hanson, S. and Fontaine, D. 2007. 'What counts as activism?: The role of individuals in creating change'. *Women's Studies Quarterly, 35*(3/4): 78–94.

Marsh, D., Hart, P. and Tindall, K. 2010. 'Celebrity politics: The politics of the late modernity?' *Political Studies Review, 8*(3): 322–40.

Marshall, P.D. 2014. *Celebrity and Power: Fame in Contemporary Culture.* Minneapolis: University of Minnesota Press.

Masciandaro, Donato, Profeta, Paola and Romelli, Davide. 2016. 'Gender and monetary policymaking: Trends and drivers'. *BAFFI CAREFIN Centre Research Paper No. 2015–12.* Available at SSRN: https://ssrn.com/abstract=2683917.

Mason, Rowena. 2024. 'Biggest Tory donor said looking at Diane Abbott makes you "want to hate all black women"'. *The Guardian.* 11 March. https://www.theguardian.com/politics/2024/mar/11/biggest-tory-donor-looking-diane-abbott-hate-all-black-women.

Mathew B.Eng (@UK_Engineer_Mat). 2020. 'I believe Singapore's response is also headed by a women epidemiologist (not some useless male ego driven politician)'. *Twitter.* April 9. https://twitter.com/UK_Engineer_Mat/status/1248216026866728960.

Matt_Oslo (@OsloMatt). 2020. 'Perhaps the women have had to work to the top instead having privilege to ease their promotion. Suffering and caring may bring better understanding than an expensive education. Elitism has little to offer when you discover you are human and fallible'. *Twitter.* April 9. https://twitter.com/OsloMatt/status/1248172798184431616&sa=D&source=docs&ust =1711039282800008&usg=AOvVaw3KeL4cENrmiSsifP4-xosS.

Mavin, S. and Grandy, G. 2016. 'Women elite leaders doing respectable business femininity: How privilege is conferred, contested and defended through the body'. *Gender, Work & Organization, 23*: 379–96.

McClennen, S.A. 2021. 'Trump's ironic effect on political satire'. *Film Quarterly, 75*(2): 27–37.

McClintock, E.A. 2016. 'The psychology of mansplaining'. *Psychology Today.* https://www.psychologytoday.com/us/blog/it-s-man-s-and-woman-s-world /201603/thepsychology-mansplaining.

McGarry, Orla. 2016. 'Repositioning the research encounter: Exploring power dynamics and positionality in youth research'. *International Journal of Social Research Methodology, 19*(3): 339–54.

McGee, M. 2005. *Self-help, Inc.: Makeover Culture in American Life.* Oxford: Oxford University Press.

McIntosh, I. and Wright, S. 2019. 'Exploring what the notion of 'lived experience' offers for social policy analysis'. *Journal of Social Policy, 48*(3): 449–67.

McLarney, E. 2019. 'Beyoncé's soft power: Poetics and politics of an afro-diasporic aesthetics'. *Camera Obscura: Feminism, Culture, and Media Studies, 34*(2): 1–39.

McLaughlin, T. H. 2000. 'Citizenship education in England: The Crick report and beyond'. *Journal of Philosophy of Education, 34*(4): 541–70.

McLeod, Douglas M., Eveland, William P. Jr. and Nathanson, Amy I. 1997. 'Support for censorship of violent and misogynic rap lyrics: An analysis of the third-person effect'. *Communication Research, 24*(2): 153–74.

McQuail, Denis. 2010. *Mass Communication Theory: An Introduction.* London: SAGE Publications.

McRobbie, Angela. 2008. 'Young women and consumer culture: An intervention'. *Cultural Studies, 22*(5): 531–50.

McRobbie, Angela. 2009. *The Aftermath of Feminism: Gender, Culture and Social Change.* London: Sage

McRobbie, Angela. 2013. 'Feminism, the Family and the New 'Mediated' Maternalism'. *New Formations, 80–81*: 119–37.

McRobbie, Angela. 2020. *Feminism and the Politics of 'Resilience': Essays on Gender, Media and the End of Welfare.* New Jersey: John Wiley & Sons.

Meadows, Ruthie. 2022: 'Queer cuarentena and mandinga times: Rita Indiana, Caribbean artivism, and LGBTQ+ social media spheres during COVID-19'. In *LGBTQ Digital Cultures,* edited by Paromita Pain, 8–23. New York: Routledge.

Meagher, K., Singh, N.S. and Patel, P. 2020. 'The role of gender inclusive leadership during the COVID-19 pandemic to support vulnerable populations in conflict settings'. *BMJ Global Health, 5*(9): e003760.

Medina-Vicent, M. 2020. 'A tendency to essentialism? Discourses about women's leadership'. *Social Sciences, 9*(8): 130.

Mendes, Kaitlynn, Ringrose, Jessica and Keller, Jessalynn. 2019. *Digital Feminist Activism: Girls and Women Fight Back Against Rape Culture.* Oxford: Oxford University Press.

Mendick, H., Ahmad, A., Allen, K. and Harvey, L. 2018. *Celebrity, Aspiration and Contemporary Youth: Education and Inequality in an era of Austerity.* London: Bloomsbury Publishing.

Mendick, H., Allen, K. and Harvey, L. 2015. 'Turning to the empirical audience: The desired but denied object of celebrity studies?'. *Celebrity Studies, 6*(3): 374–77.

Merleau-Ponty, Maurice. 1965. 'Phenomenology of perception'. Translated by Colin Smith. In *Central Works of Philosophy v4: Twentieth Century: Moore to Popper,* edited by John Shand. Routledege, 2015.

Merrik, J. 2019. 'General election 2019: Jeremy Corbyn suggests royal family should be cut in size'. *inews.* https://inews.co.uk/news/politics/general-election-2019-jeremy-corbyn-royal-family-cut-size-prince-andrew-1328995.

Merrin, W. 2021. 'Save the troll! UK social media legislation and the attack on freedom of speech'. In *Capitalism, Crime and Media in the 21st Century,* edited by N. Ewen, N.Grattan, M. Leaning, and P. Manning, 205–32. Cham: Palgrave Macmillan.

Meyer, D.S. 1995. 'The challenge of cultural elites: Celebrities and social movements'. *Sociological inquiry, 65*(2): 181–206.

Mikel-Brown, Lyn. 1998. *Raising their Voices: The Politics of Girls' Anger.* London and Cambridge: Harvard University Press.

Miller, Carolyn R. 1994. 'Rhetorical community: The cultural basis of genre'. In *Genre and the New Rhetoric,* edited by Aviva Freeman and Peter Medway, 67–78. Milton Park: Taylor and Francis.

Mirowski, Philip. 2014. *Never Let a Serious Crisis Go To Waste: How Neoliberalism Survived the Financial Meltdown.* London: Verso.

Mirza, Heidi Safia and Meetoo, Veena. 2018. 'Empowering Muslim girls? Post-feminism, multiculturalism and the production of the 'model' Muslim female student in British schools'. *British Journal of Sociology of Education, 39*(2): 227–41.

Mishler, E.G. 1991. *Research Interviewing: Context and Narrative.* Cambridge: Harvard University Press.

Mizejewski, L. 2014. *Pretty/funny: Women Comedians and Body Politics.* Texas: University of Texas Press.

Morani, Marina, Cushion, Stephen, Kyriakidou, Maria and Soo, Nikki. 2022. 'Expert voices in the news reporting of the coronavirus pandemic: A study of UK television news bulletins and their audiences'. *Journalism, 23*(12): 2513–32.

Morris, E.W. 2007. '"Ladies" or "loudies"? Perceptions and experiences of Black girls in classrooms'. *Youth & Society, 38*(4): 490–515.

Muir, Kathie. 2000. 'Tough choices: News media accounts of women union leaders'. *Hecate, 26*(2): 10–30. https://search.informit.com.au/documentSummary;dn=200106042;res=IELAPA.

Muragishi, G.A., Aguilar, L., Carr, P.B. and Walton, G.M. 2023. 'Microinclusions: Treating women as respected work partners increases a sense of fit in technology companies'. *Journal of Personality and Social Psychology, 126*(3): 431–60. Advance online publication. https://doi.org/10.1037/pspi0000430.

Murphy, M.C. and Taylor, V.J. 2012. 'The role of situational cues in signaling and maintaining stereotype threat'. In *Stereotype Threat: Theory, Process, and Applications*, edited by M. Inzlichtand Schmader, 17–33. Oxford: Oxford University Press.

Nairn, T., 2011. *The Enchanted Glass: Britain and Its Monarchy*. London: Verso Books.

Nash, Meredith and Moore, Robyn. 2019. ''I was completely oblivious to gender': An exploration of how women in STEMM navigate leadership in a neoliberal, postfeminist context'. *Journal of Gender Studies, 28*(4): 449–61.

National curriculum in England: English programmes of study 2014. https://www.gov.uk/government/publications/national-curriculum-in-england-english-programmes-of-study

National Literacy Trust. no date. *Words for Work*. Available at https://literacytrust.org.uk/programmes/words-for-work/words-work-women-leadership/ N.D.

Nauta, M.M. and Kokaly, M.L. 2001. 'Assessing role model influences on students' academic and career decisions'. *Journal of Career Assessment, 9:* 81–9.

Negra, D. and Tasker, Y. 2014. *Gendering the Recession: Media and Culture in an Age of Austerity*. Durham: Duke University Press.

Nerlich, B. 2022. 'Metaphors in times of a global pandemic'. In *Metaphors and Analogies in Sciences and Humanities: Words and Worlds*, edited by S. Wuppuluri, and A. Grayling, 421–46. Cham: Springer International Publishing.

Neumann, E., Gewirtz, S., Maguire, M. and Towers, E. 2020. 'Neoconservative education policy and the case of the English Baccalaureate'. *Journal of Curriculum Studies, 52*(5): 702–19.

Newman, Janet. 2015. 'Austerity, aspiration and the politics of hope'. *Compass.* 3 June. http://www.compassonline.org.uk/austerity-aspiration-and-the-politics-of-hope/.

Newman, Cathy. 2017. Rishi Sunak thanking 'mums' for juggling childcare and work is an insult to women – and men. *The Independent*. 28 January. https://www.independent.co.uk/voices/rishi-sunak-women-childcare-cathy-newman-b1794180.html

Newton, Esther. 1979. *Mother Camp: Female Impersonators in America*. Chicago: University of Chicago Press.

Nguyen, A. 2017. 'Presentation given at "keeping up with the Windsors: The peculiar celebrity of the British royal family'. *Celebrity Culture Club event at the BBC*. 29 August https://celebritycultureclub.com/keeping-up-with-the-windsors-the-peculiar-celebrity-of-the-british-royal-family.

Nielsen. 2019. '2019 Gender Pay Gap report'. *Nielsen News Centre*. April 2019.

Norris, P. and Inglehart, R. 2003. *Rising Tide: Gender Equality and Cultural Change Around the World*. Cambridge: Cambridge University Press.

Norris, P. and Inglehart, R. 2007. 'Cracking the marble ceiling: Cultural barriers facing women leaders. Presented at conference on women and news: Expanding the news audience, increasing political participation, and informing citizens'. Paper presented for the Shorenstein Center on the Press, Politics and Public Policy at the John F. Kennedy School of Government, Harvard University. https://sites.hks.harvard.edu/fs/pnorris/Acrobat/Marble%20ceiling.pdf.

Oakley, Ann. 2018. *The Sociology of Housework.* Bristol: Policy Press.

Obama, Michelle. 2009. 'Speech given at Elizabeth Garret Anderson School, Islington, London'. *Channel 4 News.* April 2. http://www.channel4.com/news/articles/society/michelles%2bmessage%2bof%2bhope/3064817.html.

OECD 2023. *Toolkit for Mainstreaming and Implementing Gender Equality 2023.* PARIS OECD Publishing. https://doi.org/10.1787/3ddef555-en.

Ofcom. 2021. 'Children's media lives: Year 7 findings'. April 28. https://www.ofcom.org.uk/__data/assets/pdf_file/0027/217827/childrens-media-lives-year-7.pdf.

Ofcom. 2022. 'Children's Media Lives: Year 8 findings'. March 30. https://www.ofcom.org.uk/__data/assets/pdf_file/0021/234552/childrens-media-lives-2022-summary report.pdf.

O'Keefe, Brian (@rider45). 2020. 'Is there an 'empathy' angle to this too? Are women leaders perhaps more empathetic, prioritising 'protecting lives' above anything else?' *Twitter.* April 9. https://twitter.com/rider45.

O'Malley Greenburg, Z. 2019. 'Jay-Z And Beyoncénow have a combined $1.4 billion net worth'. *Forbes.* June 4. https://www.forbes.com/sites/zackomalleygreenburg/2019/06/04/jay-z-and-beyonc-now-have-a-combined-14-billion-net-worth/#4af7c86e323f.

Oprysko, Caitlin and Luthi, Susannah. 2020. 'Trump labels himself 'a wartime president' combating coronavirus'. *Politico.* March 18. https://www.politico.com/news/2020/03/18/trump-administration-self-swab-coronavirus-tests-135590.

Otnes, C. and Maclaran, P. 2015. *Royal Fever.* Oakland: University of California Press.

Ouellette, L. and Wilson, J. 2011. 'Women's work: Affective labour and convergence culture'. *Cultural Studies,* 25(4–5): 548–65.

Parks, E.S. 2018. *The Ethics of Listening: Creating Space for Sustainable Dialogue.* Lanham: Lexington Books.

Parmanand, S. 2020. 'The dangers of masculinity contests in a time of pandemic'. *Oxford Political Review.* https://oxfordpoliticalreview.com/2020/04/18/the-dangers-of-masculinity-contests-in-a-time-of-pandemic/, Accessed 12 January 2024.

Patterson, Natasha and Sears, Camilla A. 2011. 'Letting men off the hook? Domestic violence and postfeminist celebrity culture'. *Genders,* 53.

Paule, Michele. 2017. *Girlhood, Schools, and Media: Popular Discourses of the Achieving Girl.* London: Routledge.

Paule, Michele. 2019. 'Girl trouble: Not the ideal neoliberal subject'. In *Interrogating the Neoliberal Lifecycle: The Limits of Success,* edited by Beverley Clack and Michele Paule, 67–93. Basingstoke: Palgrave Macmillan.

Paustian-Underdahl, S.C., Walker, L.S. and Woehr, D.J. 2014. 'Gender and perceptions of leadership effectiveness: A meta-analysis of contextual moderators'. *Journal of Applied Psychology,* 99(6): 1129.

Pereira, A. 2012. *Leadership: Collaborative Not Confrontational: Understanding Leadership from the Perspectives of Angami Women Leaders* (Doctoral dissertation, Creighton University).

Perloff, R.M. 2014. 'Social media effects on young women's body image concerns: Theoretical perspectives and an Agenda for research'. *Sex Roles, 71*(11–12): 363–77.

Petersen, S., Pearson, B.Z. and Moriarty, M.A. 2020. 'Amplifying voices: Investigating a cross-institutional, mutual mentoring program for URM women in STEM'. *Innovative Higher Education, 45*: 317–32.

Phillips, Louise, Kristiansen, Marianne, Vehviläinen, Marja and Gunnarson, Ewa. 2013. 'Tackling the tensions of dialogue and participation'. In *Knowledge and Power in Collaborative Research: A Reflexive Approach*, edited by Louise Phillips, Marianne Kristiansen, Marja Vehviläinen and Ewa Gunnarsson, 1–18. London: Routledge.

Pickard, S. 2019. 'Political parties, political leaders, youth policies and young people'. *Politics, Protest and Young People: Political Participation and Dissent in 21st Century Britain*, 157–94. London: Palgrave Macmillan.

Pickersgill, Martin. 2013. 'The Social Life of the Brain: Neuroscience in Society'. *Current Sociology, 61*(3): 322–40

Piispa, M. and Kiilakoski, T. 2022, 'Towards climate justice? Young climate activists in Finland on fairness and moderation'. *Journal of Youth Studies, 25*(7): 897–912.

Pineiro, F.A. 2023. 'The social media marketing goldmine: TikTok advertising revenue surges 155% in a year'. *Startups.* July 28. https://startups.co.uk/news/tik-tok-ad-revenue-155/.

Piontek, Thomas. 2003. 'Kinging in the heartland; or, the power of marginality'. *Journal of Homosexuality, 43*(3–4): 125–43.

*Pitch Perfect.* 2012. Directed by Jason Moore. Goldcircle Films and Brownstone Productions.

Pollock, Griselda. 1993. 'The politics of theory: Generations and geographies feminist theory and the histories of art histories'. *Genders, 17*: 55.

Pomerantz, S., Raby, R. and Stefanik, A. 2013. 'Girls run the world?: Caught between sexism and postfeminism in school'. *Gender & Society, 27*(2): 185–207. https://doi.org/10.1177/0891243212473199.

Pratto, F., Sidanius, J., Stallworth, L.M. and Malle, B.F. 1994. 'Social dominance orientation: A personality variablerelevant to social roles and intergroup relation's. *Journal of Personality and Social Psychology, 67*: 741–63.

Projansky, S. 2007. 'Mass magazine cover girls'. In *Interrogating Postfeminism: Gender and the Politics of Popular Culture*, edited by Yvonne Tasker and Diane Negram, 40–69. Durham: Duke.

Projansky, S. 2014. *Spectacular Girls: Media Fascination and Celebrity Culture.* New York: New York University Press.

Prügl, Elisabeth. 2012. ''If Lehman brothers had been Lehman sisters...': Gender and myth in the aftermath of the financial crisis'. *International Political Sociology, 6*(1): 21–35.

Pullen, A. and Vachhani, S.J. 2021. 'Feminist ethics and women leaders: From difference to intercorporeality'. *Journal of Business Ethics, 173*(2): 233–43.

Putnam, L.L., Fairhurst, G.T. and Banghart, S. 2016. 'Contradictions, dialectics, and paradoxes in organizations: A constitutive approach'. *Academy of Management Annals, 10*(1): 65–171.

QCA. 1998. *Report of the Advisory Group on Citizenship Final Report.* Qualifications and Curriculum Authority, London, September 22.

Quinn, David. 2020. 'David Quinn: Mass hysteria over Covid health and safety in church'. *The Times.* May 10. https://www.thetimes.co.uk/article/david-quinn-mass -hysteria-over-covid-health-and-safety-in-church-tc9qrg78g Accessed 12 January 2024.

Raco, Mike. 2009. 'From expectations to aspirations: State modernisation, urban policy, and the existential politics of welfare in the UK'. *Political Geography, 28*(7): 436–44.

Ramati, Ido and Abeliovich Ruthie. 2022. 'Use this sound: Networked ventriloquism on Yiddish TikTok'. *New Media & Society, 26*(9): 14614448221135159.

Randa, I.O. 2022. 'Integrated reporting for inclusive and sustainable global capitalism'. In *Handbook of Research on Global Institutional Roles for Inclusive Development,* edited by Isaac Okoth Randa, 175–97. Pennsylvania: IGI Global.

Randall, V. 2016. 'Intersecting identities: Old age and gender in local party politics'. *Parliamentary Affairs, 69*(3): 531–547.

Rawlinson, Kevin. 2020. '"This enemy can be deadly": Boris Johnson invokes wartime language'. *The Guardian.* March 17. https://www.theguardian.com/world /2020/mar/30/tp-captain-corona Accessed 13 January 2024.

Read, Barbara. 2011. 'Britney, Beyoncé, and me – primary school girls' role models and constructions of the "popular" girl'. *Gender and Education, 2*(1): 1–13.

Reed, E. 2020. *The Perceived Impact of Austerity on Young People of Colour's (YPOC) Psychological Wellbeing and Education in the UK.* Great Britain: The University of Manchester (United Kingdom).

Regueira, Uxía, González-Villa, Ángela and Martínez-Piñeiro, Esther. 2023. 'Selfies and videos of teenagers: The role of gender, territory, and sociocultural level'. *Comunicar, 31*(75): 59–71.

Reinharz, S. and Chase, S.E. 2002. 'Interviewing women'. In *Handbook of Interview Research: Context and Method,* edited by Jaber F and Gubrium, 221–38. London: Sage.

Rendall, J. 1999. 'Women and the public sphere'. *Gender & History, 11*(3): 475–88.

Rhee, Kenneth S. and Sigler, Tracey H. 2015. 'Untangling the relationship between gender and leadership'. *Gender in Management: An International Journal, 30*(2): 109–34.

Rheingold, H. 2008. 'Using participatory media and public voice to encourage civic engagement'. In *Civic Life Online: Learning How Digital Media Can Engage Youth,* edited by W. L. Bennett, 1–14. Cambridge: The MIT Press.

Richards, J., Woodhead, L. and Wilson, S. (eds). 1999. *Diana, the Making of a Media Saint.* London: IB Tauris.

Richards, Rebecca S. 2015. *Transnational Rhetorics and Gendered Leadership in Global Politics: From Daughters of Destiny to Iron Ladies.* London: Rowman Littlefield.

Rimke, H. 2020. 'Self-help, therapeutic industries, and neoliberalism'. In *The Routledge International Handbook of Global Therapeutic Cultures*, edited by D. Nehring, J. Ole Madsen, E. Cabanas, C. Mills, and D. Kerrigan, 37–50. London: Routledge.

Ringrose, J. 2007. 'Successful girls? Complicating post-feminist, neoliberal discourses of educational achievement and gender equality'. *Gender and Education, 19*(4), 471–89.

Ringrose, J., 2012. *Postfeminist Education?: Girls and the Sexual Politics of Schooling.* London: Routledge.

Ringrose, J. and Eriksson Barajas, K. 2011. 'Gendered risks and opportunities? Exploring teen girls' digital sexual identity in postfeminist media contexts'. *International Journal of Media and Cultural Politics, Special Issue: Postfeminism and the Mediation of Sex, 7*(2): 121–38.

Rippin, A. 2007. 'Stitching up the leader: Empirically based reflections on leadership and gender'. *Journal of Organizational Change Management, 20*(2): 209–26.

Ritschel, C. 2020. 'Prince Harry reportedly pitched Meghan Markle for voice-overs to Disney CEO'. *The Independent.* January 13. https://www.independent.co .uk/life-style/prince-harry-meghan-markle-video-voice-over-disney-royal-family -a9282216.html.

Roberts, A. 2015. 'Gender, financial deepening and the production of embodied finance: Towards a critical feminist analysis'. *Global Society, 29*(1): 107–27.

Robertson, Regina. 2020. 'Meet the comedian behind the 'How to Medical' TikTok everyone is sharing'. *Essence,* https://www.essence.com/entertainment/sarah-cooper-comedian-donald-trump-how-to-medical/ Accessed 12 January 2024.

Robson, Ruthann. 2020. 'The sexual misconduct of Donald J. Trump: Toward a misogyny report'. *Michigan Journal of Gender & Law, 27*: 81.

Rodger, G.M. 2018. *Just One of the Boys: Female-to-Male Cross-Dressing on the American Variety Stage.* Illinois: University of Illinois Press.

Rogers, L.O., Butler Barnes, S., Sahaguian, L., Padilla, D. and Minor, I. 2021. '# BlackGirlMagic: Using multiple data sources to learn about Black adolescent girls' identities, intersectionality, and media socialization'. *Journal of Social Issues, 77*(4): 1282–304.

Rorty, Richard. 1998. *Achieving Our Country: Leftist Thought in Twentieth Century America.* Cambridge: Harvard University Press.

Rose, Nikolas. 1999. *Governing the Soul: The Shaping of the Private Self.* London: Routledge.

Rose, J. and Baird, J.A. 2013. 'Aspirations and an austerity state: Young people's hopes and goals for the future'. *London Review of Education, 11*(2): 157–73.

Ross, Karen. 2002. *Women, Politics, Media: Uneasy Relations in Comparative Perspective.* Cresskill, NJ: Hampton Press.

Ross, Karen, Evans, Elizabeth, Harrison, Lisa, Shears, Mary and Wadia, Khursheed. 2013. 'The gender of news and news of gender: A study of sex, politics, and press coverage of the 2010 British General Election'. *The International Journal of Press/ Politics, 18*(1): 3–20.

Ross, Karen. 2002. *Women, Politics, Media: Uneasy Relations in Comparative Perspective*. Cresskill: Hampton Press.

Rottenberg, Catherine. 2014. 'The rise of neoliberal feminism'. *Cultural Studies, 28*(3): 418–37.

Rottenberg, Catherine. 2018. *The Rise of Neoliberal Feminism*. Oxford: OUP.

Rowbottom, A. 1998. '"The real royalists": Folk performance and civil religion at royal visits'. *Folklore, 109*(1–2): 77–88.

Roy, E.A. 2019. ''Nothing else matters': school climate strikes sweep New Zealand'. *The Guardian*. September 2019. https://amp.theguardian.com/environment/2019/sep/27/nothing-else-matters-school-climate-strikes-sweep-new-zealand

Royston, J. 2020. 'How much is Meghan Markle and Prince Harry's spotify deal worth?'. *Newsweek*, 12/16/20. https://www.newsweek.com/how-much-meghan-markle-prince-harry-spotify-deal-worth-archewell-audio-1554984#:~:text=Over%20the%20summer%2C%20they%20signed,adding%20to%20their%20growing%20fortune. Accessed 2 January 2022.

Rozsika, Parker and Griselda, Pollock. 1981. *Old Mistresses: Women, Art, and Ideology*. London: Harper Collins Publishers.

Said, E. 1978. *Orientalism*. London: Routledge.

Sales, Nancy Jo. 2016. *American Girls: Social Media and the Secret Lives of Teenagers*. New York: Vintage.

Salmond, K and Fleshman, P. 2010. 'The development of children's perceptions of leadership'. In *Gender and Women's Leadership: A Reference Handbook*, edited by K. O'Connor, 11–19. Thousand Oaks: SAGE Publications.

Sammons, P. 1995. 'Gender, ethnic and socio-economic differences in attainment and progress: A longitudinal analysis of student achievement over 9 years'. *British Educational Research Journal, 21*(4): 465–85.

Sandberg, Sheryl. 2013. *Lean In: Women, Work and the Will to Lead*. New York: Knopf.

Sandberg, Sheryl. 2014. *Ban Bossy*. http://banbossy.com/ Accessed 2 January 2022.

Sanbonmatsu, K., Carroll, S. and Walsh, D. 2000. '*Poised to Run: Women's Pathways to the State Legislatures*. New Brunswick: Center for American Women and Politics, Eagleton Institute of Politics, Rutger

Sanghera, G. and Thapar-Björkert, S. 2007. '"Because I am Pakistani... and I am Muslim... I am Political"–Gendering political radicalism: Young femininities in Bradford'. In *Islamic Political Radicalism: A European Perspective*, edited by Tahir Abbas, 173–91. Edinburgh: Edinburgh University Press.

Santoro, E. and Markus, H.R. 2021. 'How do you listen?: The relationship between how men listen and women's power and respect in the US'. psyarxiv.com. https://psyarxiv.com/4ycf7/.

Savage, M., Bagnall, G. and. Longhurst, B. 2001. 'Ordinary, ambivalent and defensive: Class identities in the Northwest of England'. *Sociology, 35*(4): 875–92.

Scardigno, Fausta. 2009. 'The informal choices of Italian young people: Between increase and erosion of family cultural capital'. *Italian Journal of Sociology of Education, 2*: 230–52.

Scott, J. 1992, 'Experience'. In *Feminists Theorize the Political*, edited by J. Butler and J.W Scott, 31–47. London: Routledge.

Scott, A.O. and Dargis, M. 2015. 'Heavy-hitting heroines'. *The New York Times.* July 5 1-L.

Scott, Kylie (@dearkyliescott). 2020. 'Ur doing great sweetie'. *TikTok*, April 15. https://www.TikTok.com/@kyscottt/video/6815758866769349894.

Scotto di Carlo, Giuseppina. 2020. 'Trumping twitter: Sexism in president trump's tweets'. *Journal of Language and Politics, 19*(1): 48–70.

Sennett, J. and Bay-Cheng, S. 2003. '"I am the man!" Performing gender and other incongruities'. *Journal of Homosexuality, 43*(3–4): 39–48.

Shaffner, J. 2020. 'Over 50 groups launch vision for U.S. Feminist Foreign Policy, ICRW'. https://www.icrw.org/press-releases/over-50-groups-launch-vision-for-a-u-s-feminist-foreign-policy/ Accessed 13 January 2024.

Shain, Farzana. 2013. '"The girl effect": Exploring narratives of gendered impacts and opportunities in neoliberal development'. *Sociological Research Online, 18*(2): 1–11.

Sheppard, L.D. 2018. 'Gender differences in leadership aspirations and job and life attribute preferences among U.S. undergraduate students'. *Sex Roles, 79*(9–10): 565–77.

Shields Dobson, Amy and Kanai, Akane. 2018. 'From 'can-do' girls to insecure and angry: Affective dissonances in young women's post-recessional media'. *Feminist Media Studies, 19*(6): 771–86. https://doi.org/10.1080/14680777.2018.1546206.

Shinew, D.M. and Jones, D.T. 2005. '"Girl talk: Adolescent girls' perceptions of leadership'. In *Geographies of Girlhood: Identities in-between*, edited by Pamela J. Bettis and Natalie G. Adams, 55–67. London: Routledge.

Shome, R. 2001. 'White femininity and the discourse of the nation: Re/membering Princess Diana'. *Feminist Media Studies, 1*(3): 323–42.

Shome, R. 2014. *Diana and Beyond: White Femininity, National Identity, and Contemporary Media Culture*. Illinois: University of Illinois Press.

Short, Lucy R. 2015. 'Still haunted: Tending to The ghosts of marriage and motherhood in white feminist critiques of Beyoncé Knowles-Carter and Michelle Obama'. *Tapestries: Interwoven Voices of Local and Global Identities, 4*(1): Article 22. http://digitalcommons.macalester.edu/tapestries/vol4/iss1/22.

Silva, E. 2001. '"Squeaky wheels and flat tires': A case study of students as reform participants'. *Forum, 43*(2), 95–9

Silva, E.M. 2002. *The Broken Mic: Student Struggles for Voice, Power and Position in Urban School Reform*, (Thesis, University of California).

Simon, S. and Hoyt, C.L. 2013. 'Exploring the effect of media images on women's leadership self-perceptions and aspirations'. *Group Processes and Intergroup Relations, 16*: 232–45.

Sinclair, A. 2013. 'Can I really be me? The challenges for women leaders constructing authenticity'. In *Authentic Leadership: Concepts, Coalescences and Clashes*, edited by D. D. Ladkin and C. Spiller, 239–52. Auckland University Press.

Sinclair, Amanda. 2014. 'A feminist case for leadership'. In D*iversity in Leadership: Australian Women, Past and Present,* edited by Joy Damousi, Kim Rubenstein and Mary Tomsic, 1–35. Australian National University Press. http://press.anu.edu.au/titles/diversity-in-leadership/.

Singh, V.S., Vinnicombe, S. and James, K. 2006. 'Constructing a professional identity: How young female managers use role models2'. *Women in Management Review, 21*: 67–81.

Skeggs, B. and Wood, H. 2008. 'The labour of transformation and circuits of value 'around' reality television'. *Continuum: Journal of Media & Cultural Studies, 22*(4): 559–72.

Sky News. 2020. 'Murnaghan D. Ellen Johnson Sirleaf: 'The real heroes in fight against Covid-19 are women''. July 18. Available: at https:// news.sky.com/ story/ellen- johnson- sirleaf- the- real- heroines- in- fight- against- covid- 19- are-women-12025762 Accessed 2 January 2024.

Smith, S.M. 1999. *American Archives: Gender, Race, and Class in Visual Culture.* New Jersey: Princeton University Press.

Smith, Laura GE, Gavin, Jeffrey and Sharp, Elise. 2015. 'Social identity formation during the emergence of the occupy movement'. *European Journal of Social Psychology, 45*(7): 818–32.

Smooth, W. and Richardson, E. 2019. Role models matter: Black girls and political leadership possibilities. *The Black Girlhood Studies Collection*, edited by Aria S. Halliday,131–57. Ontario: Canadian Scholars' Press.

Solnit, R. 2012. 'Men explain things to me—Facts didn't get in the way. *HuffPost.* https://www.huffpost.com/entry/men-explain-things-to-me-_b_1811096.

Southwick, L., Guntuku, S.C., Klinger, E.V., Seltzer, E., McCalpin, H.J. and Merchant, R.M. 2021. 'Characterizing COVID-19 content posted to TikTok: Public sentiment and response during the first phase of the COVID-19 pandemic'. *Journal of Adolescent Health, 69*(2): 234–41.

Sparkmovement. no date. http://www.sparkmovement.org/agenda/feminist-clubs/ Accessed 2 January 2024.

Spence, L. 2015. *Knocking the Hustle: Against the Neoliberal Turn in Black Politics*, 20–1. Brooklyn: Punctum Books.

Spohrer, K., Stahl, G. and Bowers-Brown, T. 2018. 'Constituting neoliberal subjects? 'Aspiration' as technology of government in UK policy discourse'. *Journal of Education Policy, 33*(3): 327–42.

Stead, V. and Elliott, C. 2019. 'Pedagogies of power: Media artefacts as public pedagogy for women's leadership development'. *Management Learning, 50*(2): 171–88.

Steele, C. and Lu, J. 2018. 'Defying death: Black joy as resistance online'. In *A Networked Self and Birth, Life, Death,* edited by Zizi Papacharissi, 143–59. London: Routledge.

Steele, C.M., Spencer, S.J. and Aronson, J. 2002. 'Contending with group image: The psychology of stereotype and social identity threat'. *Advances in Experimental Social Psychology, 34:* 379–440. https://doi.org/10.1016/S0065-2601(02)80009-0.

Steinberg, Marc W. 1998. 'Tilting the frame: Considerations on collective action framing from a discursive turn'. *Theory and Society, 27*(6): 845–72.

Stevens, H. 2024. 'We need more women in local government'. *National Association of Local Councils*. 06 March 2024. https://www.nalc.gov.uk/news/entry/2834-we-need-more-women-in-local-government

Stockton, Kathryn B. 2009. *The Queer Child, or Growing Sideways in the Twentieth Century*. Durham: Duke University Press.

Storberg-Walker, Julia and Haber-Curran, Paige. 2017. *Theorising Women and Leadership*. Charlotte: IAP Inc.

Street, J. 2004. 'Celebrity politicians: Popular culture and political representation'. *British Journal of Politics & International Relations, 6*(4): 435–52.

Strong, G. 2020. 'Meghan Markle all smiles as she is pictured for the first time since leaving the UK' Hello Magazine'. https://www.hellomagazine.com/royalty/2020011583193/meghan-markle-spotted-first-time-canada/.

Swales, J.M. 1990. *Genre Analysis: English in Academic and Research Settings*. Cambridge: Cambridge University Press.

Switzer, H. 2013. 'Post-feminist development fables: The Girl Effect and the production of sexual subjects'. *Feminist Theory, 14*(3): 345–60.

Szameitat, A.J., Hamaida, Y., Tulley, R.S., Saylik, R. and Otermans, P.C. 2015. '"Women are better than men"–Public beliefs on gender differences and other aspects in multitasking'. *Plos one, 10*(10): e0140371.

Taft, Jessica. 2011. *Rebel Girls: Youth Activism and Social Change Across the Americas*. New York: NYUP.

Taft, Jessica. 2014. 'The political lives of girls'. *Sociology Compass, 8*(3): 259–67.

Taft, Jessica. 2020. 'Hopeful, harmless, and heroic: Figuring the girl activist as global savior'. *Girlhood Studies, 13*(2): 1–17.

Tan, K.H., Jospa, M.E.A.W., Mohd-Said, N.E. and Awang, M.M. 2021. 'Speak like a native English speaker or be judged: A scoping review'. *International Journal of Environmental Research and Public Health, 18*(23): 12754.

Tannen, D. 1997. 'There is no unmarked woman'. *Signs of Life in the USA*. Boston: Bedford books.

Taylor, C. 2004. *Modern Social Imaginaries*. Durham: Duke University Press.

Taylor, J. M., Gilligan, C. and Sullivan, A. 1995. *Between Voice and Silence: Women and Girls, Race and Relationship*. Cambridge: Harvard University Press.

Taylor, C.A., Lord, C.G., McIntyre, R.B. and Paulson, R.M. 2011. 'The Hillary Clinton effect: When the same role model inspires or fails to inspire improved performance under stereotype threat'. *Group Processes & Intergroup Relations, 14:* 447–59.

The Fawcett Society. 2022. 'Sex and Power 2022'. https://www.fawcettsociety.org.uk/sex-power-2022. Accessed 13 January 2024.

The Fawcett Society. 2023. 'A house for everyone: A case for modernising parliament'. https://www.fawcettsociety.org.uk/a-house-for-everyone.

The Female Lead (@the_female_lead). Twitter account. https://twitter.com/the_female_lead.

The Female Lead. 2017a. https://www.thefemalelead.com/ Accessed 2nd January 2022.

The Female Lead. 2017b. https://www.thefemalelead.com/get-involved Accessed 2nd January 2022.

The Female Lead. 2019a. *Classroom Resources.* https://www.thefemalelead.com/ new-female-lead-society-launches-in-schools-today Accessed 2nd January 2022.

The Female Lead: About Us. 2019b. https://www.thefemalelead.com/the-campaign Accessed 2nd January 2022.

The Guardian. 2016. 'Trump 'prowls' behind Clinton during presidential debate (pooled source)'. October 10. https://www.theguardian.com/us-news/video/2016/ oct/10/donald-trump-behind-hillary-clinton-debate-video.

The Jouker. 2024. 'Covid inquiry: Fake Nicola Sturgeon WhatsApp messages go viral'. *The National.* https://www.thenational.scot/news/24075288.covid-inquiry -fake-nicola-sturgeon-whatsapp-messages-go-viral/ Accessed 13 January 2024.

The UK Test. 2024. *Life in The UK Test 1.* https://www.theuktest.com/life-in-the-uk -test/1

Tischner, I., Malson, H. and Fey, K. 2021. 'Leading ladies: Discursive constructions of women leaders in the UK media'. *Feminist Media Studies, 21*(3): 460–76. https://doi.org/10.1080/14680777.2019.1640266.

Trilling, Lionel. 1972. *Sincerity and Authenticity.* Oxford: Oxford University Press.

Trump, Donald J. (@realdonaldtrump). 2020. 'Liberate Virginia'. *Twitter.* 17 April 17. https://twitter.com/realDonaldTrump/status/1251169987110330372.

Tseëlon, E. 1995. *The Masque of Femininity: The Presentation of Woman in Everyday Life.* London: Sage.

Turner, G. 2004. *Understanding Celebrity.* London: Sage.

Turner, G. 2010. 'Approaching celebrity studies'. *Celebrity Studies, 1*(1): 11–20.

Turner, J. 2014. 'Testing the liberal subject: (in) security, responsibility and 'self-improvement'in the UK citizenship test'. *Citizenship Studies, 18*(3–4), 332–48.

Tyler, I. 2008. '"Chav mum, chav scum": Class disgust in contemporary Britain'. *Feminist Media Studies, 8*(2): 17–34.

Tyler, I. and Bennett, B. 2010. '"Celebrity chav": Fame, femininity and social class'. *European Journal of Cultural Studies, 13*(3): 375–93.

Tyler, I. and Jensen, T. 2015. '"Benefits broods": The cultural and political crafting of anti-welfare commonsense'. *Critical Social Policy, 35*(4): 470–91.

UK Public General Acts. 2022. 'Police, crime, sentencing and courts act 2022'. https://www.legislation.gov.uk/ukpga/2022/32/contents/enacted Accessed 2 January 2022.

United Nations Women. 2020. 'Facts and figures: Leadership and political participation'. https://www.unwomen.org/en/what-we-do/leadership-and-political-particpation/facts-and-figures Accessed 2 January 2022.

Utley, E.A. 2017. 'What does Beyoncé mean to young girls?' *Journal of Popular Music Studies, 29*: e12212.

van Staveren, Irene. 2014. 'The Lehman Sisters hypothesis'. *Cambridge Journal of Economics, 38*(5): 995–1014.

van Zoonen, Liesbet. 2006. 'The personal, the political and the popular: A woman's guide to celebrity politics'. *European Journal of Cultural Studies, 9*(3): 287–301.

Vesey, A. 2018. 'Playing in the closet: Female rock musicians, fashion, and citational feminism'. In *Emergent Feminisms*, edited by Jessalyn Keller and Maureen E. Ryan, 73–89. New York: Routledge.

Vicinus, Martha. 2013. 'Fin-de-siècle theatrics: Male impersonation and lesbian desire'. In *Borderlines*, edited by Billie Melman, 163–92. New York: Routledge.

Vincent, M. 2020. 'Prince Harry and Meghan Markle's first 'holiday special' episode of their £30m Archewell Audio'. *Dailymail.com*, 31.12.20. https://www.dailymail.co.uk/news/article-9100835/Prince-Harry-Meghan-Markles-episode-30m-podcast-ranked-whale-noises.html.

WAGGGS. 2017. 'Leadership and opportunity for young women'. Presentation of ESRC-funded project findings for the Fawcett Society: Gender Equality Symposium, London. September 12.

Wall, A. 2001. 'On bringing Mikhail Bakhtin into the social sciences'. *Semiotica*. https://www.degruyter.com/document/doi/10.1515/semi.2001.005/html.

Wallace, M. 1990. *Black Macho and the Myth of the Superwoman*. New York: Verso.

Walkerdine, V. 1990. 'Difference, cognition, and mathematics education'. *For the Learning of Mathematics*, 10(3):51–6.

Ward, O. 2017. 'Intersectionality and press coverage of political campaigns: Representations of Black, Asian, and minority ethnic female candidates at the U.K. 2010 general election'. *The International Journal of Press/Politics*, 22(1): 43–66.

Warrell, M. 2018. 'Raising girls to be brave leaders'. *Forbes*. October 11. https://www.forbes.com/sites/margiewarrell/2018/10/11/raising-girls-to-be-brave-leaders/ Accessed 2 January 2022.

Warrell, M. 2020. 'Seeing is believing: Female role models Inspi e girls to think bigger'. *Forbes*. October, 9. https://www.forbes.com/sites/margiewarrell/2020/10/09/seeing-is-believing-female-role-models-inspire-girls-to-rise/?sh=441567d47bf9 Accessed 2 January 2022.

Watts, Jonathan. 2019. Greta Thunberg, schoolgirl climate change warrior: 'Some people can let things go. I can't'. *The Guardian*. 11 March. https://www.theguardian.com/world/2019/mar/11/greta-thunberg-schoolgirl-climate-change-warrior-some-people-can-let-things-go-i-cant.

Webb, D. 2007. 'Modes of hoping'. *History of the human sciences*, 20(3): 65–83.

Weidhase N. 2015. 'Ageing Grace/Fully: Grace Jones and the queering of the diva myth'. In *Women, Celebrity and Cultures of Ageing*, edited by Deborah Jermyn and Susan Holmes, 97–111. London: Palgrave Macmillan.

Weil, A.M. and Wolfe, C.R. 2022. 'Individual differences in risk perception and misperception of COVID-19 in the context of political ideology'. *Applied Cognitive Psychology*, 36(1): 19–31.

West, D.M. and Orman, J. 2003 *Celebrity Politics*. Upper Saddle River: Prentice Hall.

White, Khadijah L. 2011. 'Michelle Obama: Redefining the white house-wife'. *Thirdspace: A Journal of Feminist Theory & Culture*, 10(1): 1–19.

Widholm, A. and Becker, K. 2015. 'Celebrating with the celebrities: Television in public space during two royal weddings'. *Celebrity Studies*, 6(1): 6–22.

Williams, Rebecca. 2011. 'Wandering off into soap land': Fandom, genre and 'shipping' The West Wing'. *Participations*, 8(1): 270–95.

Williamson, Milly. 2005. *The Lure of the Vampire: Gender, Fiction and Fandom from Bram Stoker to Buffy*. London: Wallflower Press.

Wilson, Julie. 2010. 'Star testing: The emerging politics of celebrity gossip'. *The Velvet Light Trap, 65*: 25–38.

Wilson, Julie. 2017. *Neoliberalism*. New York: Routledge.

Wilson, Suze and Newstead, Toby. 2022. 'The virtues of effective crisis leadership: What managers can learn from how women heads of state led in the first wave of COVID-19'. *Organizational Dynamics, 5*(2): 100910.

Wolbrecht, Christina and Campbell, David. 2017. 'Role models revisited: Youth, novelty, and the impact of female candidates'. *Politics, Groups, and Identities, 5*(3): 418–34.

Wollstonecraft, Mary. (1787) 1974. *Thoughts on the Education of Daughters: With Reflections on Female Conduct, in the More Important Duties of Life*. New York: Garland.

Wollstonecraft, Mary. 1792. *Vindication of the Rights of Woman*. (Vol. 5). In *Collected Works of Mary Wollstonecraft*, edited by Janet Todd and Marilyn Butler. London: William Pickering.

Women's Grid. 2017. 'Black and Asian women MPs abused more online – Amnesty International Report'. https://www.womensgrid.org.uk/?p=3866 Accessed 2nd January 2022.

Wood, Helen. 2019. 'Fuck the patriarchy: Towards an intersectional politics of irreverent rage'. *Feminist Media Studies, 19*(4): 609–15.

Woodgate, Roberta Lynn, Tennent, Pauline and Barriage, Sarah. 2020. 'Creating space for youth voice: Implications of youth disclosure experiences for youth-centered research'. *International Journal of Qualitative Methods, 19*(1): 160940692095897.

World Economic Forum. 2018. *108 Years: Wait for Gender Equality Gets Longer as Women's Share of Workforce, Politics Drops*. http://reports.weforum.org/global-gender-gap-report-2018/press-release/?doing_wp_cron=1560782669.2314689 159393310546875 Accessed 2 January 2022.

World Economic Forum. 2024. *Global Gender Gap Report 2024. https://www3.weforum.org/docs/WEF_GGGR_2024.pdf*

Yandoli, Krystie Lee. 2020a. 'Former Employees Say Ellen's "Be Kind" Talk Show Mantra Masks a Toxic Work Culture'. *BuzzFeed News*. July 17. https://www.buzzfeednews.com/article/krystieyandoli/ellen-employees-allege-toxic-workplace-culture

Yandoli, Krystie Lee. 2020b. Dozens Of Former "Ellen Show" Employees Say Executive Producers Engaged In Rampant Sexual Misconduct And Harassment *Buzzfeed News*. July 31. https://www.buzzfeednews.com/article/krystieyandoli/ex-ellen-show-employees-sexual-misconduct-allegations

Yelin, Hannah. 2015. 'A literary phenomenon of the non-literate': Classed cultural value, agency and techniques of self-representation in the ghostwritten reality TV star memoir'. *Celebrity Studies, 7*(3): 354–72.

Yelin, Hannah. 2016. 'White Trash celebrity: Shame and display'. In *Women's Magazines in Print and New Media*, edited by Noliwe Rooks, Victoria Pass and Ayana Weekly, 176–91. Abingdon: Routledge.

Yelin, Hannah. 2020. *Celebrity Memoir: From Ghostwriting to Gender Politics*. Basingstoke: Palgrave Macmillan.

Yelin, Hannah and Clancy, Laura. 2021. 'Doing impact work while female: Hate tweets, "hot potatoes" and having "enough of experts"'. *European Journal of Women's Studies, 28*(2): 175–93.

Yelin, Hannah and Clancy, Laura. 2024. '"I have a folder in my email called hate mail": Academic public engagement, digital hate and the unequally distributed risks of visibility'. *New Formations, 2023*(110 & 111): 187–206.

YMCA. 2020. Out Of Service. https://ymca.org.uk/wp-content/uploads/2024/08/YMCA-Out-of-Service-report.pdf

Yoda, Tomiko. 2017. 'GIRLSCAPE: The marketing of mediatic ambience in Japan'. In *Media Theory in Japan,* edited by M. Steinberg and A. Zahlten, 173–99. New York: Duke University Press.

YouGov. 2019. 'How Britain voted in the 2019 general election'. https://yougov.co.uk/topics/politics/articles-reports/2019/12/17/how-britain-voted-2019-general-election Accessed 2 January 2022.

Younge, Gary. 2020. 'I was recently mistaken for David Lammy'. *inews*. January 31. https://inews.co.uk/opinion/gary-younge-mistaken-for-david-lammy-steve-mcqueen-1381951.

Zaslow, E. and Schoenberg, J. 2012. 'Stumping to Girls through Pop Culture: Feminist Interventions to Shape Future Political Leaders'. *Women & Language, 35*(1): 97–116

Zhou, Li. 2020. 'Trump's racist references to the coronavirus are his latest effort to stoke xenophobia'. *Vox*. June 23. https://www.vox.com/2020/6/23/21300332/trump-coronavirus-racism-asian-americans Accessed 2nd January 2022.

Zulli, Diana and Zulli, David J. 2022. 'Extending the Internet meme: Conceptualizing technological mimesis and imitation publics on the TikTok platform'. *New Media & Society, 24*(8): 1872–90.

# Index

# About the Author

**Dr. Michele Paule** is Reader in Gender, Audiences, and Culture at Oxford Brookes University. She researches ways that discourses associated with gender and youth circulate in popular and institutional settings, and how young people draw on these in forming views of themselves, their worlds, and their imagined futures. She is interested in how ideas about girlhood emerge in the interstices between endorsed forms of knowledge in research, media pedagogies, and the public imagination and how historical discourses coalescing around girls emerge in contemporary contexts. Her first monograph, *Girlhood, Schools, and Media: Popular Discourses of the Achieving Girl* (2016), defined her approach to girlhood studies in terms of its interdisciplinary scope and its weaving together of face-to-face, online, and textual methodologies. Her edited collection (with Beverley Clack) *Interrogating the Neoliberal Lifecycle: The Limits of Success* (2019) extended her work on the relationship between public discourses and lived experience, bringing it into dialogue with that of other scholars and practitioner-researchers working internationally across different life stages, disciplines, and modes of dissemination. She is PI for the 'Girls, Leadership and Women in the Public Eye' project and led an international action research project for the World Association of Girl Guides and Girl Scouts (Europe) on gendered barriers to leadership in youth. Michele also undertakes consultancy work with NGOs, governments, and educational organisations. Before academia, she worked in the secondary education sector and has published for policymakers, practitioners, and students. Michele is a youth club charity trustee and a three-times-elected local councillor in the city of Oxford.

**Dr. Hannah Yelin** is Reader in Media and Culture at Oxford Brookes University. Her research specialises in the politics of visibility. She is the author of *Celebrity Memoir: From Ghostwriting to Gender Politics* (2020), a monograph examining the self-representational possibilities for women in the public eye, the curtailments upon them, and their resistant strategies for countering these. As director of Cultures of Digital Hate, Yelin researches the unequally distributed risks of visibility and how these disproportionately affect already-minoritised groups and leads collaboration with those working in law, tech, data science, activism, policy, and academics across disciplines to foster the conditions in which varied voices can participate safely in public debate. She runs the Celebrity Culture Club, a network bringing together academics, media professionals, and interested members of the public to discuss the politics of celebrity culture. She is the chair of the Creative Industries Research and Innovation Network and programmes the annual International Festival of the Creative Industries. Before academia, Hannah had a twelve-year career in the media, producing award-winning work with organisations like the BBC, UKTV, and Global Radio. Her research has been featured in the press around the globe, including interviews and opinion pieces for *Sky News*, ITV, *The Independent*, and *Grazia* in the United Kingdom.

www.ingramcontent.com/pod-product-compliance
Lightning Source LLC
Chambersburg PA
CBHW021815270326
41932CB00007B/188